Praise for the Stunning *New York Times* Bestseller

My Story

Sarah The Duchess of York

with Jeff Coplon

"What *MY STORY* has going for it is something quite rare [among] titles about the British royals—a first-person account that gives a nose-against-the-glass view of this quaint, stuffy but nonetheless fascinating institution."

—Paul D. Colford, New York *Newsday*

"It would be difficult to conjure a human being more down to earth or eager to please than the Duchess. . . . Among other things, *MY STORY* catalogs the Duchess's unhappiness with the protracted separations from her naval officer husband and the strictures of royal life. . . . *MY STORY* flails at the courtiers whom the Duchess believes assisted in her downfall."

—Joanna Kaufman, *The Wall Street Journal*

"Her treatment at the hands of palace management permanently moves one over to her side by the end of this enlightening book."

—Carolyn Jack, Cleveland *Plain Dealer*

"If Cinderella had married the prince and not lived happily ever after, one hopes she would have told her story with the Mary Poppins cheekiness of Fergie. . . . While the book is coauthored, the voice is all Fergie's. She traces her life from her horse-loving childhood through her working-girl days. . . . Fergie comes across as the one member of the monarchy you could invite over for macaroni and cheese. . . . A good-humored trip to and from the palace."

—Carolyn Nizzi Warmbold, *Atlanta Journal*

The Duchess by The Duke, 1985.

SARAH
THE DUCHESS OF YORK

My Story

WITH JEFF COPLON

POCKET **STAR** BOOKS

New York   London   Toronto   Sydney   Tokyo   Singapore

PHOTO CREDITS: *First Insert* Alpha: 4 bottom; Camera Press: 5; Srdja Djukanovic: 9 top, 11 top, 13 bottom, 16 bottom; Arthur Edwards: 15 bottom; Jayne Fincher: 14; Tim Graham/Sygma: 16 top; Lord Lichfield/Camera Press: 3; Gene Nocon: 10; Robin Nunn: 15 top; Personal Archives: 1, 2, 4 top and middle, 6, 7, 8, 9 bottom; Albert Watson: 11 bottom, 12; HRH The Duke of York: 13 top. *Second Insert* Alpha: 2 top; Camera Press: 7; Gianni Dal Magro/Press Impact Italia: 13 bottom; Srdja Djukanovic: 1 top and middle, 6 bottom, 12 top, 14 top; Jean-Daniel Lorieux/Press Impact Italia: 13 top; Robin Matthews/Camera Press: 7, 9 top; Robin Matthews/Press Impact Italia: 10 bottom; Trevor Meeks/Horse and Hound: 12 bottom; Gene Nocon: 2 bottom; Robin Nunn: 1 bottom, 6 top; Personal Archives: 3, 4, 5, 8, 9 bottom, 10 top and middle, 11, 14 bottom; Watercolor by The Duchess of York: 16; HRH The Duke of York: 15

A Pocket Star Book published by
POCKET BOOKS, a division of Simon & Schuster Inc.
1230 Avenue of the Americas, New York, NY 10020

ISBN: 0-671-00439-5

First Pocket Books printing April 1997

10 9 8 7 6 5 4 3 2 1

POCKET STAR BOOKS and colophon are registered trademarks of Simon & Schuster Inc.

Cover photograph by Greg Gorman

Printed in the U.S.A.

With thanks to my friend
David Tang,
who has taught me so much
about books and poetry

For Tine
with all my love

Contents

Contents

My Story

Rock Bottom

Of all the Queen's homes, Balmoral Castle is so special. With its ivied walls and slender turrets, it stands like some friendly colossus on the Scottish Highlands. Balmoral was born in the mind of Victoria, the Queen of queens, the woman in history I most revere. It was the Royal Family's summer home, a place for languid days and light labor.

For me it was the perfect haven, a staunch fortress against the arrows loosed my way since I entered Buckingham Palace in 1986. Balmoral was a tonic for the senses. I loved the crackle of its morning frost and the smells of its heather and peaty soil, so delicious and earthy. Even the water there was brown from the peat, carried down from the mountains by the rushing River Dee.

I loved most of all how Balmoral relaxed the man I had married: Prince Andrew, The Duke of York. On this vast estate my husband felt sprung from glaring eyes and incessant protection; he could drive about its acreage without a policeman at his side. He became easy and full of gentle fun, his truest self, and it was lovely to see.

And as for me . . . I can say that Balmoral set me free. Back in London I had become this stiffly disciplined woman, drowning in duty, cramped and shackled. But here I could take my dogs out and walk for miles. Or we would trek up into the mountains for evening picnics and barbecues, in the little huts built by Queen Victoria for her beloved Prince Albert to use when he was out stalking. When I rode at Balmoral with the Queen, with our mounts willing and the air so sharp, I would feel almost at home. As though I actually belonged there, inside this most exclusive family, in this most heavenly of places.

If ever that family needed a respite, it was in August of 1992. The Queen would later call it *annus horribilis,* the year of torn moorings and shattered peace. In April, Princess Anne entered divorce proceedings against Captain Mark Phillips. In June came the first published excerpts of *Diana: Her True Story,* a tabloid-flavored rendering of the Princess of Wales's bulimia, suicide tries, and marital problems with Prince Charles.

Not one to be left out, I'd had my own bit to contribute. From early on that year, Andrew and I had been discussing a separation—not because we'd stopped caring for one another but because I had reached the end of my royal rope. For six years I had shouldered the demands of Palace life. I'd endured the constant scrutiny of the British press and the barely veiled hostility of the Royal Household, the courtiers who run the show. Gradually, relentlessly, they had beaten me down. They were killing me by inches. It was time to save my life.

In March our plan to separate was leaked prematurely to the *Daily Mail,* that blunt instrument of a newspaper. A senior courtier publicly blamed me for the leak, an utter false-hood, and proceeded to flog me up and down. The BBC knew a hot story when it fell into one: *"The knives are out for Fergie in the Palace. . . ."* There were prompt apologies, but the damage had been done. I had been tagged "unsuitable" for royal life, and the charge stuck. I was frozen out, and not just in the Palace; the wind from all the doors slamming in my face might have knocked me over.

A stronger person might have lashed back in righteous anger—but then, a stronger person wouldn't have trapped herself in such a corner in the first place. Deep down I knew that the charge was fair; I *was* unsuitable, always had been. Just seven years before, I had been an anonymous working girl, hard-pressed to pay her rent, dodging summonses for traffic tickets. And then, with fictional suddenness, I was cat-apulted up into royalty—to be the object of cheers and curt-seys, the toast of state dinners. "The breath of fresh air," they called me.

For a while I coped with this mutation from private to pub-lic life. But I was never cut out for the job, and the harder I pushed the more things fell apart. Even at my dizzy height of popularity, I knew that the clock would strike twelve and I'd be seen for what I was: unworthy, unattractive, unaccom-plished. And finally, logically, undone.

I wasn't the only one to suffer. In my wake I had left a trail of destruction that stretched longer than the train of my supernaturally fabulous wedding gown.

But I was unsinkable, and though March had been excruci-ating, it wasn't enough to finish me off—or to make me much wiser. Though bruised I still stood upright, still clung to some small shard of dignity. But the other shoe would drop, I *knew* it would—I had written the script myself, you see, and I was hooked on sad endings.

I just didn't think my bogeyman would penetrate the thick stone walls of Balmoral—not *here* of all places. Dear God, not just yet. . . .

Two days after I arrived in Scotland, his hot breath singed my neck.

As usual, I had it coming. Just a week before, I had been on holiday near St. Tropez with John Bryan, an American who started out as my financial adviser, then became something more. If I could live anywhere in the world, it would be in the south of France—there is nothing to compare with its colors and smells and honeyed light. But this trip was a stupidity. The timing was rotten, too close to Balmoral and my time there with Andrew, a man I still loved. It felt wrong from the beginning, but I'd long since short-circuited my intuition. John really wanted to go and I wanted to make him happy, and I just went along with it. I was a puddle of water that summer. I followed the path of least resistance.

I was committing social suicide, without leaving a note.

But while our holiday was misguided, even reckless, it was not as indiscreet as would be made out. We took reasonable precautions: a private plane to a private airstrip, a rented villa on a ten-acre estate, two miles off the highway. As Beatrice and Eugenie were with me, we also had a pair of royal protection officers at our side. (As princesses who were fifth and sixth in line to the throne, my young daughters would always be safeguarded, regardless of their mother's marital status.)

Ringed by densely wooded hills and vineyards, the villa was naturally secluded. Still, I felt twinges of something amiss. At the airstrip I had seen a van and a motorbike that I hadn't liked the look of. A few days later, as I sunbathed by the pool without a top, I said to my friend Gabrielle, "I have this feeling of being watched and I don't know where it's coming from." When I got up I covered my chest with my arms, but then I felt silly and paranoid—the soft heat of the Côte d'Azur will lull one's suspicions into slumber.

After a day back in London, my daughters and I boarded a flight to Aberdeen to join Andrew and his family in Balmoral. I'd been lurching in a fog since March, not knowing which end was up, but Scotland began to work its emerald wonder —to remind me that life was a dance, not a dirge.

On Tuesday I took the first of many calls from John Bryan. "I'm afraid they've got photographs of our trip to France," he said. Rights had been bought by the *Daily Mirror,* one of the heavier-breathing tabloids.

As a grandmaster of self-destruction, I knew disaster when I saw it. Even if I saw it only after the fact.

"Now you relax, honey," John went on, in that smooth humming way of his. "I'll take care of it—everything will be fine. I'm going to the High Court, and we'll stop them there."

I urgently wanted to believe that my man of the world had everything in hand. That whole year I had needed someone to take the wheel, to steer my life and leave me on automatic pilot. John had relished the role, always knew just what to do —a magical trait to someone like myself, who wrestled with doubt every day of her life and often got pinned to the mat.

I told Andrew straightaway; I never held back from him, we were always honest with each other. "I will completely support you," Andrew said. "I knew that John was down there, and that's our business and no one else's."

I went up with heavy feet to brief the Queen. She couldn't have been pleased, but she is like her middle son; she is not easily rattled. "All right, let us see what happens," she said.

On Wednesday I got half a dozen updates, each one grimmer than the last. "We're trying our hardest," John kept saying. That afternoon came more bad news: the High Court had refused to grant an injunction, failing to see how blocking the photos would serve "the public interest." But there was one last hope, John reported. The judge told him that if the Palace were to back us before the Press Complaints Commission, we could still prevent the *Mirror* from publishing the next morning.

Forcing myself to stick to routine, I took Beatrice and Eugenie to swim in the local public indoor pool. People say that children pick up on your distress, that you cannot really hide it, but I can—I can block out my demons and live in the moment with my daughters. It is a great gift, for me as well as them.

But as soon as we left the pool I felt enveloped by a black buzzing, a swarming dread as thick as sparrows.

At ten o'clock that evening John called one last time. The deadline had passed, and the Queen's private secretary, Mr. Z, had refused to intercede. (I will forgo using his name—not to be mysterious, but because his name doesn't matter. Like all the top courtiers, he was a creature of the Palace Establishment, no more and no less.)

"They're out," John said; he'd got hold of the *Mirror*'s first edition. There were twenty-odd photos, all of them set by the scallop-edged pool at our villa, and they were worse than he had thought. Neither John nor I were the least bit out of focus.

"I'm sorry," John said. "There was nothing we could do."

"Okay," I said dumbly, and put down the phone.

With the halting voice of a crash victim, I relayed the news to Andrew. "Don't worry, we'll just deal with it," he said. This prince rises to adversity. As a helicopter pilot in the

Falklands War, he accepted the most dangerous of assignments, to serve as decoy for enemy missiles. He is brilliant under fire, in a drama—and that is the word he used that night in Balmoral. *"Brilliant,"* he said. As in: *You are still wonderful to me; we will not let them defeat us.*

But I did not feel brilliant. I had a glass of brandy to cushion my fall into shock, and fall I did, to the center of the earth. This was pain beyond description—beyond sensation, even. In Britain, where sex can never be mentioned and is therefore on everyone's mind, these photos would be the ultimate curtain twitch. I was a royal duchess and had shown affection to a man not my husband, and had been found out—end of story. No matter that Andrew and I were separated. I had been exposed for what I truly was. Worthless. Unfit. A national disgrace.

I might have blamed John Bryan, or Mr. Z, or the ruthless paparazzi or the barons of the press, but I didn't. I had a much nearer, fairer target: myself. Not because what I had done was so awful, or immoral, but because I had enemies in high places, all the good gray Establishment types who would hoist their goblets to my obliteration. Now I'd served them the opening they'd sought, and they had seized it, as jackals rip into carrion. There are no moral dilemmas on the jackal's side, only hunger; it is not a complicated transaction. And the worst part was that I *knew* all of this—I was no more a babe in these woods. I knew it like my name, but it had seemed less taxing to forget and keep wending my blind and merry way.

If you gauged me by conscious action, you might say I was not responsible for what I had done. I had let my life spin out of control long before. But at the end of the day, of course, we are all held responsible. We may choose not to answer our critics, but we must at last answer to ourselves.

The clock in the tower was chiming—*nine, ten, eleven* . . . My royal coach was reverting to pumpkinhood before my eyes.

And still I had no answer, only a mute and bewildered: *Why?*

*T*here was no question of sleep. I sipped my brandy and sat in my bedroom with Alison Wardley, my children's nanny and for that night mine as well. I was the prisoner in the dock, already found guilty and knowing what terrible sentence she was to receive, and knowing that sentence would be just. I felt numbed to my fate, resigned to it, but broken and grieving just the same. Alison never gave up on me, stayed patient with my lamentation. Somehow she kept me together.

All too soon (for summer nights in Scotland are brief and flitting things), the ink outside turned cobalt, then gray, and then Thursday's first light touched the heather and close-cropped lawns. It was my favorite time at Balmoral, all softness and solitude.

Today it would be my morning of truth, my judgment hour.

I rang up a loyal friend. "Just remember," he said, "the only person who has the right to judge you is the Lord. Ask God for forgiveness, and then just hold your head up high, pull your shoulders back, and walk proud."

Good, brave words, but I could not face the Family, and Andrew went down to the dining room alone. The Queen and the Duke of Edinburgh had their breakfast upstairs, but my husband's siblings were there: Charles, the heir to the throne; Anne, the Princess Royal; Edward, the youngest. Plus all the children, and an equerry and a lady-in-waiting or two. It would be accurate to report that the porridge was getting cold. Eyes wide and mouths ajar, the adults were flipping through the *Daily Mirror* and the rest of the tabloids. Until they saw Andrew and stopped, as it never feels quite right to be gazing at your brother's wife when she hasn't all her clothes on.

All watched for Andrew's reaction as he went to the newspapers, but he must have been a disappointment—he casually leafed through them, as though digesting the cricket results.

Then he brought a copy up to my room, and I faced the music I'd composed. John was right; it was the work of a professional. The photos were sharp and clear, in garish living color, and they strongly suggested that our friendship was more than platonic. I had been exposed, body and soul.

I am a more private person than most people know, and a part of me expired that morning.

The *Mirror*'s headline, in typical hydrogen-bomb type, read: FERGIE'S STOLEN KISSES. Nearly the entire front page was swallowed by two photographs. The smaller one caught me sitting next to John without my top; I was captured from the back at a three-quarter angle. The larger one depicted John and me lying on a blue-and-white striped lounge chair for a "kiss and cuddle."

"These are the sensational pictures the world has been waiting to see . . ." the lead story began.

There were more photographs plastered over nine pages inside; the *Mirror* had reportedly spent upwards of $100,000 for its booty and was out to get its money's worth. The shot that caused the most furor—the one that would define me for years to come—showed John planting his mouth on the top of my foot. *Toe-sucking!* went the tabloids' refrain, and you could almost hear the grown men giggling.

For the record, no sucking of toes had taken place in the

south of France, a fact soberly acknowledged by the *Los Angeles Times*. ("That does not now appear to be the case. . . .") John and I were actually playing at Cinderella when the picture was snapped—the whole scene was not nearly as intense as it was made to look.

But if you read the *Mirror*'s own back-patting editorial, you might have thought they had fingered a serial killer or busted some treasury-sapping racket. The poolside photographs, the paper pronounced, "strip away all the lies, humbug and hypocrisy that have surrounded the Duchess's relationship with Mr. Bryan. . . .

"Fergie, now staying in Balmoral, has once again made our Royal Family look a laughingstock in front of the world. For Prince Andrew it is a humiliation few men could bear. His wife and her American friend must be sent packing. . . .

"If the Royal Family is to survive beyond the Queen's reign, it cannot afford another scandal like this."

With the passage of time, the *Mirror*'s language might sound slightly overheated. You must understand, however, that the London tabloids see themselves as principled protectors of the same monarchy they love to bash. If at times they must skulk about to look through other people's keyholes, so be it—there is a higher purpose involved.

Once again, in fairness, I had made myself an irresistible target. On the bottom rung of Fleet Street, there are two sure-fire circulation-boosters: an "exposé" of a Royal, however slender in the facts department, or a picture of a bare-breasted woman.

In that light, the Bryan photos marked a breakthrough for the press: the first time they had latched on to *both* their favorite items in one foul swoop. And it goes without saying that they could not have achieved their historic coup without me.

I had turned self-sabotage into an art form—had anyone ever done it quite so well? Was there ever a more perfect masochist?

But the horror wasn't nearly over. I still had to face the woman by whose kind permission I was staying at Balmoral. She was my mother-in-law and my Sovereign, and a woman I cared about deeply—and this was how I had thanked her. I had let down a person who had never let *me* down, the last person in the world I'd have wished to disappoint.

At 9:30 that morning I went up to see Her Majesty the Queen.

The Queen was furious. I had apologized, of course, but penance and contrition have their limits—there are some things which cannot be put right.

Her anger wounded me to the core, the more because I knew she was justified. I had violated her trust. I'd betrayed the bond that we'd built ever since she had invited me to Royal Ascot in 1985, as one of the younger people she enjoyed having about. The Queen had been so saddened when Andrew and I separated. But she had never let it affect our personal ties, even as I became distinctly unwelcome at her Court. There was something special between us, and maybe that was what moved me to mount some feeble defense, instead of just slinking out of her room.

"Don't you think it's a bit weird that it keeps having to be *me* that gets caught?" I said. "Don't you think it's time someone asked, 'Why is it always her?' I can't be *that* idiotic."

(Later that day the Queen and Andrew authorized Mr. Z to release the following statement to the press: "We strongly disapprove of the publication of photographs taken in such circumstances.")

I curtseyed my retreat, then went and found the one woman who understood what it meant to marry into the Royal Family and how hard it was to measure up. I went up to Diana's bedroom and sat with my friend. She couldn't say anything, she was just there for me—and she was great.

For the rest of the day I sought out other family members and apologized to them, one by one. By early afternoon I needed another brandy, but I saw the gauntlet through. They were all very gracious—even Prince Philip, who could be stern at times, tried to console me. Lady Sarah Armstrong-Jones, Margaret's daughter, was absolutely charming. They all knew that I wasn't the first person in the annals of royalty to be caught in an indiscretion.

Still and all, I was leveled when I entered the room for dinner and saw everyone staring at me. I *knew* they must be seeing me topless, or being nuzzled by a bald American. The courtiers eyed me sneakily, discreetly. The butlers and footmen gaped, and I felt naked in their sight. I would need a *Roget's* to express my degradation at that moment and even then I would fail; there are no words for it.

For so long I'd fed into my self-loathing, until now it had turned malignant—had nearly taken form outside of me. I felt disgust in that dining room and a queasy fascination, as if they were looking at a burn victim. The sensation was strong and palpable, and I could not stave it off . . .

I stayed in Balmoral for three more days, as scheduled. Andrew spoke up for me at every turn, and Alison was staunch as Gibraltar, but I faced a trial by fire nonetheless. Three days of national derision, and more Mediterranean photos; the *Mirror* strung out its exclusive to the limit and ultimately sold two million extra papers. Three days of vile headlines—of FERGIE IS FINISHED, and DISGRACED DUCHESS OF YORK TO LEAVE BALMORAL FOR GOOD.

If anything, the Fleet Street boys were gaining momentum. "The monarchy is now reeling," the *Daily Express* wrote on Saturday, "under the biggest scandal since the abdication of 1936."

It wouldn't have been right to deny the Queen her grandchildren on holiday, I told myself. So I stayed and got stared at as a term of my surrender. I would do it for the Sovereign. I yearned to please her more than ever, though I feared it could never be the same between us.

This will sound too pathetic, but I found some satisfaction in that unmitigated hell, in my free fall of self-hatred. I was like the battered woman who gets what she's sure she deserves. I was good only for punishment, and punished I was, never fear. I pinned on my scarlet letter—mine would be a *T*, for toe-sucking—and wore it everywhere, with a sort of perverse comfort.

They all saw the true *me* now; there was no more need to hide. If you know you are worthless and a sham, a fitting object for ridicule, it relieves quite a lot of pressure when someone rips off your mask and the world comes around to the same opinion.

Or as the Americans like to say: When you ain't got nothing, you've got nothing to lose.

On Sunday, my getaway day, the tabloids carried a fresh scandal: Diana's so-called "Squidgy tape," twenty minutes of phone chat with a male friend. I wasn't the only one being spied on, that much was clear. I went into Diana's room and thanked her for taking me off the front page; it was our private, rueful joke.

I took half a Valium, the only time I ever used it in my life.

Then I flew back with my daughters to London, with no clue as to what the next day would bring.

"She faces a long, lonely exile," a courtier told the *Daily Express* that day, "and it is cold out there."

But *was* Fergie finished? I had hit rock bottom, no question. I was paying the price of an unexamined life—of a skein of wrong decisions made for bad reasons, or for no conscious reason at all. I had flung myself into one peril after the next, like a diver who never checks the depth of the pool. Finally my risks had caught up with me, as I should have known they would.

To take stock: I was a nonperson in the Family; any future I might have had there was now irrevocably ended. I had lost my husband, whom I loved unconditionally and who loved me back the same way. I had squandered the British public's esteem, a hard loss for a person who lived to please.

To make matters worse, I was building a mountain of a debt. As a single mother with few assets and less income than most presumed, I was in deep financial trouble, though I would never admit it.

In short, I had reached my crossroads. The choice was stark. I could race on in the same old direction, keep bingeing on food and spending and work. I could skirt the darkness that way, and the sad, shriveled self that lived there. I could just let my life happen, make it up as I went along, and hope I stayed a step ahead of the sheriff.

That was the road I knew, the one more traveled on.

It was also the route to insanity, or an early grave.

The other path was new to me and by far the more frightening. It was a slower, broader road, and it led to the deepest part of me, the best part. But to get there I would have to confront the broken shell of my existence—and how empty I had been even when intact. I'd have to put myself back to-

I 4

gether, when all the king's horses and all the king's men had already written the job off. Most of all, I'd have to face my pain—and my pain had always beamed like the sun to me, too intense and enormous to look at for long.

I was only thirty-two years old, but I sensed that my next wrong turn could be my last. Would I learn what I needed to solve my own riddle—and before it was too late?

On Fleet Street, and in the stale, hushed corridors of Buckingham Palace, the betting was against me.

We should note, however, that those widely esteemed, supremely well-connected, and oh-so-powerful gentlemen had underestimated me before.

I

The Pot Hunter

Many are the things I love about horses. They are large and safe, and they never answer back. I love the way they smell; I am one for whom smells are important, who follows her nose. And I adore horses' high spirits, their capacity to be difficult—and the way they fall in line when you show them who's boss.

But as a child growing up in the shires of southern England, what I loved most about my horses was their loyalty, their consistency, their companionship. They were my secret sharers, my touchstones.

For a good while, they seemed almost enough to make me happy.

At my first home, Lowood, a big white Edwardian house in Berkshire, we were a forty-minute drive from London and right in the middle of horse country. We had fourteen acres and two makeshift wooden stables. By age three I had advanced from my painted rocking horse to a real Dartmoor pony. My mother refused to baby me; when I fell, she'd make a joke about how silly the horse had been to step in such a rut. Soon I would be laughing with her. I was a tough little monkey, and I'd just clamber back on and dig in my heels.

With my sister Jane, two years older and my best friend, I'd play pretend for hours in the garden, with Jane as the "driver" and myself as the horse, snorting and prancing or pointing my toes like a show pony. Or we'd watch the great show jumping riders on television and clamor for our favorites. Horses were everywhere in my childhood; they were part of our landscape.

Though heavily Irish on both sides, my family tree claimed its quota of blue blood, with four dukes and at least three mistresses of Charles II. My father, Major Ronald Ferguson, hailed from a long line of distinguished gentleman soldiers; my mother, the former Susan Wright, came from an established family in Ireland. They once owned a grand estate near Dublin called Powerscourt, which boasted the tallest waterfall in the British Isles.

By the time I came around, we were country gentry with a bit of old money but assuredly *not* landed aristocracy. You wouldn't put me in the same category as a certain fourth cousin of mine, Lady Diana Spencer, who came out of a big ancestral home with a title in her own right.

Still, we had quite a comfortable life, with a small household staff and trips to the seaside in the summer and Switzerland in the winter. In 1969, after my grandfather died of leukemia, Dads inherited a dairy farm called Dummer Down, over the county line in Hampshire, and we moved out to *real* country. I was nine years old and found all of it wonderful. The village of Dummer was a tiny clutch of thatched-roof cottages, with a small stone church and a post office that sold good sweets on the side. A winding lane, canopied with cherry trees and just right for bicycles or toboggans, led down to our new home, a red brick farmhouse with beamed ceilings and a large country oven.

The house wasn't as grand as Lowood, but I found it quite perfect. I was always one to be out-of-doors, anyway, chafing for adventure in all weather, and now I had a kingdom to explore: more than eight hundred acres of gently swelling pasture and woodland. We had black-and-white Frisian milk cows and neat fields of corn, barley, oats, and wheat. There was a rose garden and an apple orchard, which doubled as a dog cemetery. Flowers grew everywhere: pink fuchsia, lavender foxgloves, blankets of white and yellow daffodils.

At my new home I had but two worries. If I picked the prettiest flowers, a perpetual temptation, would we get as many back again the next spring? And wasn't it unhealthy to get our milk straight from a churn in the big fridge—where were the milk bottles I'd known at Lowood?

For Jane and myself, the most exciting part of rural life was our expanded pony operation. Dummer Down featured brick-and-cedar stables and a two-sided Dutch barn, open in the middle—a sort of animal courtyard. We had an equitation "school," a fenced-off grassy circle for training the horses, and, best of all, a full-fledged cross-country course, complete with "tiger traps": three wooden poles placed over a fence.

When we weren't jumping, we'd conscript our ponies into grisly battles of cowboys and Indians—I doted on American Westerns and especially *Bonanza*. As I rode around the farm, I'd feel proud to think that all this land was ours—as far as my eyes could see, as far as my young world stretched. It seemed so vast, and yet I felt snug and protected within its bounds.

Years later I would revisit that exhilaration, on a rather larger scale, at Balmoral.

In the spacious yard by the Dummer farmhouse, I would thrill to the sight of a dozen or more horses, most of them in training for Dads. My grandfather, Colonel Andrew Ferguson, had distinguished himself as commanding officer of the Life Guards, the Queen's Household Cavalry. My father had set out on the same track and had served several postings in the Middle East. When his military career stalled, Dads resigned his commission in the Life Guards, took on part-time work in public relations, and immersed himself in his one true passion: polo, the game he had taken up while stationed in the Suez Canal Zone in Egypt.

At six feet two, broad of shoulder and square of jaw, Dads was known on the field for his "length and strength"; he became a very useful five-goal player. Through polo he met the Earl Mountbatten, then Mountbatten's nephew, Prince Philip, for whom he eventually ran the Guards Polo Club; he later became Prince Charles's polo manager.

As a result, Jane and I had frequent opportunities to practice our curtseys before the Royal Family. They were not some remote abstraction; we considered them friends of our parents.

I had little taste for polo and its roughness. I liked to ride tough and strong but gracefully as well, like Elizabeth Taylor in *National Velvet*. When we ventured to watch Dads in a weekend match at Smith's Lawn in Windsor Great Park, I would sneak to the back of the stands in mid-chukka to play tag with other like-minded truants—including Prince Andrew, who was just my age. (Young Andrew always got on well with my mum; when she visited Windsor Castle, he liked to play at squirting her with a hose.)

Mum was a tremendous horsewoman in her own right, who'd win her share of sidesaddle and working hunter competitions at the local shows. Jane was a miniature version of

Mum: the same lithe frame, soft brown hair, stunning features, and grace in the saddle. And then I came along, barreling ahead with my mop of tight red curls and my galaxy of freckles. I was a wild child, a total tomboy, the son my father never had. I hated all physical constraint; the baggier my dungarees, the better. When we rode cross-country, I'd go flat out, my horse jumping everything clear. I might not be the prettiest rider, but I'd get to the final fence in the best time.

Dads raised me to get outside, get muddy, and—most of all—to *get on with it.* If I wanted to do something, you could not stop me—it is the same with me today. When I set my sights, I don't like to muck about. You want to get from A to B, you take the shortest path, the straight one, and you deal with any hurdles as they come.

They tell a story about me in my toddler days, when Mum —who could be quite strict about such things—determined that it was time I went properly to the bathroom. Equally firm, I balked. To win her point, Mum grabbed a diaper and tied it around my front to the leg of a table in our playroom, adjacent to Lowood's kitchen. I was to stay there until I was ready to perform in a civilized fashion. Two minutes later, she found me back in the kitchen, grinning with victory; I'd untied the diaper.

"I'll fix you this time," she muttered, and now she knotted the diaper at my back, where I couldn't possibly get at it. But she was barely back in the kitchen when she saw me looking in from the doorway. Stymied by the knot, I had dragged the table with me.

I was volatile when young, no question—not out of petulance, or moodiness, but for feeling tongue-tied. By the time I could express myself, the rest of the family had lost interest, or moved on to some other subject, or left the room. I could never quite get the words out, and so my will burst out as temper. My family thought me angry when I simply was frustrated.

My mother had herself been raised in the classic British fashion, to display world-class manners and submerge all emotion. My father, molded by military discipline, was the dean of stiff upper lips. From early on I came to dread their disapproval. "When I tell you off," Mum would admonish me, "why can't you just accept the criticism and say you are sorry, and then forget all about it?" I so craved their affirmations, the big smile or the murmured "Well done," that I took Mum's advice straight to heart. They would scarcely reach mid-reprimand—in public or private, it made no difference —before I'd be making my amends: *Okay, fine, quite right . . . I shouldn't have done that . . . Wasn't I a silly fool?* And, sure enough, they would stop. Life was easier that way. By the time I was nine or ten, my protests were few and far between.

I wanted to be loved by everyone. I wanted to be the nicest, the kindest, the most clever, the most able. My parents' marriage was already cracking by the time I was born. I was the child who would caulk the fissures—it was my job to make Mummy and Daddy happy. It's an impossible job, of course, but if you're a child like me you think you can do it, somehow.

And when you are let down, when your mother moves into a separate bedroom—Dads was in too much pain after a polo injury, she'd try to explain—you have let *yourself* down. You have failed. So you fail and fail and fail and fail, and every single time you fail. And even when you think you have done well, you are setting yourself up to fail anew. No matter that my standards were unreachable; I would flay myself in ways that would have alarmed my dear parents, had they known. Even in the years when all seemed outwardly serene for me,

I lived with jackhammer stress, the worse for having to hide it.

I became The Pleaser; I was always The Pleaser.

I could never be as beautiful or as graceful as Jane, but I could surely be more tractable, less bothersome. I became my mother's favorite not for who I was but for how easily I gave in. When Jane would bridle and make a scene—she was a sensitive, searching person, my sister, no less lost than I in the thickets of growing up—I'd feel a queasy surge of pleasure as Mum exclaimed, "Why can't you be more like Sarah?"

My father's integrity is of the stubborn sort; it does not yield to fashion or peer pressure. For a time my parents were invited once each winter to join the Royal Family at a shooting weekend at Sandringham, the Queen's Norfolk estate. It was a chance for Dads to spend time socially with Prince Philip and other influential polo chums, and Mum always cherished riding with the Queen. But one day Dads went out to a different shoot, where the company brought down 550 pheasants and partridges, every last one reared for the kill from babies. Dads came home and hung up his gun, and he never touched it again.

"Those birds were beautiful," he exclaimed. "What the hell was I doing?"

There would be no more invitations to Sandringham after that, but Dads didn't care. While unflaggingly respectful to the Royal Family, he had little use for the British Establishment's conventions. If he didn't feel like getting up in a morning suit for the races at Royal Ascot, he would not go, and that was that. He had his own views and ignored his critics.

The major's younger daughter, whose sole idea was to placate all around her, could only marvel at such conviction.

Dads also had a playful side, best displayed when he took us on special outings to London. He insisted on surprising us, never revealing our destination; he would even stride past the theater where he'd bought the tickets. Or he'd pretend to be taking us for bacon and eggs, or to some bloated Wagnerian opera, before veering off at the end to land us at *Sleeping Beauty,* the pantomime we had been begging for. Along the way we had to play follow the leader; if Dads swung round the lamppost, Mum would have to do the same, then Jane and I, with our aging nanny or portly cook bringing up the rear. When Dads planned an outing, no one was excluded.

There were long stretches, though, when Dads's polo consumed him, end of story, and we'd be left with Mum—who was simply the most brilliant, zestful person I have ever met. She had grown up herself just after World War II, when it was hard to go anywhere, and now she was making up for lost time. Mum organized our ski trips abroad, and the family Christmases, and the most elaborate, colorful birthday parties. But she didn't need great events to prompt her. When she wasn't hosting a gymkhana (a local pony competition), or carting us to someone else's, she would instigate a party for a bunch of our friends from Daneshill School: swimming, ice-skating, the movies, the circus. Or we would make tracks for my all-time favorite lunch spot in London, Fortnum & Mason, where the mayonnaise was just up my street. My order never varied. First, ham salad, then an ethereal treat known as "three in a boat": one scoop apiece of mandarin, raspberry, and lemon sorbet, with raspberries and mandarin orange sections arrayed around them. You can still have it there now, if you want to.

Jane and I could invite one friend each on these adventures, and Mum would be the fifth girl, with her liquid laugh and mischievous gleam. She was the most popular mother in Hampshire, the type your friends would praise as "super-cool."

Mum just made everything happen.

Shortly after moving to Dummer, Mum and I went out to inspect a striking chestnut Welsh cross for me to ride in competition. I liked the pony at first sight—he had wonderful conformation, and his red coat shone in the sun. And you could see that he was a character, even when he was standing still; he had a precious way of crossing his front legs and looking at you sagely.

But Mum was more cautious. The high price might have given her pause, or perhaps she sensed something amiss. "Do you think there are any problems with him?" she asked the seller.

"No, no, he's fine," the woman assured her.

So I hopped on for a test drive, and as we drew up to the first fence the little horse napped—shied back and reared up on his legs like a bucking bronco. He wasn't acting startled or fearful; he knew exactly what he was about, which was to rid himself of this presumptuous midget on his back.

But he did *not* get me off; this day he had met his match. I gave him a swift one with a stick down his rib cage. We turned and ran back at the fence, and I told him he had better well jump it. He leaped it like a stag, and he never, ever napped with me again—well, he did do it once or twice, but he knew what he was in for. In the years that followed, that contrary little horse would misbehave with anyone else, but he'd give me his all.

The pony's official name was Hartmoor Silver Sands, but his stable name was Herbert, and his pet name—when I felt especially affectionate, or exasperated—simply Herbie. He was typecast for the working hunter pony, my best event at the time. You would go into the ring and jump some rustic fences, then show your pony off in some basic dressage: trotting, walking, galloping, figure eights. A winning pony needed looks and discipline, and a nimble toughness for the jumps. Herbert had the whole package, and soon Jane was not the only Ferguson girl to be bringing home rosettes.

Ponies weren't all fun and games. I hated mucking out Herbert's stall, got out of it when I could. The water buckets ate into my hands. Schooling in dressage bored me to screams. But I loved the jumping—I *loved* it. When I fell off I never complained; I just brushed myself off, got back on and rode again. There was no lack of courage in me.

For the fancy-dress shows, Herbert and I would make a grand entrance as Huntley & Palmer's Ginger Nut Biscuits, a popular cookie. We had a no-nonsense girl groom named Binnie, who would spend hours plaiting Herbert's tail, till it looked like a tube package of biscuits. Then she'd sew actual Ginger Nut Biscuits into Herbie's mane, onto each plait. I wore a white T-shirt with Huntley & Palmer's insignia sewn on the back. With our matching red hair we made a formidable pair, my pony and I. People worried when we arrived.

If you are frightened of a horse, he will know it. But if you trust him, the horse will know that too, and he will repay your confidence with his diligence. Herbert was my true friend, and I secretly enjoyed it when he acted up with another rider. I had tamed him; our bond was exclusive and so all the more real. Herbert saw me as *me*. He understood me at a time when I'd begun concealing the best parts of myself—the creative, assertive, expressive parts—from the people in my life. With my horse I could relax; he would not judge me.

After I turned eleven, I began working with a second horse for show jumping, where the fences are higher and the competition more democratic. Here a pony's looks and breeding counted less than heart and bravery and sheer athletic talent. Spider was strong and thick, black and muscular; when we shaved his mane, he would look like a Roman war horse. He was solid as mountain rock, steadfast, and reliable—all the qualities I most prized.

When you reach a fence some three feet high and three feet across, horse and rider both must take a literal leap of faith. The two must team up, in the deepest sense; you must earn your horse's confidence, his trust and his love. If you are firm but also gentle, if you are his boss and yet his friend, then he will do anything for you within reason, and sometimes beyond.

It was not difficult for me to love my horses. I talked to Spider all the time, I would sit in his box with him and treat him to carrots. And Spider would never disappoint me in the ring—though his flair for the dramatic could test one's nerves. Spider would lazily traipse into the arena, creep up to the first fence, and just barely skim over the red and white poles. That was my pony's way, and there was no pushing him for extra. Somehow Spider knew that all he needed was a clear round to advance to the jump-off, where the format changed. Now he would be racing against the clock. To win he would need a second clear round, and in faster time than the rest.

If you hadn't seen Spider compete before, you would have given him little chance in the jump-off. But he became a dif-

ferent horse then, as though he'd tuned in to a higher fre-
quency and said, *All right, boys, now I'll show them.* He
would take off like a missile, slowing only to cut each corner.
Was it the buzz of the crowd or the keen body of his young
rider that put Spider into a special gear? I only know for
certain that I loved those all-out moments. When you have so
much horse under you, one so clever and true, it is a thrill like
no other.

So willing was Spider that I frequently worried he might
try to clear a fence too big for him. At the Hampshire Horse
Show that year, the rain fell in sheets. My trainer, Dick
Stillwell, asked me if I still wanted to try. The grass was slick,
but I was a "pot" hunter, always gunning for the trophy, and
I replied, "Yes, of course." Good old gung-ho, slap-her-on-
the-back Fergie wasn't about to be defeated by the weather. I
might be shadowed by fear from dawn to nightfall, but in
the show ring I was intrepid. Spider always jumped, never
faltered. Spider would never let me down.

We had a good start, my pony gripping the turf with his
studded shoes, but then we took a corner too tight. Spider's
feet began slipping from under him as we reached the fence,
and a great triple fence it was, too. But my horse was so kind
and diligent—he wasn't going to stop, as I hadn't asked him
to—that he jumped, even as he slid out of control. He took
off and crashed into the fence, and the last thing I remembered was that loyal, thick-necked pony tumbling down on
top of me.

Spider was unhurt, but I was knocked cold with a major
concussion; I had to spend two days in bed, a jail term for me.
To this day I have severe back problems from my mishaps on
horses. But that was how I lived my life from childhood on:
setting great goals, taking high risks. I strived to be perfect,
to make every round clear.

If anyone could do it, I could do it.
Even when I couldn't.

When I was twelve, it was my year to shine. With two fabulous ponies—a *fleet* of horses, to my mind—I was collecting cups by the dozen. Mum, ever thoughtful, took each one to the jeweler to have it inscribed with my mount's name. At show jumping meets I might win $50 or more at a crack, and I spent every penny on Spider—a new rug or bridle, a fresh set of bandages.

I was fiercely competitive but not a bad loser; Mum taught me that from the start. I'd find solace in a bag of crisps and a can of Coke, and my consolation prize if I got one, and on to the next show. I never blamed my ponies. When I fell short, I figured it was probably my fault.

My high-water mark came when I qualified in working hunter pony for Peterborough, a British championship. It was a huge coup just to get there, and I knew I had a strong shot to win, for I had been facing and beating the same girls all season long. The grand champions would go on to the Royal International Horse Show, my dream of dreams.

Two weeks before Peterborough, I was playing bicycle tag with Jane around the farm. One of us would coast off and hide, while the other counted to fifty before setting off to chase her. The sun had sunk low that summer afternoon, and I'd been stuck with the little bike all day. Since I'd grown as tall as my big sister by then, I thought it only fair that we swap. But Jane refused to cede the larger bike, and I pedaled off in a grump.

In my pique I'd put on speed by the time I swung round a corner on the gravel drive. I didn't see the newly pegged string of barbed wire, planted to keep the cows from straying, until I was on top of it. I skidded straight through the barbs, chest-high, and it was the most extraordinary feeling; I felt like I'd been sliced in two.

I walked my little bike down the hill to the house, the blood seeping through my shirt. I went into the study; my mother was chatting away on the phone, her back to the door. "Mum, I think I've cut myself," I said.

Mum turned around and told her friend she would call back, as if nothing were amiss, and then she said, "Okay, we better go to the doctor now." I was taken by her calm. I got in the car, on Dads's knee, holding on to his thumb, and I nearly broke it on the way when the pain came through.

Mum said my screaming in the doctor's office, as they cleaned me and sewed me up, was worse than anything for her—it was so high-pitched, I was in such hurt.

For me it was a double blow. I couldn't ride at Peterborough, which crushed me. I had been so proud, and Mum and Dads and Jane were all coming to watch. Dads had bought a new horse box for us to camp in—a real family occasion. I was bringing us all together, getting everyone's approval. Doing just what I was supposed to do. Until I had failed us all, again.

Worse yet, my poor twelve-year-old's chest had been gashed to smithereens; I still have the scars.

By the following year I had outgrown game little Herbert, and we sold him for three times what we'd paid; we could not afford to keep him. I hated our parting—he was my friend, you see, and I had few enough of those.

I would never forget the day I rode into the barbed wire. But what I'd recollect most vividly in years to come, as my family scattered to the edges of the globe, wasn't the pain, or the doctor's stitches past counting, or even the disappointment of my missed chance at Peterborough. What I'd remember the clearest was sitting on Dads's knee, squeezing his thumb for all I was worth. And wondering whether life would ever be right again.

It was one of the last times I would see Mum and Dads together.

2

Green Socks
and Mockery

*T*hat next summer, in 1972, my parents flew out on holiday to the Ionian island of Corfu. There Mum met an Argentinean named Hector Barrantes, and the ensuing quake would rattle Dummer Down and the lives of all who lived there.

A onetime rugby star and Golden Gloves heavyweight, Hector was an eight-goal player at polo, one of the very best in the world. He was large and round and powerful—"a great bear of a man who used polo sticks like telegraph poles," as his patron, Lord Vestey, once put it. They called him *El Gordo,* "The Fat Man." But when he got on a horse he lost fifty pounds, he rode with such touch and finesse.

At that time, Hector was also a terribly lonely man; he had recently lost his wife, eight months pregnant, in a car wreck. When he met my mother they connected with the power of things preordained. At summer's end my parents came home together, but also apart.

Mum was ripe for a big change—I had seen it building in

her for some time. She'd been groomed as a perfect Lady of the Shires, with a tyrannically strict upbringing; a limited education, followed by secretarial school; a debut before the Queen at Buckingham Palace; a marriage months later, at the tender age of eighteen. She was the liveliest, most vivacious of girls, but fifteen years later she had been ground down by a foundering marriage, by a husband who'd been gone too often and strayed too far. I never heard my parents argue— Mum was never unhappy like that. Only there would be fewer of her sunbeam smiles and more and more of her time spent riding, out of the house.

She organized one last family Christmas, complete with paper hats and crackers and much contrived jollity. Soon thereafter she began shuttling to London, where my family owned a small house in Chelsea, and to trips with Hector. By the following autumn she would move out of Dummer for good.

In the meantime, I had my own transition—and trauma— to deal with. To that point I'd been sheltered at Daneshill School, with close friends I still claim today. Claire and Lulu called me "Ginge," but I was known generally as "Fergie," the less than delicate nickname first attached to my grandfather. I was the ringleader, scattershot and untamed; my hair was all over the place, and I always had on the wrong-colored jersey. But Daneshill was a forgiving place with a loving headmistress in Miss Vallence, and I thrived there.

When it came time to pick a senior school for me in the fall of 1972, Daneshill was closing down. My parents settled on nearby Hurst Lodge in Sunningdale, where Jane was already enrolled. I was to be a weekly boarder, with weekends back at Dummer—and I was devastated. My friends had moved on to St. Mary's Wantage in Oxford, a much better school academically, and what was wrong with me that I hadn't been accepted?

Originally established as a ballet school, Hurst Lodge was still ruled by its diminutive, ancient, and absolutely intimidating founder, Doris Stainer, who was the actor Leslie Howard's sister. The school had a strong drama division, as well; Juliet Stephenson studied one form above me, and my best friend there was Florence Belmondo, daughter of Jean-Paul.

Never was a fish more out of water. I was a country girl, a sporting girl, a wild thing who loved fresh air and running free. And here I was plunked into a rambling old mansion in the middle of a town, with no grounds to speak of, pressed to keep pace with kid sophisticates from show business families. I used to run for miles, but now I never ran because the urban fumes choked me. I had always slept with my windows up, cocooned by layers of bedclothes, but here it wasn't safe to open windows at night, and so I parboiled in the bed and cursed the central heating.

Of the one hundred girls at Hurst Lodge, I was convinced, ninety-nine were more comely and competent than I. I was achingly self-conscious. My bottom was too wide by half, my freckled face absurdly spotty. "Just look at the state of me!" went my anguished refrain.

When you have an adolescent weight problem, ballet school is not quite the place to be. Hurst Lodge was populated by a colony of sylphlike creatures, impossibly slim and supple as they did their splits, with mirrors everywhere—and here came good old Fergie Form, bobbing along, wincing at her own reflection. It didn't help when I received the occasional chirpy letter from St. Mary's Wantage: "We're all here having fun, Fergie—what are you doing?"

Here is what I was doing, as my roommate Florence would

attest: I was eating too many pieces of toast and crying myself to sleep.

I lived for my weekends at Dummer, but these turned disappointing as well. It couldn't be nearly the same without
Mum, without her high standards and the fresh flowers she'd
arrange to make the farmhouse sparkle. It felt as though the
color had drained from our lives, as though we had gone from
Oz to Kansas.

Dads hired a series of housekeepers. There was one who
could be wonderfully funny but also very harsh. Put in charge
of my wardrobe, she bought nylon tights and heavy shirts
with wool in them, though I was allergic to both. I itched all
the time, for years, but no one listened. There were ghastly
skirts, too, with pleats that billowed out to make my hips look
even bigger. And I remember my first party and *needing* to
buy a dress in London, and getting one homemade out of
material from Basingstoke instead.

I wouldn't be the belle of that ball nor any others in those
days. I'd pour my heart out to sweet Florence, but she was
French and gorgeous and had the finest shoes and skirts—
how could she possibly understand?

When I brought my plaints home to Dummer, the house-
keeper would denounce me as too serious and having lost my
sense of humor. No part of me stood immune from her zeal
for reform. She even changed my handwriting; it wasn't
"right and proper," she declared, and proceeded to make it
rounder.

Predictably, I struck back. I shattered the peace of Dummer
Down—shouting and screaming, dashing upstairs and slamming my door. But mostly my rebellion found more passive
form: I ate, compulsively. The weekend menu at home had
suffered in Mum's absence; Dads's best recipe was scrambled eggs with cheese sauce. Moreover, my craving for sau-

sages had entered the toxic stage. I would load half a dozen into the Aga—they always smelled better cooking in that old oil-fueled stove. I'd have sausages for breakfast, for a snack at 11, then again after lunch, and at tea as well, when I'd round out the plate with white toast and butter and boiled eggs. I feasted alone at the scrubbed pine table in our country kitchen, drunk with food.

In my Daneshill years I had been a sturdy little girl, perfectly normal, but now I always felt fat and always wished I wasn't. I felt hideous and ugly, like some lump of a larva with no butterfly inside. I was certain no boy would glance twice at me.

By the time of my fourteenth birthday, Jane mostly steered clear of the glum scene at Dummer. After leaving school for secretarial college, she minded a shop for a time and lived with Mum in our house in Chelsea. Soon she would flee further still to marry Alex, the lanky tractor driver who'd once built our equitation school, and settle on his sheep ranch in Australia. She was crying out, I think, for the same missing sustenance as I. But where Jane fled as far as she could go, I burrowed in deeper, to hunt blindly—for what, I could not tell. My sister might be living in the outback of New South Wales, next door to snakes and lethal spiders, but it was hard to say which of us had landed in the stranger place. For I'd been shipwrecked with Dads on some alien isle, past the margins of any map known to us.

As Mum receded from his life, Dads became rather a recluse; there was his polo, of course, but not much else. In society he was often misread as reserved, even aloof, when in truth he was deceptively shy. For all of his can-do bluster, Dads was laced with insecurities. I knew that he'd had a brother, the favored son, a gifted artist who had died of food poisoning at the age of twelve and so become frozen in all his perfect potential. Dads couldn't possibly measure up, nor, it turned out, could he fill the spit-polished boots of his father, who'd served with Monty in World War II.

Though set in his ways, Dads had great generosity of heart; he was a deeply feeling person if you could only tap into it. He treated everyone with respect, social class notwithstanding, and wouldn't mind soiling his hands. If there were a problem with a pipe in the middle of a lake and the plumber announced he could go no further than his job description allowed, Dads would just roll up his trousers and wade in.

At a time when my own relationship with Mum seemed frail and sporadic, Dads never mentioned her in any but glowing terms—he owned not an ounce of bitterness. I was grateful for that and for how well he and Hector got on together in their polo summers here. I so respected the way he had dealt with Mum leaving, how brave he'd been about it all—how he ignored the scandalized whispers that hung heavy in the local air. I remember how smart he looked on special days in his Brooks Brothers suit. He stood out in any crowd of fathers—he was the coolest and best-looking by yards.

Dads could also be a major-league romantic. When I was a small child, he would flood me with birthday cards—not just from him and Mum, but also "signed" by the cat, the dog, the ponies, the house, the car. Now, at Hurst Lodge, the deluge came on Valentine's Day—cards posted to me from Birmingham and Glasgow and Manchester. Dads had mailed them ahead to friends to forward on to me. He wanted all the girls at school to think I had endless boyfriends—a far-fetched fancy, I thought, but delicious nonetheless.

Dads knew how I pined for Mum and all her small touches. One Christmas morning at Dummer after she'd left, he realized that nobody had done me a stocking. In honor of the driving test I'd just passed, he hustled off to the garage with a pillowcase and stuffed it full of sponges and antifreeze and Clean-Your-Windscreen-With-Anti-Fly-Repellent, with all the prices left on. Dropping the bundle at the foot of my bed, Dads grandly declared, "There's your stocking!" It was such a lovely thing, such a kind thing to do—Father Christmas had been via the garage!

But Dads was over his head as a single parent. I know firsthand the demands of that role, and I'm sure he felt totally boggled by it. He was a very, very tough father. I didn't mind so much that he made me do my own washing and ironing and the cooking of our dinner; the chores kept me well grounded, and I'm glad of that today. But it was more than just strictness with Dads. He had his own agenda, and if he didn't want to do something he'd dismiss it—the dark side of that integrity I'd admired. When my demands became a bore, he would call me selfish and spoiled, and—hated word —an "encumbrance." No daughter of his would get above herself, he'd vowed; he would keep me in my place. What Dads didn't see, couldn't see, was that I was hard-pressed to hold on to what tenuous place I had.

Like many fathers, Dads underrated the weight of his words. He didn't intend to put me down, for he was not a cruel man. His reproaches were born of fatigue and a leaden sadness, heavier still for being unspoken. But we are literal-minded as children. I looked up to my father completely, and so I took it on board that I was selfish and spoiled and an encumbrance to people when I was thirteen. I would never stop believing it, really—I received those hurtful words like doctrine, held on to them like faith.

In our friendlier moments, Dads raised me like a boy. When we weren't watching war movies together or setting off for a polo match, it was: Feed the animals, walk the dogs, get out in the air, change the car's oil and water. Dads liked it that I managed so well and rarely complained. He didn't realize how hard I worked to try and get it all right, how I never allowed myself to *be* myself: a fragile, painfully tentative teenage girl.

I had no social skills to speak of, no idea about which skirts required a petticoat underneath or what I should do at dances —how was I meant to dance with a man? As a weekly boarder I was betwixt and between, the out-of-touch commuter. At Hurst Lodge I felt backward next to the smart city girls, who went home on weekends to London. In Hampshire I was too infrequent a presence—and too lacking in confidence—to fit into the "right" set, the Ascot set, where Mum had starred for so long. I would stay at Dummer instead, playing hostess and dutiful son to my Dads.

Then there were the dreaded Female Questions. I knew less about anatomy than auto mechanics, and Dads was not one to be asked about the facts of life. He came straight from the old school: Keep a clean reputation, and don't do this and don't do that.

Oh, I led a gray life. Even my riding fell off. I didn't do it as properly as I used to; Mum's leaving stole much of the fun of it. As I got older, the iron nerve that had won all those pots in the jumping ring began to corrode. My one cell of hard confidence had left me.

I had so many fears then, whole constellations of them, but my oldest, strongest fear was of the dark. One night I woke up in a small terror. I crept out to the hallway, to Dads's room —which was very brave in itself, to hazard that bit of corridor in that very spooky house—and when I got there I found Dads in bed with a girlfriend. She promptly accused me of checking up on them, of knowing full well what was going on. It was untrue; I was just spooked and wanted my Dads.

I would remember that episode later on, when more formidable critics would hang me for premeditated malice in doing this or that, and I'd think to myself, *They have no idea what I'm about.* It wasn't only that I meant no one any harm—I *couldn't* premeditate, for I lived in a state of unconsciousness, of unexpressed fears and longings. I never knew what I was doing, not really. I was just stumbling along in the dark, hoping to last until morning.

The saving grace of that hellish era was my grandmother, the Honourable Doreen Wright—that dynamic, chain-smoking, fiercely loyal woman whom Jane and I knew as Grummy. Then well into her seventies, Grummy came to help look after me on weekends after Mum, her baby daughter, had left her "ex-son-in-law," as Grummy referred to him. People thought it was funny and strange that my grandmother kept coming to the farm. But she and Dads were very close, and she would allow no one—Mum included—to say a nasty word about him. It was as if she refused to acknowledge their separation; she had never given a divorce to her own husband, a leading entrepreneur in the steel industry, even after he'd gone off with another woman.

Unconditional love was a core principle for Grummy, and I was a prime beneficiary. She had been a hard, unyielding mother with Mum, and there still was no getting one over on her, but we could talk about anything, from religion to the Pill. When I got older she'd be okay with all my boyfriends, in contrast to Dads's stern disapproval. Because she never judged me, I confided in her freely, even let the real Sarah peep out now and then.

Like Mum, Grummy relished a good time. On Sunday

mornings we had two rituals: first the church service (for she was a great supporter of the Church of England), then a stop at the post office for sweets. Grummy held that God had a sense of humor and therefore we must always laugh—and laugh we did, like hyenas, until we'd break out into a little jig and laugh some more. But she also owned a great stillness about her. You could just put her in a chair and she would needlepoint away for hours, never demanding a thing. It was a comfort to me just to know she would be safe there.

From Grummy I learned the grace of life, the treasure of each moment; the importance of manners and the urgency of goodness; the prize of humility and the necessity of compassion. When I was feeling down and fat and lonely, she taught me to train my sights outward. Her favorite prayer was from St. Francis of Assisi: "Seek to love, not to be loved; seek to understand, not to be understood."

Slowly I did come to understand—that it was self-indulgent to sink into misery, that I must give to others to find my own happiness. "Don't always wish for more," she would tell me. That was Grummy's creed, a noble and enduring one—and a perfect tool for The Pleaser.

But St. Francis had his limits. He could inspire great deeds and lofty thoughts. But he could not help me find out who I was in those bitter, tear-stained days. Or, more crucially, what I was meant to do.

Late in 1973, Mum returned from a stay in Argentina with Hector, to see if she could live there for good. She came out to Dummer one weekend, and Jane and I could see the purpose in her stride, the way her legs moved in her brown velvet trousers. She walked straight into the drawing room to see

Dads and shut the door. My sister and I stood mute and rooted in the hallway, waiting on a decision we had no say in.

Suddenly the door wheeled open and Mum came back out, walking even faster, like someone making her escape. She was so caught up in her huge decision that she couldn't notice that we'd both just had our hair cut. She just left.

Not long after, my parents were divorced, and Mum went to live with Hector in Gloucestershire for the polo season. That summer she returned to our farmhouse one more time and told me, "I'm going, and I'm going to be with Hector." I was lying in my four-poster bed when she said it, and I thought, *Good, I'll get more Christmas presents.* I actually felt relieved. To my child's mind, the responsibility for Mum's happiness now fell onto Hector instead of me.

Mum asked me which bedroom I might like to move into after she had gone. She'd be glad to do it up for me. I chose a cozy, quirky upstairs room that followed the roof line, not a right angle in it, and that was fine.

"So you don't mind, then?" Mum asked me.

Seek to understand. . . . "No, no, it's perfect, that's great," I said, in full sincerity. Indeed, I didn't mind, because Hector did love her, and I got on well with him. And deep down I was relieved that Mum was happy. It would be easier all around. For the first time I could remember, I wouldn't have to worry about her. Years earlier, when she'd gone out to a dinner, I had left her a note saying, "Mummy, you are coming back, aren't you?" I suppose I had been thinking of a car crash, but maybe it was something vaguer and more ominous, even then.

I never felt anger toward Mum. I never stopped loving her. Abandonment is relative, and I would not risk losing what claims I had left. I could still cruise around with Mum to polo and smile at the sloe-eyed Argentine men and stay with her and Hector on some weekends. Though I wasn't sure she was definitely with *me,* because Hector came first, and you wouldn't want to be in the way. You had to be quiet for his siesta before the game. You had to be a good girl.

Mum and Hector were married a year later, and that was that.

My mind was anywhere but on studies in the summer of 1974. Mathematics eluded me, and I labored on my English but couldn't concentrate. "Although enthusiastic and anxious to please," my form mistress reported at the close of summer term, "Sarah has not yet learned to channel her energies in the right direction. Both work and behavior are erratic, and she needs to exercise greater control over both. . . ."

I was at loose ends, to be sure. Once I applied Super Glue to the seat of a teacher's chair—I'd long played the joker to get attention, to hide my shyness in the general laughter. But I was also earnest in my way. I had a brain in there, somewhere, had some teacher been willing to hunt for it and give me the attention I needed. I loved geography and history, particularly of the British kings. In one essay I considered whether the Royal Family was "necessary" or "a waste of money," and came down on the side of both monarchy and the pursuit of honest pleasure.

While the Royal Family might be expensive, I conceded, "without them who would we try and succeed for, who would give us hope? . . . We cannot cut out all our traditions. Life is to enjoy—we cannot be too depressing. . . ." For some reason I'd crossed out a paragraph at the end, one I might have restored had I foretold my future: "They are not too wealthy, and the money is used for clothes, etc., which are needed for a good example."

By autumn I had settled down—"Sarah is making much more effort in academic work"—and began to explore a new outlet: acting. I could throw my voice, throw my weight, pull any face you liked—I was good at losing myself in character, you see. In our production of *Alice in Wonderland,* I was typecast as the Queen of Hearts: lots of humor, big bottom.

If you are really good at pleasing people, if you put their concerns before your own, you can become quite the popular person. I'd absorbed Mum's sterling manners and Dads's brusque efficiency and Grummy's philosophy of St. Francis, to the point where I never had to examine *my* feelings, much less assert them. When Florence Belmondo wanted our room's window shut tight, I was quick to capitulate, even as I starved for oxygen: "Quite all right, whatever you say . . ." (Though I confess I would fling the window wide open as soon as dear Florence's breathing grew steady.)

After a thousand such concessions I was named prefect and then, in my fourth year at Hurst Lodge, I was voted head girl, the equivalent of class president. "I was so uncontrollable," I'd explain, in a typical put-down, "they *had* to make me head girl so I would start behaving." I was accountable for prayers and assembly, and to represent the student body in talks with the teachers. If a girl broke curfew, I was meant to turn her in, but I would not play the rat—I was too busy breaking rules myself. One thing I kept an eye on was any bullying at prep time; when I saw unfair play, I'd get angry and stop it.

Yet despite my apparent acceptance in school, I never felt I quite fit in. I was a piranha at tennis, as fast a swimmer as any, and center and captain of the school team in netball (a version of basketball without the backboard). Netball was my favorite—I thrived on team spirit, on belonging to a group. I kept the whole court running on attack and had a few good tricks defensively; you couldn't get past me very easily.

But games were an afterthought at Hurst Lodge, which would always be a temple for dance. I had superior control at ballet and was often put at bar one, to model for the rest, but it wasn't my top priority. One afternoon I had a netball match scheduled just after ballet class. I feared I wouldn't have time to change out of my tights and leotard, so I wore my gray gym shorts and white T-shirt, and my smart green rugby socks (sent from Mum) inside my pink ballet shoes.

Ballet is a form of huge discipline, first and last. I was making mockery—*mockery!*—and it was my poor luck that Doris Stainer herself stopped by to observe that day. Her eagle eyes lit upon me, and she said, "Miss Ferguson, would you please come with me?" We stepped through a squeaking door and into the corridor. The tiny doyenne craned her neck, the better for those steely pupils to bore into my own. *"Never,"* she hissed, with contained but unmistakable fury, "are you allowed to do ballet again!"

I would truly miss my ballet class, but when Doris Stainer passed sentence on such rank subversion, there could be no appeal.

Many years would have to pass before I could laugh at my green-sock fiasco. At the time it seemed the signature of a girl who lacked all confidence or discipline, who just didn't know which end was up.

"I am back at school," I wrote to a friend in March of 1976, "and for some reason I am feeling so dreadful and depressed (again!) . . . I am so longing to leave . . ." I went on to discuss some weekend plans at Eton and my "need of a boyfriend," and ended by apologizing three times for complaining ("Sorry to go on about this").

Two months later I left Hurst Lodge, for good, though without any sense of completion. I felt utterly aimless. I had no specific ambition, no notion of what to do next.

My classmates wondered about their head girl, too, if one sentiment scrawled in my yearbook was indicative: "So don't worry, Sarah, things are never as black as they seem."

I packed up and came home to Dummer. I found comfort in pushing my pony hard through the fields, riding for the freedom of it. When I was galloping, wholly in the moment, no one and nothing could catch me. I could even outrun my loneliness.

But you cannot gallop forever. On July 26, 1976, Dads hosted a wedding reception for Jane and Alex at the farmhouse. Mum came, of course, and everything was fine till the party was over, and those two women we loved so much had gone, and just Dads and I remained in the house. The caterers had left raspberry stains all over the kitchen floor, so we got down on our hands and knees to scrub the linoleum, and that's when I saw Dads crying for the first time in my life. I felt so sad and so sorry for him—it was a huge bond for us, that moment. I was all he had left.

I was sixteen years old, and that is when I let go the last shreds of my childhood, when I vowed to take care of my father, to stand by him come what may.

Shortly after the wedding, I set off on that time-honored interlude before I was meant to settle into humdrum respectability: the trip abroad. I had no idea what I would do in Argentina. My motive for going there was simple: I missed my mum. I wanted to see her, as any girl would, and I needed to see her in Argentina, to make her new world concrete for me.

They met me in Buenos Aires, and we drove three hundred miles southwest, across the great green prairie of the pampas, to Hector's farm outside a town called Trenque Lauquen. The air was pure and the sky unbroken; I could breathe again. I galloped world-class polo ponies and flirted with the gauchos, but most of all I went everywhere with Mum and Hector. I loved how they were together, how Mum had retrieved her magic.

I had adored Hector from the start; he was so warm and gentle with me, so large and cuddly, one of the first men I felt comfortable hugging. In Trenque Lauquen I came to really know him, to know how lucky Mum was. Hector was endearingly bright and funny—opinionated, to be sure, and intolerant of my less presentable boyfriends, but kind and intuitive as well.

Hector and I spent hours on his terrace, watching "the discothèque" move in, the thunderstorms rolling over the grassy plate of the pampas. As we listened to the rain—Hector had a corrugated iron roof put on his house, the better to hear that driving percussion—we'd talk on and on about anything, from politics to ponies. We'd share some wine and his cigarettes (I started smoking in Argentina), and laugh about our weight problems. It was just as Hector had told me at the start: "I'm not your father; I'm not your stepfather. I'm your friend."

After a five-month reprieve, it was back to England to sort out my future—or, more accurately, to find some respectable niche for my holding pattern. Dads announced that I would go to Winkfield Place, where I'd learn to fix flowers and cook a meal without ptomaine. Winkfield was one of those fashionable venues for up-and-coming Sloane Rangers, that well-connected set of smug, socially ambitious preppies. It was the perfect place to become the perfect young lady and hence the model trophy wife.

Well, I might not have known what I wanted to do, but I knew that I didn't want *that*. Though I craved Dads's approval, something in me recoiled. Some tiny voice inside peeped out that a "finishing school" was no place for a person who'd yet to find her starting gate. My heart was still on Buenos Aires time, in the land of open spaces and open minds. I felt positively antisocial. I was *different* from that—couldn't Dads see?

No, the poor man couldn't; I'd surpassed his understanding, not to mention his patience. He put his foot down, but with an option: I was bound either for Winkfield Place or secretarial school. One or the other, take it or leave it.

I took Queen's Secretarial College in South Kensington, the lesser of two evils, though not by much. I moved in with Aly Brown, my friend from Lowood days. She warned me that the course was a horror, and she wasn't joking. As soon as I cracked the textbook, I knew the next nine months would be intolerable; every boss in the sample readings was a man, every woman his good girl Friday, so ardent and willing that she practically wagged her tail. At Queen's the highest virtues were neatness and subservience. I was uneven on the first count, impossible on the second.

I would not conform. I copied off my neighbor's shorthand and cheated on my typing tests, and when I really got vexed I threw two of those antique pecking machines straight out the second-floor window and into a dumpster below. I'm surprised that I wasn't expelled.

Aly looked after me like a sister—without her I wouldn't have managed. She drove out to collect me each afternoon, and we'd sail into uproarious spoofs of my prim instructors.

But I was a hard one to keep afloat. I missed Mum and Hector terribly, felt down all the time.

I graduated in December 1977, with a reasonable typing speed and several fines for breaking typewriters. "Bright, bouncy redhead," went my final report, in a tone that could send you to strangle someone. "She's a bit slapdash. But she has initiative and personality, which she will use to her advantage when she gets older."

The bouncy redhead herself wasn't quite so optimistic. "What's the point," I wrote to my sister, Jane, "of going on?"

3

Fine Art and
Kedgeree

I entered the working world with a well-used Mini Clubman Estate, a boxy little car handed down from my stepgrandfather, and an allowance of $150 a month from Dads. I would mostly survive on what I earned and was proud of that, though it wouldn't be easy.

I took a temp job at a flat-sharing agency before hiring on as a secretary to Neil Durden-Smith, a friend of Dads's, at his public relations firm in Knightsbridge. My starting salary: $6,000 a year. I hurled myself into the whirl of London, into the wine bars and restaurants and music clubs—and into the dating game that threw me for a loop.

I look around today and see how eighteen-year-olds manage their affairs of the heart, and they seem so grown-up by comparison. I was so naïve, so uncertain. I had no idea what I was doing or how I should be doing it. Shall I ring him today or ring him tomorrow? Will he ever ring me again? Should we go to the Italian place or the French bistro? To the reggae bar or the disco? *What was right?* I'd get poleaxed by indecision, unable to do anything without three outside opinions—begging for reassurance, trusting none of it.

Who would give me the time and care to help show me the way? Mum wasn't there and Dads was too busy. By then he had remarried, to a wise and gentle woman, and I rang my stepmother, Susan, about five times a day. Until Dads would get exasperated and tell me I was being a bore.

I would be always, always fretting so much that I had upset people. That if I *didn't* go to dinner I'd be unpopular, and then I would have no friends. My whole life had been a beauty contest, and though I knew I had no shot at winning, I could still be Miss Congeniality. But only if I never tripped up. Only if I never frowned once.

As a result I was immensely popular—can you imagine how many friends I had? Of *course* I was popular; I was all things to all men. (Except when it came to bedding down, where I was most conservative, having swallowed Dads's warnings about a Nice Girl's Reputation.) I catered totally to their demands, their interests—which wasn't so hard, since I would have been hard-pressed to name my own. I ran an approval-seeking marathon. I wanted everybody to love me, I suppose. I was crying out for love.

Of course it blew up in my face. I was trying too hard. I understood no limits, no boundary between the *me* and the *you*. I would inundate people with my neediness—suffocate them, really. No reasonable man could stand it, and so he would run away, or go chase after someone with more self-respect. I set myself up for rejection and got permanently hurt and stunted.

At cocktail parties I was great fun—completely wild, playing the fool, wanting to make people laugh. But I hated those convivial evenings. People would be saying, "Great party," and I would think, *What is a great party?* I didn't know what "fun" was, didn't grasp the concept—it was like Sanskrit to me.

Finally I found a real boyfriend, a man a few years older who worked in the City, London's financial district. He brought me into a new social set, and I loved him very much. But he was also full of teasing, which I would feign to chuckle off, though I'd be injured to the quick. It was always good fun to tease good old Fergie, she would laugh and bounce back. It was the only way to deal with her, to fend off her smothering. To keep her at a safe distance.

I worked hard and played hard, five days a week, and then I'd load the Mini Clubman with dirty laundry and drive home to Dummer for the weekend, away from London's smoke and stress. To switch off and smell clean air and find some peace.

*I*n 1980 I dropped everything and set off with my good friend Charlotte Eden on another New World journey. We stopped first to see Mum and Hector and plant cedar trees at El Pucara, their new ranch, then set off on a two-week bus trip: to São Paulo, Guaíra—the site of the largest volume of falling water in the world, where Charlotte and I spent the night on a bench—and finally Rio de Janeiro. In that great sprawling city I got my first brush with real poverty. The sight of so many homeless children unsettled me. One day, I thought, in the formless way of the young, I would do something about it.

From Brazil we flew to San Francisco. We had next to no funds, and Dads didn't believe in credit cards for young women. After a few hours of sleep in a bus station, we reached Squaw Valley in the high Sierras, flat broke.

To raise money to keep going, Charlotte and I put our energies to work. From 6 to 10 A.M. we cleaned the urinals and lavatories at our youth hostel. From 10 A.M. to 4 P.M. we served as human chairlifts, carrying disabled children up the mountain and skiing down with them, then up again. And from 4 to 10 P.M. we toiled in the local strudel house, making apple strudel and hot chocolate and swabbing down the machines. The lifestyle had its drawbacks—I got hugely fat from eating strudels—but after six weeks we'd raised $600 apiece.

Much later, when I would travel in comfort and be grateful for it, nothing rankled me more than when the tabloids made me out as some inveterate food fighter, a thrower of buns. That was not me. I would not do that sort of thing, for I knew firsthand what hard work it was to clean up after people.

Our earnings took Charlotte and me by bus to the Grand Canyon, to New Orleans, and finally to Palm Beach, Florida, where Hector and Mum had polo friends. Wanderings done, we went to play tennis at one of those exclusive clubs, and I remember Charlotte and me watching a men's doubles game on the next court and cackling at how absurdly funny everything seemed in Palm Beach after months of Greyhound bus stations.

Then I stepped on a tennis ball and broke my ankle. The men I'd been laughing at had to ferry me off the court.

Which was something to consider: I had passed through all those bus shelters at four in the morning, and no harm had ever come to me. I'd spent hours next to the rootless and indigent, and they were honest within themselves and looked down on nobody. It wasn't pretty in those shelters, and I was eager to escape them, but every day was real there—the world made sense to me.

Then I got to Palm Beach, where I was perfectly protected

—bathed in luxury, back under the wing of our suitable contacts. And everything seemed unreal, out of whack, and I felt so disconnected that I landed in a cast.

If I had been inclined to read below the surface of things, I might have wondered just where I belonged.

After six months abroad, I returned to London to make my way. Everyone assumed I would have my own flat, like other girls from my background with rich-enough families. But our family's house in Chelsea had since been sold, and I rented a room for $50 a week from Carolyn Beckwith-Smith. The two of us shared a small two-bedroom south of the Thames. Once a solid working-class district, Clapham had been invaded by the white-collar types who were priced out of Chelsea or Belgravia; it was dotted with fabric shops and sidewalk cafes. But the neighborhood remained "on the wrong side of the river," and muggings were common. We lived on Lavender Hill, near a graveyard, and it unnerved me whenever I parked next to it.

Number 40 Lavender Gardens was a nondescript brick townhouse like thousands of others in southwest London. I had a single bed and a chest of drawers, and a bathroom around the corner, and that was it. But I also had Carolyn, my best friend, my guardian angel. She had the patience of Job, and every day she'd listen to my problems, which were as legion and twisted as ever—I might have seen a fair swath of the world, but still I was far from worldly.

I needed to find work but detested going through an agency; they would test you first for typing and shorthand, where my skills could not pass muster. It was frustrating, because I knew I could bluff my way into a job and manage, if only I could get around the test.

Then I saw a listing for a personal assistant at an art gallery in Covent Garden: "Twenty-eight and over apply." I rang up and said, "I am not twenty-eight, I am twenty-one and you need me. I know I'm perfect for this job, and I am coming down for an interview." Such amazing boldness—I seemed so confident and strong that they hired me on the spot. It was a lesson I'd keep resisting—that when I went after what I wanted, I could indeed make myself happy.

My new boss was a lanky perfectionist named Bill Drummond, and his high standards made the gallery a wonderful place, with its rich wooden floors and serene music for background. Like Hector, he really *talked* to me; he'd launch into long and passionate discussions about art and its relationship to the environment in which the artist worked. Bill was wonderfully witty as well, alive to the gossip that resides in a painting. He opened my eyes to look at pictures in a different way, to take in the wealth of color and form in the world.

I must have done a good job as I stayed on for four years. I should have had a great time, but I couldn't really enjoy myself, couldn't quite relax. Deep in the sanctum of myself, I knew I was letting someone down. Most of my friends were account executives or some such, so I had to be falling short in Dads's eyes. (Now I think he was quite proud of me, though he never would show it.) And though I worked so hard to please my boss, I chronically worried that I had bungled some invoice or muffed a press release. It was ridiculous, really, but I couldn't help myself. I didn't realize that *everybody* "cheats"—that when people write a press release they probably get five other people to help them and still take the credit without a second thought.

Later on, when I became an instant celebrity and the press

rushed to compile my thumbnail biography, my boss from another job I'd held briefly would wax on about how competent I had been, how I "wasn't afraid of anybody" and was remarkably "up front."

In truth I feared everyone and their shadows. I lived in chronic fear—but I knew I must take a deep breath and *get on with it*. I might hyperventilate, but I would cope.

I worked like a fiend for that gallery, running late all the time, gulping black coffee like spring water. (The Mini Clubman had expired of natural causes, and I had bought myself a similarly decrepit Volkswagen and finally a more reliable used BMW.) I ate on the run—Carolyn and I were always dieting, at least when we weren't bingeing. Once she'd been on fruit for six weeks and was finally allowed a bit of chicken. When I came home that evening and opened the fridge, there it was: a tasty little drumstick on a dish. Not realizing this was Carolyn's big night, I devoured it. Carolyn absolutely freaked out when she found it was gone—we nearly fell out right there over that chicken leg.

I had horrific migraines, aggravated no doubt by the stress of juggling my meager finances. Though I took a second job on Saturdays, as a salesperson in a maternity shop, my ends barely met. I piled up parking tickets by the handful—I was rushing around, no time to check the meters—and there was no way I could pay them off *and* cover my share of the phone bill. Some mornings there would be a knock on the door from the Parking Gestapo—*Is Miss Ferguson in, please? We have a summons for her*—and I'd say, "No, I'm sorry sir, she's gone to work," and ease the door shut on them.

What money I had went toward tanning salons, restaurants, and jazz bars. I loved to be bathed in sound and rhythm, though I was an inhibited dancer, thinking that everyone was watching me and they must think I looked stupid. There was very little cash left for my wardrobe, which was definitely bohemian, sort of upscale Salvation Army. I had my trusty beige boots (Aly's rejects) and a well-cut man's dinner jacket from an antique shop, which I'd wear every day. I refurbished a couple of secondhand skirts—I'd rescued them from a friend's dustbin on their way to the trash, sewed up the cigarette marks, and they were fine. I never had any "outfits"; I just pulled things together.

I could brush up quite nicely if I wanted to, however, with clothes lent by my angelic stepmother. And some brushing up was called for whenever I got hooked into that notorious Sloane Ranger preserve: the shooting weekend in the country.

The Sloanes are quite an astounding species—they will give our future anthropologists a run for their money. What makes them special and distinct is that they think they are *frightfully* upper class when actually they are not, and so they must try harder than those at the very top. (The Court at Buckingham Palace is full of them, but more on that later.) They all went to the same boarding schools, where little Muffy and Daphne played *frightfully* well together and became lifelong *chums,* or *muckers.* Their dress code was rigid, if eccentric: Laura Ashley shirts, with a frill up top and pearls over the frill; a *cardy* over the shoulders; tweedy skirts, trailing down near the calf; navy blue tights; practical shoes without heels. Slightly scruffy, in other words, but expensive.

Sloanes have the most riotous nicknames, and especially the males of the species, with their *spiffing* sense of humor. A man with a red face would be Pinky (also applied to anyone whose surname was Salmon). Dads would be called Perky, because he was always pale. A man named Roger Marsh was invariably Swampy; a Freddie Gosling would answer to Quack-Quack.

The shooting weekend would start on Friday with, "Are you getting a lift down with Henry?" And you would get a lift down to the country house that afternoon, where you'd been invited to stay because Camilla's Mummy and Daddy were giving a little dance on Saturday night.

You'd be offered a "G and T" on arrival—"Would you like to take your drink up to your bath with you?" After that you would change for dinner, but it was *frightfully* relaxed on Friday night, just trousers or a skirt and a shirt. Then it was, "Would you like breakfast in your room or will you be down with the boys?"

After Saturday breakfast would come the challenge that separated the more precious Lady Sloanes from the unvarnished manhunters: "Will you be going out with the guns?" If you'd resolved to bite the bullet, as it were, you would pull on your corduroys and your green Wellington boots, and you would stand in the pouring rain for hours—that was the thing to be done. Then back to the house for a glass of sherry before lunch, to ward off the grippe, and then if you were *really* after the man, you would follow the guns out again, to watch the sky rain dead pheasants.

Back to the house for tea, then perhaps a bit of *telly*—it would be rather jolly to watch *Blind Date,* or something like that. Then you'd go upstairs for a bath, and another G and T, and you would put on your long dress for Camilla's dance.

For Sunday breakfast, at which you'd be dreadfully but comically hung over, you would be treated to a lovely plate of kedgeree, an ensemble of rice and eggs and cream and fish all mixed together—it would be *awfully* good, thanks to the leftover salmon from dinner. Then it would be off for a morning constitutional and some fresh air before you drank your Bloody Mary over the Sunday papers. You'd pretend to be frightfully intelligent and digest *The Sunday Times* when you hadn't the foggiest idea of what you were reading. (If no one was watching, you might steal a glance at *News of the World*, Mummy and Daddy's grown-up equivalent of the comics.)

"Would you like another *Bloody* before lunch?" You would have a *huge* lunch, eat far too much, before you all piled in to drive back to London with Henry in his car. And on Monday you'd recount the lurid events to your office chums, with a long-suffering but good-natured air: "It was frightful, I can't tell you what a bore, it rained the entire day and then my dog Tiddle picked up the wrong birds!"

I confess to having spent weekends just like that one and coming back for more. And it was easy for those awful thumbnails to whittle and wedge me into the Sloanes' box: right breeding, right schooling, proper horsey background—"Tallyho with Fergie and her jolly japes," and all that. But the truth was just the opposite, much to Dads's chagrin. (Though my father was a nonconformist himself, he would have swooned in relief had I only come out at the Debutante Ball.) My attitude was all wrong. I didn't grasp the rules, and even when they were put to me, they simply made no sense.

After one country weekend, I sent a thank-you gift to the lady of the house, a mixed flower arrangement that might have wreathed a racehorse. And the woman later told me, "You know, you really don't need to send a huge bunch of flowers—just a letter or a little posy is fine." She must have thought me terribly pretentious for a young person who was living on a thousand dollars a month, at most. But I wasn't meaning to be grand; I wanted her to like me and I just didn't understand. Unconscious, once again.

The fact was that I never got along with the real British Establishment. I had no patience for those arrogant twits who sat there with their fat tummies and pale faces and made huge whopping great statements on "foreigners" and "morality."

I never sought to gain entry into the "right" set. I had lots of different friends from different sets; I've always wanted a smorgasbord in life, not just a plate of kedgeree. I had Argentinean friends through Hector, and French friends through Florence Belmondo, and artist friends through Bill Drummond.

And I had friends, as well, from the fast lanes of the Swiss Alps and of international motorcar racing.

I first skied in Switzerland at the age of four, when I'd stand between my mother's legs and whoop for more speed as my own limbs bowed like india rubber. The next year I decided I could do it on my own and took off with my big sister. Jane skied like she rode, like a ballerina. But I would get down the mountain first—no cautious snowplow for me, just full-bore ahead from point A to point B. I was chuffed I could do it, proud to be following Mum, thrilled to be going so fast.

As I grew older and more contained—stuck in my stale room at Hurst Lodge, then clogged by the fumes of Clapham —I longed for the tonic of Verbier. I would go into debt to fly there, but it was worth it; I felt loose and free, as though I'd shed my coat. When I skimmed down the mountain's most perilous "black" runs, with the cold air alive on my cheeks and nose, I blew away the cobwebs of central heating and pollution. I felt clean again, from the inside out.

It was in Verbier, in 1982, that I found Paddy McNally. Some twenty years older than I, he had an immense chalet, referred to locally as "the castle," overlooking the town. He hosted a continual round of parties and business dinners, all with superb wine.

Paddy was probably Dads's worst nightmare: not the right age, not in the Household Cavalry, just a man named McNally in motor racing. *Here she goes again.* . . . But I loved Paddy for all the things he wasn't—for the phony graces he rejected, the airs he'd refused to put on, even after he had done quite well for himself. He had a sharp, practical mind, a large and open heart—he was just himself, straight down the line.

Paddy showed me a different way. He never strived for effect. And he took each day head-on, without flinching. He taught me to open my bank statements, even when I knew I had an overdraft.

Much of my time was spent with Paddy's two sons, Sean and Rollo, who were eleven and nine when we met up. Soon we were acting like family; I was their nanny and their friend. I took them to the slopes or the video store and helped put them to bed at night, and it felt good to be needed, to belong to people. Those children meant the world to me, and they taught me quite a lot, not least my need to toughen up. Boys of that age are always calling you strange names—fat or thin, ugly or smelly—and you gain ground when you stop taking it personally.

Through Paddy I also met Richard Burton, another urbane ex-racing driver who now published fine art books. In 1984, I left the gallery in Covent Garden to become Richard's acquisitions editor in London—a dream opportunity. Though my salary was never much (topping off at $18,000 a year), I was virtually my own boss. I could set my own hours and spent a lot of my time close to Richard's home base in Geneva.

Here, surely, were the basics for fulfillment: a creative job, with frequent travel; a mature man who cared about me; a widening circle of exciting friends. And yet . . . I lived each day with anxiety. I always thought Paddy was going to dump me and that to keep him I must be the perfect girlfriend. When he saw someone else or failed to call me, I could never bring myself to ask him, "Why did you do that?" I was terrified that he might turn around and say, "Well, okay, stuff you and I'm off!"

I worked so hard at being Paddy's ideal partner. I desperately wanted to marry him, though I never dared to broach the subject. Even as he kept saying, "I must do the decent thing," deep down I knew he didn't really want to get married. We were at such different times in our lives, but I was afraid to let the relationship go—to be on my own, in my void—and so I just carried on.

Yet I still sought *more,* still hoped that someone out there could give me what I needed. Not seeing that the incompletion lay most within myself.

4

"Just Keep Smiling"

Given Dads's polo connections, my orbit continued to inter-sect the Royal Family's every now and again. It was a normal part of my life, until I reached the age of self-consciousness and promptly got intimidated. I will never forget the first time I met the Prince of Wales at a Guards Polo Club drinks party. I was eighteen years old, and by the time Dads introduced us I was so fevered with anticipation that my tongue felt too big for my mouth. I'd had it all planned out; I would talk to Charles about the mountains, something a prince would find interesting. But now that he was *here,* in the flesh, I blurted out something about rabbits—totally and utterly opposite. I could have gratefully died at that moment. I wanted to vanish into the wall.

With Diana, whom I had known from adolescence, it was different. I ran into her a year before her wedding, during one of Charles's polo matches, when Diana was nineteen years old and still teaching kindergarten. Our mothers had been in

school together, where Mum and Frances held some legend-
ary burping competitions. Diana and I hit it off, and soon we
were lunching together once a week.

Diana invited me to her wedding, a very big deal, and
thoughtfully gave me some material to make up into a dress
—needless to say, I had nothing suitable in Clapham. I went
to the ceremony on my own, in a very big car. I walked up to
St. Paul's and in on my own—to Dome A, Row A, Seat 4—
and walked out the same way, nerves ringing at every step.
Diana's flatmates were all included for wedding "breakfast"
at the Palace, but I had not been invited. My feelings were
hurt—there was nothing like a grand occasion to make me
feel fat and unworthy.

I stayed close with Diana, kept having lunch with her each
week, though now I'd be zipping off from the gallery to see
her in Buckingham Palace. (On one occasion, Bill Drummond spied the safety pins on my cuffs and lent me his gold
cuff links.) I knew that Diana had very little social life. She
never went out, never did anything except to be adored. She
was (and is) the most beautiful, perfect princess. But perfection came at a cost, even for Diana. She was two years
younger than I, and I strove to support and protect her as I
would a younger sister—as I still do today, as a best friend.

It was only natural, then, that I'd get invited to the occasional cast-of-thousands dance at Windsor Castle—for Andrew's twenty-first birthday, for example, and later for
Edward's. But the big one came in the spring of 1985, when
I found a heavy bond envelope in our postal slot. It was from
Lieutenant-Colonel Sir Blair Stewart-Wilson, Deputy Master
of the Royal Household, requesting "the pleasure of your
company at the Queen's house party at Windsor Castle during the week of Royal Ascot."

Now I could make coffee nervous. Royal Ascot wasn't so

formal as in Mum's day, when each evening was a white-tie affair. But it required a real wardrobe—hats and gloves and real shoes and clothes that looked right together. My androgynous dinner jacket would be out of its league there. I was in a state; I didn't know what to do. I finally borrowed clothes from my ever-tolerant stepmother and had a few things stitched together.

I wasn't ready, I could *never* be ready for this, but here I came nonetheless.

On Tuesday morning, June 18, Paddy drove me the twenty miles to Windsor; he was like that, he would do anything for me that he could. A footman met us at the castle's private entrance, to take my luggage. A lady-in-waiting led me through a maze of corridors to my room, a major bit of exercise. We stopped at a suite in the Edward III Tower, to be met by this lovely, friendly young girl, a housemaid named Louise Penn. She shared a laugh with me, which I sorely needed. Then she helped me unpack and organized my clothes for pressing, a great luxury. Louise would take care of me the whole length of my stay—pointing me in the right direction, making sure my hat stayed on. I doubt I'd have made it through without her.

On my bedside table was a card embossed with the Queen's cypher, listing the four-day schedule of mealtimes, along with a seating plan for the day. For lunch I had been placed between a vice-admiral and Prince Andrew, then on leave from his duties on HMS *Brazen*. More jitters. I had seen Andrew on occasion since our childish games of tag, and one of those occasions had left me red-faced. We had been invited to the same weekend at Floors Castle, the regal home of the Duke and Duchess of Roxburghe. I'd felt out of my depth, and when I walked down to Sunday breakfast I silently cursed my heels as they squeaked over the wood floor.

I entered the dining room, into a load of men with their newspapers —"Morning! Morning!"—and I longed to sit down quickly with my half grapefruit and be ignored. I hurried toward a table with some newspapers, something I could hide behind . . . and there was Andrew, standing next to me. So much for safe havens! I was ultranervous now, and as he reached across the table to get a paper, I somehow thought he was leaning toward me for a good-morning kiss. So I gave him one, and he looked at me and said, "Oh, thank you very *much!*"

"Oh, I didn't mean to do that!" I cried, which he must have found quite hilarious. It honestly hadn't been deliberate, just another Fergie fiasco. And now, just my luck, I was seated almost on top of him, where I'd be at the mercy of his famous needling. (I had yet to suspect that matchmaker Diana had engineered this.)

I stepped into the Green Drawing Room at 12:45 on the dot for drinks. At 1 P.M. I took my place at a table long enough for shuffleboard: thirteen people on each side, one on each end. For the duration of the meal, conversation followed basic protocol; following the Queen's lead, the ladies would speak to the man on their right or their left, alternating with each course. When I turned to face Andrew, I was struck by how handsome he was in his morning suit, and soon my worries had flown. Andrew was easy, and I felt relaxed with him, for me a rare condition—even though I addressed him as "Sir," as per protocol.

We both knew the same idiot jokes; we both loved a good prank. When the chocolate profiteroles came around, I tried to pass—I was on a diet, as usual—but Andrew claimed that refusing them would be improper etiquette. Then, when it came time to take his portion, he refused—"No, thank you very much!"—and I indignantly swatted him on the shoulder with the back of my hand.

Out of such humble beginnings came a great and lasting friendship, one that endures today.

As I came to know Andrew that week, he seemed like a very charming, gentle giant who had sprung magically from the woodwork. Now a lamp shone into my forest, and I'd been rescued by this great-looking man with a blinding smile.

Small gifts began to flatter me in Clapham: a rose cut from the Palace garden, a romantic letter. Later that summer I was invited up to Balmoral: more terror. I hauled up my poor stepmother's wardrobe; I'd be changing three times a day, for lunch, tea, and dinner. Andrew was there with a friend, a girl, and I was anxious because Nigel Dempster's "Diary" in the *Daily Mail* had just noted my involvement with Paddy. Would Andrew write me off?

I took him aside and told him that I'd been going out with Paddy, and I hoped he didn't mind, and he said, "Why should I mind? I like you! I couldn't care less about that." That was a very good reaction, I thought. Here was a man taking me as I was, without prerequisites or conditions—who knew what *he* believed and didn't mind what others thought. Nor was I ever jealous at the gossip of Andrew with some other lady. He cared for me, and that was enough.

Our courtship was still mostly unspoken, but we got closer that week at Balmoral. I cast myself into Andrew's every pursuit. I gave him the same fervent support I had once lent to Paddy's business deals or to Dads's polo. I could be whatever Andrew wanted me to be—I was the chameleon queen! I would dazzle the assembly at lunch with my slapstick and then run up every hill, go out with the guns like a seasoned infantryman. I didn't shoot, but I was always out there, brimming with energy and gumption.

Today I would be less enthusiastic at such sport. My sympathies lie with the bird; I know what it is to be hunted. I couldn't have been so different back then, barely a decade ago—where was the *me* in all this? Where were my feelings? Did I stop and think about myself at all?

Of course I never did. I was still running on my treadmill, like Alice's rabbit, still speeding pell-mell for reasons lost and mysterious.

*A*s Andrew would acknowledge months later, on television, our romance was no "thunderbolt." It was more like a plant with good southern exposure: growing slowly, but thriving by the day. On occasion I would join him for dinner at the Palace; other times he would park his green Jaguar (protection officer included) outside 40 Lavender Gardens, and we'd dine in my tiny kitchen. The locale didn't matter as long as Andrew returned my phone calls, and he did, every time. He was constant. He showed *interest* in me—what a remarkable phenomenon!

At first it was hard to fathom that I was serving baked beans to the Sovereign's second son, but that distanced feeling soon passed. From a life lacking in all sureness and conviction, I began to feel confident of something huge: that I loved Andrew, and he loved me back. I was swept away and gave myself up to it, as to the ocean's surf. Here was this amazing person, who needn't compete with anyone for being a prince, and he wanted *me*. We played silly games; we acted like children together. We *liked* each other before we loved.

I had dinner with Paddy that autumn and broke it off. He

let me go freely and graciously—it was, I think, what he had hoped would come to pass. Because he felt that Andrew was a better man for me and that I should be with a younger person, who could give me what I needed.

In December of 1985, *Brazen* docked in the Port of London. Diana convinced me to come out with her to visit Andrew—brazen indeed, as the press was still blind to what was going on. (In fact, they would ignore me for some while longer; in their eyes, I probably wasn't Andrew's "type.") To make me feel stronger in my first public appearance with the Royal Family, Diana lent me a smart black-and-white checked coatdress. At one point, when the photographers were upon us, popping questions and clicking shutters, I looked over at my friend in befuddlement.

"Just keep smiling," Diana whispered.

And I did, as I would for long years to come. I always felt safe in mimicking Diana—she was so far ahead of me on the learning curve, such a deft ambassadress for Britain and the Royal Family. No situation fazed her. She gave no hint to me or anyone of the problems she shouldered at the time. (A bulimic must be highly secretive, so as not to be found out.) Diana simply went out each day and did an exceptional job in what people now realize was a most difficult position. I will always respect her for that.

When I lived in Clapham, Diana helped me by giving me all her shoes (and, less happily, her plantar warts)—we wore the same size. I tried to copy Diana's clothes, as I had Carolyn's before her. I thought Diana had all the answers.

For one who had so little sense of self, fashion was just another morass.

*   *   *

*F*or New Year's, Andrew invited me out to Sandringham, the Queen's private estate in Norfolk. We were getting serious, all right; a few weeks before, Andrew had asked me to address him by his first name. (For six months I had kept calling him "Sir," as per protocol, though more and more lightheartedly.)

Sandringham was my first time to be with "just the Family"—though the Royal Family, in all its genealogical extensions, could fill a small auditorium. I had been nervous before but never like this. I allowed four hours to make a ninety-minute trip—what if the car broke down or I ran out of petrol and was late? With two hours to kill, I stopped at a local pub and changed from my grubby driving clothes into something sort of smart. Then: Should I have a drink? What if they smelled it on me? But I needed something to soothe me, considered vodka (easiest on the breath), settled on a substantial gin and tonic.

Finally I set off for my firing squad. As my car pulled up the great drive, I had gravel fever—I wanted the gravel to be silent, so no one would know I had arrived. I hadn't worn a jersey despite the cold, and my fright had left sweat rings on my smart silk shirt, great parabolas of embarrassment.

Then Andrew staged his sneak attack. As I got out of my car, on that first crisp day of 1986, he said: "I love you." I felt like jumping back in the car and getting out again, because I knew what I wanted to answer but my tongue was knotted, and so I actually screamed. And when Andrew laughed in response, I just crumbled at the knees.

I still had to pass through the creaking front door. I still had to greet the Family in its gigantic drawing room. People were immediately charming, but I was the last arrival and the in jokes were flying, which made me feel even more the outsider. To this day I remember that bizarre, Martian sensation, and so I always make an effort to welcome people into a room, to be the first to extend my hand.

My entrance was suitably grand. No sooner had Andrew brought me a drink than I tripped over the piano leg and sent it splashing over the sofa. Then, as I curtseyed to the Queen, my boyfriend's mother, I kicked one of her dogs. It was a glancing blow, but corgis are a melodramatic breed, and you would have thought the little yapper was bound for the Royal Kennel in the sky.

My main concern was protocol. At bottom, protocol is simply good manners, what Mum taught me at home, no more and no less. You stand up when people come into the room and so forth. But that day the stakes were higher, the rules more complex. There seemed to be hundreds of people in that room, and it was a safe bet, or so I thought, that all were of nobler birth than the redhead from Clapham. I knew that one must curtsey to members of the Royal Family—and not with just a bob of the head, either, but as low as you could make it without bumping the coffee table or crashing to the floor.

Then there were the titles. Whom did I call Sir or Ma'am; who went by Lord or Lady; who could be addressed by their actual first names? When uncertain, I decided, it was better to err on the respectful side.

Whenever I went some place new, it wasn't enough for me just to smile and fit in like a normal person. I was that pathetic shy type who would compensate with noise and bustle. I could carry it off, so you'd think that I knew exactly what I was doing or wearing or saying and everything was fine. I was the life of every party, the house comedian—good old Fergie Form, she's a guinea a minute.

But inside the laughter dwelt my own worst critic, my hanging judge, the self-hating core of me.

Inside, good old Fergie was dying.

*I*n February I joined Charles and Diana at Klosters while Andrew was at sea. I was in my element. I knew everybody from past holidays there, and after years of skiing powder at Verbier I could get down the mountain faster than most men. Looking back, it must have been hell for Diana. She was going through one of her rough patches, didn't ski that well anyway, longed to stay inside—and there was rosy-cheeked Fergie, hearty to the last, always in crashing good form. I must have been maddening to her—especially after Charles prodded her (and not for the last time), "Why can't you be more like Fergie?"

As they say, you must be careful what you wish for, for someday you might get it.

Later that month, traveling under an assumed name, I met Andrew for a tryst at Floors Castle, the scene of my crime—where I'd first kissed him over the newspapers. As snow began to fall that night, I wasn't at all surprised to hear Andrew propose, and I accepted with all my heart, toasted our future with champagne. Yet at the same time I thought he must somehow be teasing, that he could not possibly mean it.

And so in the most romantic moment of my life, I looked the man I loved straight in the eye, and said: "If you wake up tomorrow morning, you can tell me it is all a huge joke." Whenever people promised me something, I always gave them an out, so they wouldn't feel trapped—never be a nag or a bore, as Dads said. I honestly didn't want Andrew to regret what must have been some reckless impulse.

Which is quite a large and sobering thing to look back at—that I had so little confidence, such a spindly sense of worth.

To his credit, Andrew held firm the next morning. As the Queen was on official tour in Asia, he couldn't get her permission for three weeks—a formality, but a real and legal one. In the meantime our engagement would be our intimate secret, to be shared with no one. I rather liked that; I was an inordinately private person, anyway, about matters close to my heart.

But true privacy, as I'd find upon my return to London, was but a memory. Ever since Sandringham the press had suspected that *something* was afoot between Andrew and me, and now the Fergie Beat was in full bloom. There were eight major tabloids in London, and it seemed that each one had put a photographer on my case, twenty-four hours a day.

Few can understand what it is like to be an ordinary private person and then, overnight, to plunge into a public life. There were no stages to the process; it happened abruptly, relentlessly. Those photographers lodged by my doorstep each evening. When I drove to my small office in Mayfair, I would be trailed by five or six cars and a motorbike or two. The journalists set upon my favorite coffee bar like urban anthropologists. They ferreted through my dustbin, found a sketch of my ruby engagement ring and reproduced it—did the same with some idle scrap of doodling. When I went to the Palace to see Andrew, I would park at the tradesmen's entrance and take the service lift up, quiet as a spy. And if I *really* needed to fool them, I would hide in a laundry basket in the boot of Carolyn's car, and she would take me where I needed to go.

But for the most part I didn't slink away from the press. I just went along. I took their attention in stride; I rather enjoyed it, actually. Remember, we are discussing a woman who lived with fear. I feared parking tickets and taking wrong turns, and most of all I feared the dark—I would sprint to my apartment at night with my shoes in one hand and my keys in the other, as weapons against lurking assailants. But now my world had changed. Now I could stop the car anytime and go back to a press person to ask for directions. Or I could park at night by that sinister cemetery and stroll home without a care, because all these people were with me. "You can wait out there for as long as you like," I would tell them, before shutting the front door, "but look after my car for me, please." Once I even came back out and served them coffee.

Besides, I had nothing to hide. I was just *me*—the country girl. And I'd fallen in love with this very sweet man who ate M&Ms off my table, and who happened to be a prince. I was a perfectly normal woman pitched into an extraordinary situation: the classic fairy tale.

In those giddy days leading up to my wedding, the press and I had much in common. We were both quite taken with this creation called Fergie. We both seemed to like her quite a bit, in fact.

And we were both quite ready to rip her to pieces, as soon as it came time to change the tune.

On March 15 the Queen gave Andrew her consent. Four days later—a delay which allowed the budget to go to the House of Commons and still get front-page play—our engagement was announced. I awoke with a withering migraine that day, but I perked up, on cue, for the BBC. With Andrew at my side, I felt at ease before the TV cameras. He taught me by example; I just watched him and then I jumped in.

From where I sit now, I was astoundingly naïve. I told the

interviewer that I'd keep working at my publishing job, of course. And how I would "cope" with all the new demands upon me. I could handle anything, because Andrew and I were a team, "a good team," and nothing could defeat us.

Fergiemania had exploded. When I walked that afternoon from my office to a nearby hotel, the herd nearly crushed a woman bystander into a railing. Policemen lined the street to keep some semblance of order. I had slept my last night in Lavender Gardens; my old routines would be too dicey now. The next morning I would wake up in Buckingham Palace, and Andrew's personal protection officer would drive me to work in my man's Jaguar, with a police car tight behind us. I had never felt so alive and open to adventure and yet so safe.

That feeling filled me up. It stilled all my yearning, left no room for discontent. I could neatly sidestep the obvious question, the one that would swell inside me like an aneurysm, till it nearly burst and did me in: *What on earth am I doing here?*

5

Through the
Looking Glass

Of the more than six hundred rooms at Buckingham Palace, my life would be contained in fewer than six of them. My new residence was Andrew's old bachelor quarters in the East Wing. I just moved in with him, though that was hardly the "done" thing. It was never an issue, which makes me think about how the Palace was run—that it could bend and ignore things when it cared to.

Our apartment was on the second floor, on a corridor that overlooked the chipped-stone quadrangle where I parked my car. The corridor was papered in green silk and carpeted in deep red, and it stretched so long that one could hardly see the end of it. It was lined with wardrobes and china cabinets and oils of British victories at sea. On each door was fixed a typed card within a brass holder, naming the royal residents therein.

The pervading atmosphere, wrote Ingrid Seward, "is that

of a gentleman's club on a wet afternoon; quiet, understated and slightly faded."

Inside our suite one found comparable ambiance. There were five rooms and two baths in a line, with interconnecting doors: a spacious railway flat, but hardly grandiose. The rooms were done with Victorian density, much the same as when Andrew had lived there alone and Charles before him: damask curtains, pleated lamp shades, bland carpeting, brownish wallpaper.

The exception to the color scheme was my dressing room, on one end, which Diana redid in pink and white when she briefly lived there. Of ordinary size, it was crammed with massive oak and rosewood wardrobes, a dressing table, and a large canopied bed. Next in line came the dining room, where we'd entertain guests at the long mahogany table or work at our separate desks. But when Andrew and I dined alone, we would move next door to the sitting room and set up at a small serving table by the television.

Finally there were Andrew's bedroom and dressing room, an absolute time warp. Dozens of stuffed animals blanketed the bed, while pink teddies hugged each other atop a lamp. Boys' guns and bachelor bits lay all over—and I accepted it all as it was. I didn't mind the weighty furniture, or the museum-piece clocks from the Royal Collection, or the sad electric fireplaces. I saw the apartment as a transitional perch before the proper home we would get for ourselves. Watch a movie, have a glass of wine, and don't worry over the sofa being green or pink. As one who'd never had her own flat, I wasn't used to taking over places and making great changes.

When you're in love, anything goes. Your field of vision is lit from within. Drab wallpaper did not matter; I put out my own throbbing glow. Our apartment faced out on the Queen Victoria Memorial—the "Wedding Cake"—and the Mall. It had a grand view of London: the City to the right, the West End to the left, bright flags and geranium beds dead ahead. Several times a week at 11:15 they would change the Guard. The clatter made phone calls impossible, and I'd just watch the show when I could and enjoy it. How amazing to be seeing it from inside out, from here within the Palace, the place I now called home.

Over the four months that led up to our wedding, I swept along with the tide. Every person I met seemed powerful to me: the ladies-in-waiting, the protection men, even the housemaids. I figured they must know what to do, as they'd all been at it much longer than I. I followed their advice without question—wouldn't that be the way to please them, to win their acceptance?

Most of all, I looked to Andrew. My first official engagement came in April—Daffodil Day, the Queen's birthday. I was slightly panicked and moaned to Andrew, "What do I say, what do I do?" And Andrew, who was trained for this from birth, simply said, "You will learn."

And I learned! I had no idea what to do but I did it: *I can manage, fine, I will be on the balcony, right, here I am on the balcony*—Fergie thrived on challenges, everyone knew that. I stood on that Palace balcony—the massed faces blurred below me, my spectacular almost-in-laws all around me— and I watched Diana, and I smiled very bravely and waved very gingerly. Good technique for the royal wave, I deduced, was like screwing a lightbulb. It was all in the wrist.

I was wearing the famous Fergie bow in my hair and a handsome suit. Unfortunately, the day had turned hot, which meant my hair curled up like Little Orphan Annie's, and my fearsome sweat rings spread like lava. Plus I had a banana bow at the back, which emphasized my bottom—self-sabotage at its finest, there. And soon my inner voices lost their cool élan: *Wave, don't wave? Oh my gosh, Andrew, what did I just do? Has anyone noticed I don't really belong here?*

When they let me off I dashed away to ring up Dads, to find out if he'd seen me on television.

In the end it was fine because Andrew was there, and I just loved him totally and completely and utterly adored him. There was no coyness in me, no holding back. You could see it in my face in the photographs he took of me, when my eyes would open wider than for anyone else.

Andrew was my knight, my brilliant one—he had come and saved me from unhappiness. For the first time in my life I felt secure; I didn't have to fret about the phone bill. I had Andrew to help me, and he was like a rock. Someone like me needs a rock, to stay firm and consistent when the gales blow through.

Andrew lived in London that year, for officer training at Greenwich, and so I saw him all the time. I couldn't understand couples who were getting divorced or separated. For that matter, I couldn't see how my friends survived their husbands' two-day business trips—didn't they miss their men desperately? Nothing could take me away from Andrew. "No one will ever part us," I insisted over and over in public.

No one will ever *part us,* I told my inner skeptic a thousand times.

Though in the end, of course, we let them do just that.

*I*t was around this time that the newspapers began to refer to me as "the breath of fresh air." They couldn't get enough of this fabrication called Fergie; I even got my own wax effigy at Madame Tussaud's. (At the unveiling, a less than chivalrous journalist hurdled the rope with a tape measure, then shouted out the size of my hips.) A tour company led walking lectures, at up to $15.00 a pop, to my Mayfair office, the coffee shop I'd patronized, the jeweler's that had fashioned my engagement ring.

The tabloids treated me as though I were the greatest thing since sliced bread—or at least since Diana came around. They praised my humor and lack of airs, my resolve to stay at my job, my loyalty to old friends, my old clothes, even my old figure—no crash diets for me, I'd vowed.

At twenty-six years old, I was incredibly gullible and naïve. I understood nothing. I lived on the surface of things. Worst of all, I believed my own press. I believed it when they said I was a wonderful, fresh, clean page for the Royal Family—that "great-fun Fergie" would sponge away the mildew, like some Mary Poppins crossed with Cinderella. I *needed* to believe it, because for so long I had feared I was no one at all, and how could a no one ever be loved, much less marry a prince? The newspapers crafted me a persona, and I confused it with identity.

A more secure person might have glimpsed what the press was about. Once, when I still lived in Clapham and my car had broken down, I took a suitcase full of dirty laundry on the train Friday night, to be washed and ironed in Dummer —by myself, I might add. And the newspapers announced, FERGIE MOVES IN WITH ANDREW FOR THE WEEKEND. Now here was a puzzlement. They had categorically said I was spending the weekend with Andrew, and I was categorically going home with my dirty washing. I should have worked it out then and there, put the press in its place. But I just laughed it off instead. No harm done, after all.

* * *

On July 15, a week before the wedding, Andrew had his stag night at Aubrey House with the likes of Elton John and Sir David Frost. I desperately wanted to gate-crash, but the fortress was impregnable: high wall, single entrance, guards with major biceps—no go.

As a fallback, Diana and I staged a hen night. With a few coconspirators in tow, we donned gray wigs and dressed up in authentic policewoman outfits, down to our regulation dark stockings and lace-up shoes. After assembling just outside the Palace, we pretended to arrest one of our friends (chosen for her fabulous legs), who was playing the promiscuous lady.

The duty police at the gates thought this very strange. They called out the parks police, who proceeded to arrest the lot of us—even our protection officer, who played along—for causing a scene outside Buckingham Palace. They ushered us through some barriers and into their police van, and this was the worst part, because the other women slid slimly between the barriers, but I got wedged at the hip.

Diana and I had no intention of resisting. We thought it hysterically funny. We'd turned our engagement rings wrong side around, and it had worked, they hadn't recognized us.

After the van drove off and we sat down like little convicts, Diana asked the driver what kind of crisps he had on board and would he share them, please? Soon she was chomping away at these smoky bacon-flavored crisps. By the time we reached the end of the Mall, our cover must have worn thin —we heard one of the policemen say, "Oh my heavens, it's the Princess of Wales in drag!"

We got the van to drop us off near Annabel's, the big nightclub in Berkeley Square. And the people at the door said, "Sorry, we don't allow policewomen in here, it is a place for

Mum and Dad at their
wedding in 1956—
the Life Guards officer
and the perfect lady.

Above: For Dads (striking the ball,
at right), polo was a great love—
and how we made the royal
family's acquaintance.

Dads receives a polo
prize from the Queen,
Smith's Lawn, Windsor
Great Park.

My red curls resisted
management from the start.

My first horse show.

At the seaside, two years old.

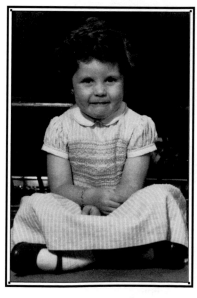

My determined look.

As a child, I strived to be the kindest, the most clever and the most able.

Jane (left) was my big sister and best friend.

Jane (right) was more elegant on skis, but I'd be first down the mountain.

Passing time at a polo match at Smith's Lawn, where the children would often play tag. From left, me, Andrew, Jane, the Queen, Edward and Sarah Armstrong-Jones. Andrew and I were ten years old at the time.

Taking my leap of faith with Herbert, the naughtiest of ponies; he would misbehave with everyone but me.

Spider always came through for me in the ring; he never met a fence he would not jump.

At Daneshill, school photograph day. The usual suspect forgot to wear her official jersey. Also in the picture are two girls who remain among my best friends. On my left in the photograph, Clare Westworth-Stanley, and second from left at the front, Lulu Hutley.

Mum flanked by her two daughters, with Jane on the right. My mother was absolutely brilliant, the most zestful person I've ever met.

At Jane's wedding, with fellow bridesmaid, my first cousin Venetia Salmond.

Jane's wedding party, in front of our home at Dummer Down. When she moved to Australia, I felt that I was all that Dads had left.

By the age of nineteen I'd established a lifelong rhythm; work hard, play hard.

On my twenty-first birthday I tried to look the part, but Dads was a knockout in his Brooks Brothers suit.

With Diana at Smith's Lawn. Friends as teenagers, we'd later support each other.

With my man in Klosters, Switzerland.

Nothing could ever drive Andrew and me apart—
or so I was convinced at the time.

Opposite: The slimmed-down
bride with her astoundingly
handsome groom.

Fergiemania strikes! On March 20th, 1986, the day before our engagement was announced, I was surrounded by the press outside the Mayfair office where I worked.

Our wedding day was filled with pomp, but I missed
out on several little things that meant so much.

When Andrew took my picture, my eyes opened wider than for anyone else.

Royal Ascot, June 1986, where hats got more notice than horses.

No one could ever fault us for lack of enthusiasm on our 1987 Canadian tour, whether dressing Western in Calgary or fighting claustrophobia at a gold mine in Yellowknife.

On our 1987 canoe trip in Canada's Northwest Territories, the toughest physical endurance test of my life.

By the time I toured Australia in 1988, the press went out of its way to make me look awkward.

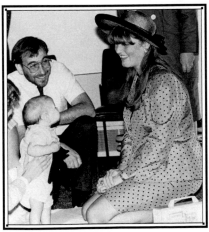

Meeting a baby in Canberra—it made me miss Beatrice, back in England, all the more.

I learned to fly so as to share even more of Andrew's life—and wound up loving the freedom of it.

At Amanda Knatchbull's wedding with three royal brothers:
Andrew, Charles and Edward.

everyone to enjoy themselves." We coaxed our way in and pushed on to the bar—where whom did we find on their working night out but some eagle-eyed executives with the *Daily Mail*. We stood there shoulder to shoulder with them —ordered a round of orange juice, drank it down—and still they didn't cotton on.

Going out, we stopped traffic in Berkeley Square—we were having a wild time now—and headed back to the Palace near two o'clock in the morning. Knowing that Andrew was due home from his own little revelry, we told the duty police to get out of the way—and then we closed the gates. As it turned out, Andrew had just phoned from his car in advance of his arrival. When he saw the shut gates, he properly took it as a sign that something was very wrong. He flicked on his car locks, rammed the Jaguar into reverse, and screeched out around the Wedding Cake. He thought he was being set up.

It was about then that I wondered if we had gone a bit too far.

The morning after found me at breakfast with Mrs. Runcie, the wife of the Archbishop of Canterbury, who was to marry us. I could hardly see straight; I just barely made it through. (I do adore the Runcies; they've both been of such great support to me.)

Later I confessed our hen night to the Queen, and she thought it was reasonably amusing. We had got away with it clean—I'd been as naughty as I could be, and still I was adored by all. They were playing flush into my complex. I was wonderfully, extravagantly, madly brilliant. I could shoot a stag and hook a trout, and dance to *Swan Lake* in my wellies for good measure. I could do no wrong.

Even madly brilliant people have their detractors, granted. Jean Rook of the *Daily Express* called me "an unbrushed red setter struggling to get out of a hand-knitted potato sack."

While the "First Lady of Fleet Street" wasn't alone in faulting my fashion sense, her tone put her out front of the pack, gave me a sneak preview of the battery acid to come.

Then there was *Burke's Peerage,* the aristocracy's old-guard mouthpiece, heavy on the starch. While pointing out that I had more blood ties to the ancient royal families of Britain than Andrew, *Burke's* warned that my "private life" had been "unorthodox"—a euphemism, no doubt, for my tragic deflowering.

My marriage to Andrew, the publication concluded, "will open a Pandora's box of problems that will alter Royal etiquette and protocol beyond all recognition."

Little did they know . . .

As my wedding day approached, I lived in a frenzy. Rising early and late to bed, I buzzed through a whirl of appointments and consultations. (I was on the Royal Wedding Diet: there was no time to eat.) I would start at seven in the morning with a massage or an acupuncture for my trick back. Then I'd meet with my dress creator, Lindka Cierach, for a fitting, and then with the bridesmaids and the florist. There were inquisitions to be fielded about china and glass and cutlery—I had to appear expert about things I'd never really thought about.

Presents poured in from all over the world—two thousand by the end, so many that they were stored in the Palace ballroom, which is roughly the size of Madison Square Garden. It took four people to catalogue and organize the gifts. They ranged from the breathtaking (a sapphire and diamond necklace) to the thoughtfully unusual: a dustbin with "A" and "S" and our picture on the front. One little lady up north crocheted a tablecloth for us, and I thought of how many hours went into that gift, how much generosity of heart.

I received these people's love as a sweet echo of Andrew's. For a bride it was a feeling to float on.

I normally write all my own thank-you notes, but I couldn't keep up with the landslide and felt badly about it— I hate not returning someone's thoughtfulness in kind. I did insist that each letter be written properly by the Palace staff and signed by me.

On July 21, two days to go and counting, my father and stepmother threw a brilliant dinner and dance for us. The following night I stayed at Clarence House, the Queen Mother's residence, as per wedding-eve tradition. I wish I had invited friends in, or gone out to dinner, but I sat there alone— what was wrong with me? I remember Her Majesty the Queen Mother's footman serving me out of a silver dragon decanter. And I thought that was very nice till I sipped the wine, which tasted like formaldehyde. (I'd become something of a wine snob from Paddy, who bought cases of fine red Bordeaux from Sotheby's.)

I guzzled it down anyway, to feel less alone. I wasn't nervous—what are nerves? What are feelings? I can do anything, because I am just Miss Super-Cool Perfection. All night long I heard the people camped outside my window in the Mall, less than sober themselves, screaming "Fer-*gie!* Fer-*gie!* Sa-*rah!* Fer-*gie!*"

I slept for two hours; it is not easy to sleep with people calling your name. I awoke before seven with fuzzy sight in my right eye. I knew what was coming, and soon enough here it was: a killer migraine, the monster child of all the pressure I'd soaked up and repressed. So I ordered up a comfort of my childhood, finger-sized buttered white toast "soldiers" dipped into soft-boiled eggs. This is actually about the worst thing you can eat for a migraine, but I didn't know that then and just bunged it all down.

In the middle of breakfast the troops began rolling in: the hairdresser and manicurist and beautician, with Lindka Cierach on hand to advise on the makeup to best complement my dress and my mum there for moral support. Out on the Mall the people cheered on, spirits high despite morning showers. Fortunately I had caught my headache in time and taken my pills, so the pounding was no worse than a Sousa march at twenty paces.

My headdress—a fragrant crown of gardenias, Andrew's favorite flower—was affixed. My veil was arranged. I was inserted into my ivory wedding dress, an exquisite creation I'd lost twenty-six pounds to fit into. Lindka was a genius; I knew she could make the most flattering gown ever, and she had. It was amazingly boned, like a corset. We'd chosen duchess satin because it is the creamiest material in the world. It never creases. It is smooth as glass and hangs beautifully, without a single bulge; it made my reduced figure look even better.

Woven into the design was the emblem from the coat of arms I'd chosen: a black-and-yellow bumble bee, an anchor, and a rose. The motto I'd adopted seemed perfect: *Ex Adversitas Felicitas Crescit.* Out of Adversity Comes Happiness.

Being the blithe spirit, I thought I had already survived a lifetime of adversity. Surely my pain was over and happiness must follow. I had Andrew now—how could I not be happy?

The fond object of my thoughts was heading toward his own prewedding ritual at Buckingham Palace. At ten o'clock the Queen conferred upon Andrew the title of Duke of York.

A few minutes after eleven, the gates of Clarence House swung open to release a matched pair of bay horses and their special freight, the Glass Coach, so named for the large windows on either side. There were but two passengers: myself and my father, who looked dashing in his own father's dark green morning coat. The crowd outside loosed into a raucous version of "Here Comes the Bride."

We made our ceremonious way along the Mall to Westminster Abbey. With nearly a million people lining the one-mile route, Dads looked desperately flustered. But I was just cruising, screwing lightbulbs right and left—"Do we wave here, Dads? This is *fun.*"

It isn't so hard to enjoy mass adoration; the tricky part is understanding that it has nothing to do with *you*, and that it rarely outlives an English summer. But on my wedding day all I knew or cared about was that Fergie was in glorious vogue. And as for *Sarah,* that ugly, valueless, unglamorous creature? No one had seen or heard from her for some time, which was just as I wanted it.

As we reached the Abbey's West Door, Lindka and Dads made some final adjustments to my dress—a seventeen-foot train is not easy to keep straight—and to my floral coronet. We took our places, heard the first notes of the processional. It was time to start down the aisle, for Dads to give me away. It was that poignant moment between father and daughter, a time for poetry and murmured tenderness.

And here is what my romantic Dads said to me as I lifted my satin slipper: "Let the horse take the strain." Trot on, old girl! He meant it as a joke. *Do I look like a horse, then?*—but then I thought of how nervous he must be. "It will be all right, Dads," I said, and we were off.

As I moved down that rich strip of blue carpet in a four-minute dream, my hair looking like a gardenia bush, I blocked out the 1,800 guests in the Abbey and the half a billion people watching me on television. I gave no thought to the fact that all Britain was on de facto holiday—that factories had stopped the assembly lines so that their workers could watch on big screens. All I could think about was my perfect groom, awaiting me with pride, so fantastically good-looking in his gold-braided uniform, sword hung at his side.

No one could possibly disapprove of me this day, with this man.

I stayed calm—I was anesthetized, really—right up to when Robert Runcie looked at me with his big eyes to lead me through my vows. In that moment the immensity of it all pierced my cloud of cool. My nerves kicked in. I had been drilling my lines, and in particular Andrew's middle names (to wit, Albert Christian Edward, which I remembered as *ACE*), but in the moment of truth I stammered over "Christian."

Much was made of the fact that I opted for traditional marriage vows. Diana had taken the modern route, omitting the bride's pledge of obedience, and people expected me to follow suit—I probably went the other way to be different. Meek I am not, but Andrew and I had always been of one mind, and the issue seemed moot. To obey him was merely to hear my own soul.

We plighted our troths and exchanged our rings, and the congregation burst into "God Save the Queen." In a trice I had become Princess Andrew and the Duchess of York, as well as the Countess of Inverness and Baroness of Killyleagh. (Killyleagh is a place in Northern Ireland where I have ancestral links.)

In the order of royal precedence I now outranked Anne and Margaret. Among the women I would stand fourth, behind the Queen, the Queen Mother, and the Princess of Wales.

While we signed the marriage books, I replaced the flowers that had anchored my veil with a diamond tiara for my return trip down the aisle. It was my time to be Cinderella. I had stepped up as the country girl; I would walk back as a princess.

But titles and diamonds counted for little against the man whose arm I took as we strode through that elegant wedding crowd. I was so intensely proud—not that I was now "a Royal," but because I had married Andrew and he was such a wonderful man. I married my man, and then I got my prince.

I was so deeply attached, so profoundly in love. I didn't realize that in getting my prince I would have to give up so much, not least the man himself.

*B*ack to the Palace, our coach drawn by the stately Windsor Greys . . . up to the balcony for our public appearance (so awkward three months before, it now felt like my natural habitat) . . . people calling for Andrew to kiss me, and our cupping our ears as a tease, as if we couldn't hear them . . . the great round roar that carried to Trafalgar Square when our lips finally touched. . . .

I was in a complete daze, an altered state, and I absolutely loved it. For those minutes I erased all my fears, muffled my dark commentary. I'd never felt so secure and good about myself in all my life.

Inside the State Dining Room, as I sat between Prince Philip and ex-King Constantine of Greece for our wedding "breakfast" of lamb and lobster, I came back to Royal Reality. You could count a hundred highborn people in that majestic room—there had been some big arguments about who should be there and where they should sit, and mostly I had lost.

It was lavish and proper and dull, that lunch. At one point we raised a glass, yet no one made a toast, for that was not traditional! I felt suddenly washed by regret. All the pomp had been fine, but I wanted to be a regular bride—I wanted Andrew's best man to get up and make a funny speech, and for someone else to say what a jolly good person I was or how badly I'd ridden my ponies. I had somehow missed out on the little, vital things. Like candid snapshots of the bride-to-be in her hair curlers; no one had thought to bring a camera to Clarence House that morning. Or my sweet eight-year-old godson, Harry Hadden-Paton—he should have been a page, but I lost track of it somehow. I'd just slid through the whole thing, and now my day was nearly done.

As I went upstairs to change into my honeymoon clothes, a nest of ladies-in-waiting hovered about me, jostling for position. They all wanted to be on the right side of the Queen's new daughter-in-law, and I fell for it, took them as sincere. But where was my mum and the people who loved me? Where was Carolyn?

We waited upstairs until the official photographs were processed; Andrew wanted to choose which ones to release to the press. The delay stretched to an hour, then an hour and a half, and I felt so embarrassed that people might think I had taken so long to change. I wish I had told my husband I was unhappy, that I'd simply said, "No, let's go." It was the first of a million swallowed objections, not to Andrew so much as to my new station.

When we finally did return downstairs, I thought people looked rather cheesed off—Royals are not used to being kept waiting, and there was polo to be played that afternoon. As Andrew and I climbed into our horse-drawn carriage, to the ritual shower of confetti, I wanted to shout back, "I didn't take that long to change—it wasn't my fault!"

We were bound for a Queen's Flight helicopter to Heathrow and then a jet to Lisbon. The carriage had wheeled around the Wedding Cake and off down the Mall when I saw the two of them, standing alone: my father and the young son he'd finally had, from his second marriage. Dads had wanted one last look, and now he was waving—he was really my father for that minute, he was there just for me. I was headed for places he could not follow, and my mind flashed to raspberry stains on the kitchen floor, and a strong man weeping.

So much happened on my wedding day, and so little would I remember. But through the passage of years I have never lost that last image: of Dads waving gamely in his old-fashioned morning coat, and no one else around, and when I think of it today it breaks my heart.

*I*t was the first night of our honeymoon when it fully dawned on me that ours would never be a normal marriage—that to marry a prince was to wed an institution. We were having dinner on the royal yacht, HM Yacht *Britannia*. Serenading us from below was the Royal Marines Band, complete to the last tuba, two dozen men marching up and down and playing that dreamy, swing-era number: "Pennsylvania six-five-oh-oh-oh!"

And then, for a romantic change of pace: "Chattanooga choo-choo, won't you come and choo-choo me home!"

There is the unusual, and then there is the surreal. The *Britannia* is a 5,700-ton pleasure craft. It takes 276 people to run and maintain it. On its main deck you could land a small plane.

And the passenger list for this five-day jaunt around the Azores consisted of precisely two: the Duke and Duchess of York.

That first dinner was our most intimate. From then on Andrew invited the ship's officers to join us; that is what the Queen did, that is what he thought was expected. I longed to tell him that he didn't need to do it, that he could just be with me, but . . .

Our cruise was most memorable for mishaps. Being the Remarkable Fergie—I was like the Helen Reddy song in those days, just spilling over with invincibility—I decided that we must go waterskiing, despite the miserable weather. Driving our speedboat was the ship's captain, Rear-Admiral John Garnier. When we looped around the yacht I fell into a swarm of jellyfish and got whipped across the leg really badly.

"What the———*happened?*" I howled, loud as a wolf. John Garnier will never forget it; he'll tell you that he "didn't think a princess was meant to swear quite so badly!"

After five days off the Portuguese coast, the *Britannia* swung north to pick up my new in-laws for their annual excursion to Balmoral. I recently saw a photograph of this leg of our trip, a vivid piece of time travel. There was Andrew on the deck, handsome and self-assured . . . and there was me, standing timidly behind him, in this awful dress with fluffy white bits everywhere and this huge hairdo and red face, looking literally like a baked potato. And I remembered that whenever Andrew made the slightest move, I would copy him exactly. Andrew turned, and I turned; Andrew waved, and I waved too. It was touching to see it—it reminded me of how much I placed my trust in him.

If I had been scouting for signs of coming trouble, I might have noted that we'd been booked to spend three times as long with Andrew's family as we'd had on our own. But it wasn't a time to be rocking the boat, especially one as grand as this. Far easier and more pleasant to go with the flow, no questions asked.

In fact, I looked forward to Balmoral. What better place for a "breath of fresh air" than the pristine Scottish Highlands? And what better time than this, when Fergiemania had shot off the charts? My trip with Andrew might be over, and I didn't know then just how rare an opportunity it would be. But my honeymoon with the Windsors was just entering full swing, and I was determined to make the most of it.

6

Reality Bites

As commoners go, I must have seemed like a promising addition to the Royal Family. We had brushed shoulders often enough beforehand; they figured I knew the ropes. I was a country girl, robust and jolly and not too high-strung. As the Queen Mother once said of me, in highest praise: "She is so English."

Though I too was now "Her Royal Highness," rules of protocol still applied within the family. I would curtsey to those higher up on the scale: the Queen, the Queen Mother. While we would call each other by our Christian names, there was one obvious exception: When I met the Queen in public, she was always Your Majesty.

In private the Queen and I were different, though; in private I called her Mama. And it meant so much when she spoke of me as "my daughter-in-law," as she did from early on. While I would not presume today to think that the Queen regards me as a daughter, we had—and still have—a special tie.

Our common interests and acquaintances dated back to Smith's Lawn days with Dads. The Queen and I both doted on horses and dogs, on farming and open air. I loved riding with her, as Mum had before me—I felt the happiest with her. When she waved me to sit next to her in the car or at church, I felt favored and blessed.

But our bond was more than that. In her integrity, her dignity, her devotion to husband and family and the Church, the Queen was all that I admired. She was so *solid,* so steadfast —a person to be relied on, first and last.

And so I wanted to make her happy; I *knew* I could make her happy. Mum was far away in Argentina, but the Queen and I could be close and caring.

In Balmoral that summer, I shone brighter still when held up against Diana, who felt so wretched then in every way. Diana wasn't so fond of Balmoral; she had shied from riding ever since a bad childhood accident. She was teary and reclusive and out of sorts, and then up cantered the perfect daughter-in-law, Mrs. Bubbly, Mrs. Good Form, Mrs. I-Can-Do-Anything-Better-Than-You. I was so ecstatic with Andrew, so content with my new life, and the press was on my side and everything was all right—I was a glowing ball of happiness.

How annoying I must have been.

The Queen probably thought, *Goodness, at last we have a sensible person around here,* and I believed it, too. I was sensible and cool and incredibly nice—to Diana as well, of course. I'd watch out for her, be strong for her; I was so hearty and well grounded, built to be leaned on.

In short, I was a sublimely considerate sister-in-law, and I'm sure I made a bad time for Diana positively nightmarish.

But even in my fleeting glory I knew that I tiptoed a tightrope and that Royals never worked with nets. Yes, yes, of course, I could hunt and fish and be wonderfully jokey and fun. I could ride the wild horse and ski the black run and keep everybody happy. I could do that—I could do anything.

But what about me? What about Sarah? Who *was* Sarah? She was still just The Pleaser; she needed to prove it could all be okay. She was no better than her next challenge. Without the challenge, in fact, she might not exist.

Looked at from some distance, joining the Royal Family was nothing less than my ultimate act of self-sabotage. I am very intense. I play for high stakes, do nothing by halves. For someone like myself—so desperate to fit in, so terrified of rejection—what greater gamble could there be than to enter the most powerful family in the world?

Consider: You have a fiercely private person who hates the way she looks, who always thinks she's too heavy, and now she is one of the most photographed women in the world. You have someone who fears she is not quite up to speed and who now must keep up with this glamorous Court. You have this spontaneous, impetuous, guileless woman, who lives moment to moment and heart-on-sleeve, and now she is pressed into a realm of rigid agendas and bottled emotion, where duty and decorum mean all.

And, most of all, you have this insecure woman who needs frequent reassurance from the man she loves—and who is about to be wrenched apart from him.

In short, I had set myself up, and right royally this time.

All my life I had been jumping where the grass was too slick. Rejected and abandoned—that role was familiar to me. I felt comfortable in it.

All too soon I would revive it.

* * *

$\mathcal{T}$he honeymoon absolutely ended just a few days after we came back from Balmoral to Buckingham Palace. To that point Andrew and I had spent only one night apart since our engagement. To that point I had enjoyed a perfect fairy-tale existence—but now the prince was leaving, and the princess would revert to a toad. Having completed his course at Greenwich, Andrew received his new assignment, a weapons-instructor course at Yeovilton, Somerset, 150 some miles from London.

In theory I had understood that Royal Navy officers weren't homebodies, that Andrew would often be gone. In our engagement-day interview on the BBC, when asked how I would cope with becoming a royal duchess *and* a naval wife at the same time, I was typically nonchalant. "I'm going to enjoy it immensely," I said, adding that I had "very strongly" advised Andrew to continue his Navy career.

Don't worry about my feelings; I'm all right, Jack. Dads is waltzing on air because I've got him the perfect son-in-law. Mum's thrilled to see me living out her fondest fantasies. Everyone's happy that I've done so well. Could I manage? How could I (dare to) fail?

But while I knew Andrew would be leaving, I had never really thought it through—it was abstract and dreary, like a dental appointment six months off, and what point could there be in dwelling on it? It was easier to pretend that life would go on as it had while Andrew worked in Greenwich. It was especially easy for me. All my life I had lived for the day. I paid no heed to ramifications, let the future mind itself. You need confidence to plan things, to count on A leading to B in predictable lockstep, and confidence is what I was missing.

So it happened that Navy widowhood crashed down on

me: five days out and two days back. On Sunday night Andrew would be off to Yeovilton (or later to Portland, in Dorset) and locked into his ship. Friday night he'd come home to our apartment, fresh from the wardroom, tired and grumpy. On Saturday he would get nearly human, but by Sunday lunch he'd get edgy again, because he had to get ready to go to work and he didn't want to go.

An early dinner, then off to his car. He would make a wide sweeping arc as he left the quadrangle, waving all the way. I'd wave back from the corridor window, then run into our apartment and wave some more as he passed through the Palace gates toward the Mall. And then I would put the window down and turn to Michael, my husband's valet, with tears in my eyes. I was twenty-six years old, and I would sit in my dressing room, with those stately oils of Queen Victoria staring down at me, and I would break. I would cry softly, resignedly. There were no hysterics. I would just cry my quiet rivers . . .

Late into the night I would fight sleep and hear the people driving down the Mall toward the Wedding Cake. They thought it was funny to toot their horns and shout, "Oy, Fergie! Oy, Fergie!"

On Monday morning Michael would place a rose on my breakfast plate, to keep me company.

Five days out and two days back—a scenario that has killed many a marriage. For me it was worse than for most Navy widows, as my officer was also a prince. On weekends the naval officer became the Duke of York again, and I'd join him on some gray engagement in the hinterland—there was always something. Worst of all were his tours overseas, which could steal him for months at a stretch. I would see him off at the gangplank, wave bravely and smile, then limp back to the Palace and nurse my wounds.

Through all our time of living "together," Andrew was home for an average of forty-two days per year.

His absences gradually destroyed me. I was a romantic, sensual newlywed who loved her man—he was mine and I was so happy. And when he left I lost not just my lover but also my mentor and staunchest ally on the crucial matter of being royal. I looked up to Andrew completely. I could ask him anything and didn't care if I sounded foolish, for he was always *with* me; he would never put me down. But now I had no one to say yes or no and was terrified unto paranoia of my next gaffe. The simplest decisions unhinged me: Should I leave the dining room door open? Was I meant to go downstairs and visit the Queen? I had to learn—I *had* to get it right. *What was a princess meant to do?*

It was a lot to take on. I was adrift in the Palace, my anchor lost, tossed from whitecap to jagged reef. And when Andrew did come back on Friday, tired from his own busy week, I would be so keen to see him that we'd never speak of my problems from Tuesday or Wednesday or Thursday. Just as I would muzzle my complaints on the telephone or in my sunny letters.

I would not be a nagging wife, Dads had drummed that much into me. And I would never look back anyway, because that is not what I'm about—what was done was done, and I just had to get on with it.

*I*n my first months as a princess, I asked my closest friends to warn me if I ever became "too royal," too spoiled or full of myself. But my greater hazard was in fact the opposite: not feeling royal *enough* to hold together through the day.

Isolation makes a fertile field for self-doubt. With Andrew

gone, there was no one to counter my worst suspicion—that I was counterfeit, as bogus an impostor as Twain's young pauper. A *fraud*. If anyone seemed to respect me, it was because they didn't really know me, and it was only a matter of time before they found me out.

Later, when I took my swan dive out of favor, it was popular to paint me as this fiendishly clever, premeditative creature. I had bewitched a poor gullible prince and used him to gain what I *really* wanted: a title, a place in the Palace. It is a neat little theory and a role that the young Bette Davis might have played to a turn.

But it had nothing to do with me. The truth is that I was uncalculating to a fault, in all things. No reality was too obvious for me to dodge: the implications of Andrew's naval duty, or what it meant to become a public figure. Only after the fact did I see that in saying my vows, I had enlisted in "The Firm," the Royal Family as business and institution.

If you wanted to defend me, you might say that illusions about royal life were more viable in 1986—before the revelations about Diana's plight, before my own sorry mess exploded. But the truth is it wouldn't have mattered. More data would not have helped me. I was oblivious to concern because I didn't know how to *think*. I loved Andrew, he was my whole reason for being there. And when he went off I was left with the Palace and the *Burke's Peerage* set—with all the trappings I had never cared or thought about.

And you can't cuddle up at night with trappings, no matter how royal.

*T*o be a proper royal duchess is a more than a full-time job. Modern royalty is expected to sing for its supper, earn its keep. Each day, at the back of *The Times* and the *Daily Telegraph,* they post the "Court Circular": a listing of the prior day's engagements for each member of the Royal Family. It turns into a competition, a numbers game. The press keeps a running tabulation and is all too gleeful to point out when someone lags in the standings.

But I had no need of outside prodding. As in every other job I'd held, I was driven by my own compulsion to excel and thereby ensure my acceptance—to be the best Duchess of York I could possibly be.

I had just one problem: I had no clue as to how to proceed. In our BBC interview, I had babbled on about "much looking forward to carrying it out or whatever I'm supposed to do." Now it was time for the doing—and with Andrew gone, I'd have to find my own way. I had no compass or direction, and it soon became apparent that I'd get little help from the senior courtiers or the Queen's ladies-in-waiting. They weren't overtly unfriendly for the most part, just standoffish, as if waiting to see whether I'd prove up to snuff.

I responded in my timeworn manner—I vaulted into the fray. I glued myself to duty. I would make Andrew proud of me or bust.

Royal work has three components: official engagements, charity projects, and high ceremonies like Remembrance Day or Trooping the Colour. Andrew and I were scheduled at least six months in advance, based on joint household meetings in December and June, when our top staff people would excavate through mounds of invitations and recommend the ones they thought best. There was no set pecking order within the Royal Family as to what you could do, but it was understood that one didn't raid existing franchises. (Anne, for example, had cornered the market on Save the Children; Margaret had tied up The National Society for Prevention of

Cruelty to Children; Charles had an exclusive on architecture and the inner cities.) In the main you could follow your preferences—as long as you met the unwritten quota.

I now shared Andrew's private secretary, who coordinated our public lives, and his equerry, the number-two man, an officer on secondment from the military. But I worked most directly with my lady-in-waiting, my personal secretary, my dresser, and a lady clerk or two. Also at my service were two protection officers, the household valet, my chauffeur, and various Palace butlers and footmen.

I had always done for myself, and having a staff took getting used to. But I did get used to it. At bath time the dresser would pour the hot water, then fold my robe on the mat stool so I might pull it up around me after I sat down. Once—a few months, a lifetime ago—I had rented a room for $50 a week, with a bathroom off the hall. Now life could be so blissful, such a miracle of luxury, that I would slide into a dream state. This didn't seem quite real, but who was I to object?

Besides, it soon grew clear that I would require every one of my staff people—that the demands before me were insatiable, and I would need all the help I could get.

My day normally began at six o'clock. I was met by my dresser, who had already extracted the outfit for my first appointment, no simple job. My wardrobe, nonexistent a year earlier, had mushroomed exponentially, thanks to a monthly clothing allowance from the Queen and a steady parade of representatives from the most au courant shops, presenting their fashions for my approval. My dressing room was crammed with cupboards and chests and free-standing oaken wardrobes, and all of them were packed. More wardrobes overflowed into the corridor—one for skiing, another for

Balmoral, and so forth. The inventory just kept growing, as though in Manifest Destiny.

I would ultimately collect 15 fluffy, formal ball gowns, for state affairs and top-tier dinners; another 25 long dresses for slightly less formal occasions; 40 cocktail dresses; 150 day suits; 60 hats; and 200 pairs of shoes. With numbers on this scale, you couldn't just reach into a closet and pull out what you fancied. My wardrobe had its own file of seventeen folders, with hundreds of color sketches of my dresses and suits. Alongside each sketch, my dresser would jot down the name of the designer; the name and date of the function where I had last worn the item; the color of the hat and shoes and gloves we'd matched with it.

Fashion "rules" are overrated; in high society they make them up as they go along. There is no Grand Arbiter to prohibit you from wearing the same outfit twice in the same month. But my records would save me from needless embarrassment, such as showing up in the same gown two years running to the same charity ball, where the paparazzi would be out in force.

I took care to be correct in what I wore. I stuck to convention; I took the job of Duchess of York very seriously. Where Diana had balked at wearing gloves, I donned them willingly —long gloves for a long dress, short gloves for a suit, just as Mum had taught me. And I made sure that my lady-in-waiting packed the mandated contingency items in her bag: spare pairs of gloves and tights; a needle and thread and safety pins; a handkerchief and makeup bag.

It could take up to an hour to change my clothes, until I got the knack of it, and I would change two to four times a day. It played hob with my nerves, made me chronically almost late, but I took it as part of the course. Trot on, old girl . . .

By seven I was out the door, a bit of fruit in my hand to eat on the fly, then back before lunch for another change, a look at the mail, and a consultation with Helen Spooner, my lady-in-waiting. I had met Helen shortly after moving to London, when we both worked for Neil Durden-Smith, and I knew she owned all the essentials of a right-hand woman: an efficient mind, a loving heart, and an even temper to bear the buffeting of the royal redheaded tempest. Helen had a desk in our Palace office, but it sat a quarter-mile from the flat, and we often worked side by side in the dining room instead.

Staff relations for this Duchess have always been most informal. I rely on my people's loyalty and friendship, and we've been known to share a glass of wine at work's end. But there were still the demands of protocol. Like everyone else, Helen greeted me with a curtsey: "Good morning, Your Royal Highness." She would thereafter address me as "Ma'am" until leaving for the day, when she'd curtsey again and wish Her Royal Highness a good night.

I found these rituals less bearable with old friends. "Don't do that—you don't have to *do* that!" I would plead as they curtseyed. "I'm still just Fergie!" It took me a year to feel right about saying, "It's the Duchess of York" on the telephone. Whenever my protocol wavered, as it often did those first months, the Queen's lady-in-waiting took me aside to remind me of what was expected.

Lunch was often geared to a meeting with some board in the dining room. Then back to the dressing room for another change and the hairdresser and new makeup, and a briefing by Helen on my next appointment. For formal London engagements, or smart dinners, we would order a Rolls-Royce. These official cars were all more or less the same, all black with some age on them.

As we rolled smoothly on through the streets of London—we'd have three or more policemen from the Special Escort

Group whizzing about on motorbikes, halting traffic at the intersections precisely as we passed—Helen and I would go over her foolscap notes, reduced to the size of index cards. They included my agenda, any relevant correspondence, the key people I'd be meeting. I would skim through once and that would be enough, especially if I'd met the group before. I had a gift for recalling names and husbands and children and ages; I could spot a face in the crowd months after our last encounter.

For engagements outside the city, we would generally take a private vehicle—at first Andrew's Jaguar, later my own Ford Granada, large but not too ostentatious. Or if the way was far, or the itinerary heavy, we would commandeer a helicopter or a fixed-wing plane from the Queen's Flight—the only way to get to five places in Wales, for example, all in one day. We might open a hospital, send off a ship, present an export award at some factory, visit a special-needs school or a hospice. At each stop I'd try to meet not just the managers or board members, but also the secretaries. I had been among their number not long ago and knew full well their importance.

I would be expected to say a few words—it might be to five people or five thousand. I had little background in public speaking, but I watched Andrew and the Queen on video and, at first, I copied them. Soon I found ideas popping into my head and I started ad libbing, working with my audience, making jokes, doing my thing. I might completely die the day before a big speech and be foul to people out of nerves, but when the time came I would fly by the seat of my pants and bring it home.

My biggest thrill came when I represented the Royal Family at a military ceremony in Berlin. When I was young, Dads took me every year to Albert Hall for the British Royal Legion Festival of Remembrance, where we paid homage to those who died for our freedom. I'd been partial to pomp and tradition ever since. One of the great days of my childhood was when Herbert and I carried the flag for Britain at International Polo Day; it was nice enough to watch a pageant, but far better to be part of it.

Now I was part of it all the time. When the band played "God Save the Queen" I would feel incredibly proud, standing up like a man as Dads had taught me, with shoulders back and arms down by my sides. I always wondered if Dads were watching me on the television, watching me stand upright and tall like a good old soldier.

After my full day's round of events, more often than not I would have an evening function—a charity award reception, or a dinner at the Mansion House, thrown by the Lord Mayor, or a gathering of the Freemasons or some other traditional group. In any case, it meant another change of clothes, another hairdresser, another briefing. With Andrew away I would also carry the ball at state dinners, not known for their brevity, and it could be midnight or later before I'd get back to the flat.

But still I was not done. There could be dozens of thank-you notes for our hosts of the day—not just the officials, but the young girl who had given me flowers, impromptu, or some valiant patient in his final fight. Not for me to simply sign a letter written by my staff. I would do my own, by hand, to the last thoughtful comma, as if the public would somehow know this and love me more for it.

I'd fall into bed with nothing left, into sleep with no twilight.

Then I would begin all over again the next morning.

Official engagements were etched in stone, in those biannual-Stonehengian blocks. I was like the postman—through hail or snow or freezing rain, or any state short of a coma, I would be there. And if something wonderful cropped up a month or two beforehand—a godchild's birthday bash, say, or an old schoolmate's thespian debut on the West End—and it conflicted with my commitment, I sent my regrets to something wonderful and carried on.

Even minor changes were fraught with complications. To move my hair appointment from ten o'clock to eleven would affect the driver collecting the hairdresser, the footman who must be downstairs to escort her, and my dresser. I had no flexibility—except in dates with friends, which I canceled right and left until they'd grow vexed with me. I would keep to my schedule, come what may. I would be on time, dressed like a model duchess, getting each name right—I might feel like a week-old posy inside, drooping and wilted and nearly dead, but I would plant the most genuine smile on my face and it would not fade.

They say if you want something accomplished you should give it to a busy person, and that was me in spades. I can get an extraordinary amount done in a day. I can orchestrate and decide things, keep five balls in the air. It was not uncommon then to catch me at home shouting some business over the telephone, even as I called out instructions to the hairdresser, got a briefing from Helen, and drained my fourth cup of tea.

No one demanded this of me; I did it to myself. To succeed in the Palace, I would return to my workload each day like Sisyphus to his rock. I didn't dare stop pushing uphill, for that would mean I'd stopped playing the game—I'd be cheating The Firm, and that rock might roll back and crush me.

I would go seven days a week (unless Andrew came home, when I'd clear the whole weekend to watch videos with my man). I'd work sixteen, eighteen, twenty hours a day—when

I look at my royal diaries today, at the dense clots of entries on their oversized pages, my manic intensity makes me sick.

I've been blessed with great stamina and could somehow recharge overnight. But it was harder for the people around me. I would send my protection officers home at four in the morning, and they'd have to be up again at seven. My staff pandered to my insanity, got caught up in it. I would call in from my car to change my schedule half a dozen times a day, each change demanding half a dozen more phone calls, and sometimes at the end we would wind up right back where we'd started.

I am proud to say that most of my staff have stayed with me for years (proof I can't be *that* bad), but it's also true that most have taken leave for R&R at one time or another.

Consumed by hyperactivity, I never stopped to take a breath. I must have wanted it that way, to keep myself from peering at the lonely person within, the one I doubted and despised. Because a moving target is tougher to strike. Because I feared consciousness most of all.

But the damnable thing about a treadmill is that it never gets you anywhere. The more you do, the greater the expectations; the more you do, the more there is left to be done. (I might as well have done nothing for what satisfaction I got.) *Have we sent the flowers to Lady Pinkerton just to make her happy? Have we thanked Lord Bloat for his deadly pompous introduction? Am I keeping up with my quota?*

Where is Andrew, and would he think this is right?

Is it right?

What was I supposed to do?

And meanwhile my spirit was slowly seeping away. Like the air from a balloon you're huffing into with all of your lungs, but it's been pricked by just the tiniest pin, and you know that the prick will prove mortal.

As the most alienated person at Buckingham Palace, I had found the perfect den. Our apartment was larger and grander than anywhere I'd lived since Lowood. It was also about as cozy and personal as a railway hotel. I hadn't noticed this deficiency when Andrew was there each night—why quibble about the view when you can't wait to douse the lights?— but now it was becoming oppressive.

The flat had stayed unchanged since our wedding, with two exceptions. Sir Michael Timms, the kindly Assistant to the Master of the Household, had somehow finagled some funds to get me new curtains and wallpaper for my dressing room, in blue and white.

The second change was an addition to Andrew's stuffed animal family: the jumbo-sized teddy bear, a wedding-gift from Edward, that had sat on the back of our going-away carriage when we left the Abbey.

Other than that, I had added my bits and photographs, but they were buried amid the clocks and paintings and furniture that were here before we were born and would stay long after we'd departed. We were "living above the shop," as my father-in-law, the Duke of Edinburgh, once put it, and you could not easily forget it. The housemaids would come in and clean the heirloom silver and put everything back in exactly the right place. This palace was built for an Empire, and if you looked around our rooms—at the nineteenth-century battle paintings, or the leopard skin sprawled by the false fireplace—you might think we had never lost India.

The East Wing served as headquarters for the Department of the Environment. The good bureaucrats arrived at 9:30 A.M. and left at six o'clock sharp. At any time in between they might be strolling down the corridor—along with the footmen, the mailman, the royal plumber, and that nice fellow who repaired the telephones. When your dining room is your office and its door is often open, there is no stepping out of the bedroom half dressed, unless you want to make new friends.

Which went to show that one didn't need privacy to feel isolated.

Heat was rationed according to Environment's standards. In the spring the radiators went off, no matter if the streets stayed glazed with ice. You did not argue; you just found a second sweater. In September the steam came on again, Indian summer notwithstanding. Which would not have been so bad, except that our old sash windows would open six inches but no farther.

The windows were mostly off limits, anyway. As one of London's leading tourist attractions, Buckingham Palace must stay postcard-perfect at all times. As our apartment faced out on the Wedding Cake, we were barred from drawing the curtains all the way back, or from ever disturbing the sheers. As a result, the sunlight—or as much as we got of it from our northeastern exposure—would always be filtered and muted.

Our chandeliers and standing lamps contained mainly forty-watt bulbs—a prudent economy, no doubt, but a bit squinty for desk work in the computer era. On an overcast day it would get so dark in our sitting room that Jane Ambler, my personal secretary—she is from Liverpool and shoots straight from the shoulder—would remove those heavy pleated lamp shades just to cheer me up. It was so startling to see the naked light, even from a dim bulb, that people would pop into the room and say, "What is going on here?"

The perpetual gloom wouldn't have been so bad if there had been some flowers and fresh air for relief. Here you might interject, if you know London well, that the Palace contains a large and quite wonderful walled garden. There was a catch, however. I'd have to walk down my Olympic-sized corridor and past the Duke of Edinburgh's offices, descend to the ground floor in the lift, come out and turn left, and go a hundred yards past more offices to the garden itself.

It could take ten minutes to reach it and another ten to get back, and rare was the day when I had twenty minutes to spare in my schedule. I was an outdoor person trapped in the most indoors of places, and I cannot count the times that I longed for the gentle fields of Dummer, or the sheer slopes of Verbier.

In past chapters of my life, my antidote for the glums had been food and more food. But bingeing wasn't easy at the Palace. When Andrew and I got married, we received hundreds of fine dinner plates and crystal glasses, dozens of antique silver serving dishes—but not a single electric blender, that most traditional newlywed appliance. To rectify the situation, a legal firm in Washington, D.C., dispatched a first-rate blender to our door.

There was only one problem: We had nothing to blend.

As befitting the former cave for two bachelor boys, our flat had no kitchen. Nor did we have a toaster, or a coffeemaker, or so much as a kettle. There was a hot plate to keep tea or coffee warm for visitors after delivery by a footman, and a tiny refrigerator for our Schweppes.

For all else we relied upon the Palace kitchen. Lunch and supper had to be ordered from our menus the night before, or at latest, first thing in the morning. Suppertime was 7:30, but by the time the meal arrived, the footman would be weary and my grilled fish invariably cold, for the kitchen sat in a different, distant wing of the Palace, a mile away.

Then the chef would finish for the night. Had I been out that evening, had I dodged the rubber chicken at some banquet and fallen prey to a midnight pang, I was out of luck. I would fantasize about the all-American household I'd seen in the movies, where Dad and Junior raided the kitchen in the middle of the night and talked about Football or The Future over a tub of ice cream and some milk and cookies.

My sister, Jane, once suggested that I longed "to be able to do something ordinary, like just eat out of a saucepan." In fact, I would have been gratified to assemble a cheddar cheese sandwich or spoon into a raspberry yogurt.

I had certain options, of course. I could make the home front less grim by having friends over for supper, but it would require at least one day's notice, plus a menu summit between my secretary and the deputy master. Then there were the discouraging logistics: a call to security to get people's names on the Privy Purse Door, someone on hand for coats, a footman to escort them to our flat. It usually didn't seem worth the trouble, especially when Andrew was away.

Conversely, I could go out for dinner, but once again only if I'd planned ahead. I normally sent my policeman home by seven o'clock, to be with his family. I felt guilty if I kept him out at night, guiltier still if I'd asked the chef to make my supper, which would now go uneaten. Plus I had my little inquisition to contend with: Should I join our friends at restaurants without Andrew? Could I have a glass of wine in public? *How would my husband want it?*

So much for spontaneity.

For so long I had been the Anti-Planner. I'd avoided time clocks like the plague, reveled in life on the spur. Now my whole workday was programmed down to the millisecond, and I found it abhorrent to have to regiment my social life as well. My solution was simple—for a time I just stopped going out. I would sit and eat my lukewarm supper for one, and hope I'd feel better the next day, and sink into dejection.

Loyal Jane Ambler would hate to leave me in the gloaming of that apartment and often would hang on well past dark. I'd never complain to anyone else. I would tell myself how lucky I was to be in the Queen's house, to have service at all—*I must accept things the way they are done.*

But alone with Jane, my tears would well up and I'd soften my stiff upper lip. The real Sarah would peek out; she was an abjectly miserable soul. "Jane, I don't want this," my true self would say softly. "I don't understand."

Jane would get upset and feel useless; you cannot help someone who is digging her own grave, even if you grab the shovel and slap her in the face with it. But later at night, after she had finally gone home, I would ring her up and ask, "What exactly are you doing now?"

At first Jane would laugh, but then she learned to go along with me. She might be putting the dishes in the dishwasher or ironing a shirt. And I would think, *You are living a real life —this is real.*

7

Higher Callings

Sir Robert Cooke was dying.

Six months earlier he had been the picture of vigor, bounding up to my sixth-story Mayfair office two steps at a time. Now he could barely walk or write, his body little more than a crumbling husk for the keen spirit I'd come to cherish.

I had first met Sir Robert in 1984, after Richard Burton asked me to look into a book about the Palace of Westminster, the mother of parliaments. First I established that there was a hole in the market—that little of note had been written about this architectural splendor, whose genesis dated back to William the Conqueror.

Then I went hunting for an author. When I went to my friend Anna Butcher, who worked at the Houses of Parliament, she didn't hesitate. "There is a man called Sir Robert Cooke who is a former MP," Anna informed me, "and he knows exactly which ashtray sat on Margaret Thatcher's desk."

That was the kind of authority I wanted, and Anna arranged for us to meet for lunch. At first take, Sir Robert seemed a typical British upper-class gentleman: polite, well bred, fastidious. Then in his mid-fifties, he was a well-built man with a high forehead and hooded, piercingly intelligent eyes. He heard out my presentation but held back. My project would be too much work for him, he said—he didn't really want to do it.

It was only after I coaxed him into signing on, and we began meeting weekly on the book, that I realized what a wonderfully eccentric and creative author I had landed. While his manners were flawless, he owned not an ounce of pretension. Though his friends called him Robin, the nickname seemed off to me—he was *Sir Robert,* a man of special dignity. *The Palace of Westminster* was the first book I ever assembled, and Sir Robert made it a pleasure.

It was shortly before my wedding that I suspected something was wrong. Those six flights of stairs seemed to be taking more out of my friend; he'd be winded, even stumbling, by the time he reached my door. When I asked him what was wrong, he would smile and say, "Got to get a bit fitter," and turn the talk to our work.

Over the next few weeks there were more disquieting signs. Sir Robert's handwriting grew unsteady, his gait more wobbly. Eventually he asked me, "Would you mind if we met downstairs next time?" So we did, and finally Sir Robert confided that he'd been diagnosed with motor neurone disease (MND), known in the U.S. as Lou Gehrig's disease.

Motor neurone disease kills three people a day in Britain, more than AIDS, yet I had never heard of it before—it cried out for more public awareness. Once it hit close to me I became insatiable in learning all I could. I found out that MND can strike adults of any age, that there is no cure or treatment

—that we don't even know how it is triggered. (Recent research has focused on environmental toxins, but findings remain inconclusive.)

What we do know, from sad experience, is how ruthlessly MND destroys the nerves that govern movement, how inexorably it wastes the muscles. Little by little, one is robbed of the ability to walk, to speak, to swallow, and finally to breathe. Professor Stephen Hawking, the world-famous cosmologist, has lived with MND for more than a quarter of a century, but he is the exception. The majority die within two years of diagnosis.

The cruel irony is that MND spares the mind and senses; you are all too aware of your own decay. Your body becomes a prison, a private death row. Before he died of MND, David Niven remarked, "It's awful, I can no longer tell a joke—but I keep remembering them." It is, I believe, the most frustrating disease in the world.

Sir Robert was lucky in one respect, as he kept his speech to the end. I was shaken nonetheless by his steep decline; each time I saw him, he was markedly worse. That autumn he became homebound. Much of his work was assumed by his wife, Lady Cooke, who did without sleep to change him and shift him in bed at night. (In the saddest of family tragedies, Lady Cooke would die of cancer a few years later, after marrying Sir Edward Du Cann.) I saw firsthand how MND assaults the independence of even its proudest targets, how much help their families needed, and how little they were getting.

With the quiet bravery I would come to see so often among people with this disease, Sir Robert never complained. On January 6, 1987, he dictated the final paragraphs of *The Palace of Westminster* into a tape recorder. His assignment completed, he died that same day, at the age of fifty-six. Sir

Robert's work remained impeccable to the last sentence; his brain had stayed as good as on the day he was born.

When I asked Lady Cooke what I might do for her, she requested nothing for herself. Instead she made me an invitation: Would I be the royal patron for the Motor Neurone Disease Association?

I had already linked up with more than a dozen charities; they were part and parcel of one's life within the Royal Family. But the MND Association was the first one that I would champion as my own.

I somehow hung in as the flavor of the month through the first year of my marriage and then some. As it had with Diana, The Firm was counting on me to revitalize a somewhat dog-eared monarchy—to invigorate not only its bloodlines, but also its popularity among the taxpayers. I had the golden touch, it seemed. Everyone loved it, for example, when I turned on the Regent Street Christmas lights with the shortest speech on record: "I only hope there won't be a second Big Bang."

Off my initial success I became a heroine, this simply wonderful person, the perfect addition to the Royal Family. My new in-laws, *The Sunday Times Magazine* related in July of 1987, "know where they stand with Sarah—she's a completely conventional girl who lets her hair down in the loud convivial way that they themselves do in the heart of the family."

Even my ordinariness worked for me! I was swept up in this huge stream of approval, sailing on the wind, swinging from the rafters. So *this* was life—this was what it was all about, and wasn't it just brilliant? I felt like an Israelite come home after forty years in the desert. I had always ached to be wanted and loved, and suddenly the whole wide world was for me—*yippee, here we go, just look at this country girl now!* I was going to make the most of it, and in a sense you might say that I did. Absolute adoration, it would seem, corrupts absolutely.

Looking back, I committed a public figure's cardinal sin. I believed my own press—a habit that would prove hard to break, even after the raves turned to pans.

I worked so hard to meet expectations, every minute of every day. Royalty never takes a holiday, never relaxes; you are always on display, even when *en famille.* At the opera you stifle your sneezes and sit still to the end; you cannot get up halfway through and go to the loo, no matter how urgent your need. On Sundays at Windsor Castle, you are down by 8:30 for breakfast (regardless of how much you long to sleep in), in church by 11, back for drinks at 12:30.

But no day was more exhausting than Christmas at Sandringham. At first light I would dress for breakfast: a long tweed skirt with a smart blouse and matching cardigan. The plates were barely cleared before I'd be upstairs again to change for church, something *very* smart, a dress or a suit under a long coat (it gets biting cold in Norfolk), with hat and gloves, of course.

Then back to the house, off with the coat and hat and gloves, on with a silk dress and change of shoes for lunch. If I planned to stay in that afternoon, I could move into something more relaxed—a cotton shirt, perhaps even trousers, but definitely not jeans. If I were going out for a walk, it would be a long country jacket, a walking skirt, and either leather ankle boots or the old reliable walking shoes. In either case, I would need another change for tea, something similar to breakfast: probably a long silk skirt with matching top and flat shoes.

Finally came drinks and dinner, a formal affair that demanded either a long, straight gown or a full skirt. By that point my poor dresser's tongue would be dragging, but I never questioned what I was doing, much less resented it. It was par for the course, the accepted local custom, and I'd never have dreamed of deviating.

At any family get-together, punctuality was next to godliness. If dinner was set for 8:30, you'd be expected down for drinks at eight o'clock. You absolutely *had* to be there by 8:15 sharp, when the Queen would promptly enter. You never let the Queen beat you down to dinner, end of story—to come in any later would be unimaginably disrespectful.

I was not, by track record or temperament, a religiously punctual person. In my sad commuting days before Clapham, when I went home from London every night, Dads would warn, "If you miss your train, I'll drive off from the station," and so he did more than once. I was one of those women who'd allow plenty of time, be all ready to go— until I saw something wrong with my dress or hair or makeup, or (most resistant to touch-ups) my figure. I'd get delayed in my panic, and many were the times at Windsor or Sandringham that the Queen would be coming in one door and I would be *flying* through another in a sweat, tripping over the carpet and pretending that I'd already been there.

But while I tried my hardest to blend in, it never really worked. At the family's weekend shoots, some ladies would have their own dogs, to retrieve any birds that her man's dog had neglected. Timing, however, was everything. There were three "drives" in the morning and two more in the afternoon, and at each one you had to wait until the beaters beat the woods to put the pheasants to flight. In the meantime you sat very quietly, with your dog silent at your feet—you wouldn't dare twitch for fear of disturbing the birds before the guns were set.

To everyone's chagrin, my dog had the timing of a drunken polka dancer. He would run at the woods, and the pheasants would scatter in the opposite direction, and the drive would be wasted. Worse yet, where the other dogs were all black, mine was cream-colored—there would be no way to blame someone else. I loved my retriever, who'd been given me by Andrew. But he was, indisputably, a nonconformist dog for a nonconforming Royal, and he'd make the Duke of Edinburgh rather cross: "Can't you keep your bloody dog under control?"

For the most part, though, everyone laughed at my misadventures: "Good old Fergie, typical her, she has a crack at everything, she even ruins the drive." I was very much an "in" then, even when I played court jester.

It was true, I would have a crack at everything—I was Wonder Woman, and what couldn't I conquer if I tried? It wasn't enough to swim and ski and ride—I had to water ski as well, and in the summer of 1987 I would strain the medial ligament in my knee in the process. (Andrew was quite wonderful in clucking about his hobbled wife, tuning in to my every need—I would find him a man to rely on, in matters large and small.)

And it wasn't enough to be the liveliest player at charades; I had to try four-in-hand carriage driving, Prince Philip's latest passion, as well.

My nerviest endeavor came after a reporter flippantly asked if I planned to follow Andrew and take up flying, and I thoughtlessly shot back, "Of course I'll learn to fly a helicopter." It was a ridiculous sweeping statement to make in front of all the press, but once I had made it I had to be a woman of my word.

Besides, I wanted desperately to please my distant, beloved husband, to show my interest in the Royal Navy, to share Andrew's life and his dinner conversation. I wanted to bowl him over fiftyfold with pleasure—it was not every woman who could become a pilot, after all, or even who would try.

I had no idea of how hard it would be. Before taking on the helicopter, I learned to operate a fixed-wing craft. I cut my teeth on a Piper Warrior, and straight away I saw the difference between cars and planes; you can stop the car anytime and get out, but you have got to *land* the plane. This called for more than technical competence, especially when going solo. I had to put my fear in its place, keep it from overriding me.

With flying thrown into the mix, my daily schedule became a circus juggling act. I would go out to the airfield for a 7:30 lesson, fog permitting, and stay in touch with my staff by mobile phone, rattling off directives to my secretary like a country auctioneer. But after I earned my license, and a shower of praise from the Queen and the Duke of Edinburgh, I knew it had been worth it.

Then I advanced to phase two. Where fixed-wing planes are designed to offset pilot errors and stabilize themselves, helicopters depend entirely on the operator. They are more complicated, and more dangerous. To hover one is like sitting on a golf ball (not that I ever have); a tiny movement either way can cause the machine to dip or lunge. A helicopter landing demands total synchronicity, a jeweler's precision, a gymnast's grace.

As I slowly gained proficiency, I felt new pride in my naval pilot husband, in how strong and brave he must be.

By the time I received my helicopter license in November 1987, I'd won more than mere applause. I had started off doing it for Andrew, to cement my acceptance in the family, but flying had grown into its own reward. Here I was, a person who had always struggled with her math, and I'd gone out and achieved this great discipline. (Though in darker moments I wondered, daft woman that I was, if they had given me the license because of my title.)

I flew for myself now. I would climb into the cockpit in clothes that felt right, a sheepskin jacket and long silk scarf. I'd launch into the sky, till the buildings were toys and people were dots, and I could breathe again—the press of duty seemed less of a vise. Flying required so much concentration that I *had* to immerse myself in the moment and cast aside my anxieties. It was the best therapy I could imagine.

There was freedom in a helicopter, and release, and total privacy. In that cockpit I felt as I had in full gallop back at Dummer—that no one could catch me, and so I must be safe.

*I*n July 1987, Andrew and I were off to Canada, to embark on our first big overseas tour together. We went full bore for ten grueling days, from Toronto to the rodeo at Medicine Hat, Alberta.

On that sort of trip you were on review every minute; my only breaks came on the plane, where I played Scrabble non-stop. It took a lot for me to get it right—to be okay and on time and always look the part. In the cities we were followed by a mass of journalists, including forty-five hard-core veterans from Fleet Street. I had taken some heat in the newspapers just the month before at Royal Ascot, where Diana and I had poked my old school friend Lulu in the bottom with our umbrellas. We were just having a laugh, with no offense taken, but a photographer caught us in the act. The press made us out to be virtual hooligans, and I knew that my slightest slip in royal decorum would make headlines.

In Canada my dress requirements alone would have sent a saner woman off screaming to the nearest exit. We had packed at least half a dozen ball gowns in their "coffins," the large metal wardrobes used for transport, and after ten days of ceaseless changing I was ready to burn the lot of them. We averaged five engagements a day, with perhaps two hours between them back at the hotel. Andrew changed in half an hour and so had plenty of time to rest. But I would be hard pressed to finish in ninety minutes, especially on tiara nights. Tiaras are heavier than they look and tend to slip when one takes leave of a carriage or car. The grips must be secured so that the tiara stays absolutely centered in line with the wearer's nose. As the slightest imprecision would make for a lethal photo opportunity, my hairdresser would readjust the finicky thing a dozen times.

Meanwhile, I'd be running through my next speech, working all the time, not a moment to rest. The early returns were positive and spurred me to work even harder. The people liked my informality, the way I plunged into crowds and shook hands all around. Though reviews were mixed on Fleet Street, the Canadian press deemed our tour a great success— "an unabashed love-in for the woman known to admirers as Fabulous Fergie," one magazine gushed. No one knew how much strain I had endured along the way.

By the end of it I wanted nothing more than to collapse on a beach, but Andrew had a different idea for our "holiday": a two-week canoe trip with six other hearty souls down the Hanbury River, in the remote Northwest Territories.

Andrew had made similar excursions with friends back in

his Ontario school days, and he hankered to share with me the joys of white water. Touched by his eagerness, I said yes —not knowing I'd signed on for the most massive endurance test of my life. The pilot who flew us into Yellowknife predicted he would have to pull me back out within forty-eight hours; he even kept his seaplane on standby.

For the full flavor of my back-to-nature saga, let us turn to my diary.

"*Monday, July 27.* I thought it was all really amusing to get up in the Indiana Jones gear; the handkerchief around my neck, the floppy hat, khaki jeans tucked into the Maine hunting boots, with the knife precariously dangling from the leather belt. How wrong could I be . . . ?

"I was expecting a scene similar to Switzerland. Instead, I saw a barren mass of tundra. All the crew had beekeepers' nets on, signifying bad bugs. We got off the aircraft and immediately a net was put over my head and was glued to me throughout the trip.

"We paddled for three miles, which for me seemed an eternity. I think all the team wondered what a bad-tempered, uncoordinated imbecile they had agreed to take along. The setting up of camp was deadly and took ages. Once inside the tent, it sounded like rain as the bugs hit the tarpaulin.

"The men were dying for the women to fail or give up. . . . As soon as I heard that, I knuckled down and proved that I was not a WIMP and would not be defeated!

"Have you ever tried eating with a bug net on? I forgot on several occasions and steak or carrots fell down the front of my shirt. The end of a really eye-opening day. I will win, I will for Andrew.

"*Tuesday, July 28.* I am alone with my husband and the water is serene in its cold travels. What more could I ask really? You can't have everything in life—I nearly always do, so BUGS are to teach me how not to be spoiled and take anything for granted, when there is so much good around me.

"*Wednesday, July 29.* We awoke surrounded by festoons of savage mosquitoes and black fly. Swarms of the enemy lay in wait as we made our way to breakfast. The eggs looked like they had ground black pepper on them—in fact, they were black fly. I grandly declined breakfast and offered it to a less fussy crew member. . . .

"Eventually we came to some rapids. Sadly the water was too low, so we could not go through in canoes. We portaged with seventy-pound packs on our backs across rocky ground, stone-stepping. I don't envy a mule or donkey; I certainly looked like one. . . .

"Lunch was the same as the day before, actually the same every day for twelve days. By the end of the tour, the salami was strong and the cheese mature.

"*Friday, July 31.* Today passed without too much hassle. I was totally exhausted but struggled on and never let Andrew know that secretly I wanted to go home. I am very spoiled. Rapidly becoming unspoiled! The campsite was on a white sand beach. The freezing winds blew through unceasingly, but even they could not stop the mad Yorks from taking their evening dip. I heard an eerie cry—the call of the WOLVES barking on the horizon.

"*Saturday, August 1.* Time to go home, I have done my wilderness touch! Flies up my nose, mosquitoes when I pee, and paddling thirty miles a day. The fun bit is bed after vodka and a powdered orange drink. I do love my boy so much. We grow closer together hourly, and for that I thank this trip.

"*Wednesday, August 5.* When they talked about a river, I

naturally thought of Scotland. This was not the case. The River was enormous, always another bend, and the scenery never changed. It was such a lethargic river, very soul-destroying. We gave our strength to the River, and it did not respond. . . .

"*Thursday, August 6*. The going was tough today, battling straight into Arctic rain and wind. My hands and feet were numb, and my face felt burnt from the wind. . . . I was so snug in my tent. Andrew was asleep beside me. My wonderful husband, we had grown so completely inseparable now.

"*Sunday, August 9*. At last the day of return. We were home to The Explorer Hotel, and as I sank into a hot bath, I drifted back into the tundra. Now I appreciate my experience; it did me the power of good."

*A*nd what can we infer about the author of these earnest passages? On the one hand, she appears to be a terminal, teeth-gritting trouper, driven to prove her doubters wrong and get on with it at any cost. On the other, she reveals a newly-wed's affection for her husband (her heart even fonder, no doubt, from absence), a man she would follow to the seventh circle of hell if they could only share a tent there.

My lunatic tenacity got no praise from Andrew. Canoe trips were like official engagements; you got feedback only if you did something wrong.

I felt gratified, however, when Princess Margaret picked up my diary, shut it almost as quickly, and said, "I don't want to read any more—it is too gruesome."

* * *

*T*he more I felt hemmed in at Buckingham Palace, the louder came the Alps' siren call. Where the Palace dripped with intrigue and volatility, the mountains stayed safe and constant—very much like Her Majesty, actually. When the walls of my bedroom closed in on me, I would count the days until my next trip to Switzerland.

But mountains are not to be trifled with. You must be careful; you must treat them with respect if you choose to play with them. And if you are wise you will put yourself in the hands of someone who knows them, who will lead you correctly and out of harm's way. At Klosters, the ski resort favored by the Royal Family, I went nowhere without Bruno Sprecher, a guide I called "the mountain goat."

Even Bruno's talents were not fail-safe. On a morning run in March of 1988, when I was four months pregnant with our first child, I somehow skied into a stream and fell headfirst. I chipped the hangman's bone in my neck, and for a second went unconscious. To my great good fortune, the Prince of Wales was close by and jumped in to rescue me. As his boots filled with icy water, Charles pulled my head clear. "Come on, Fergie, you can do it," he kept saying, until I regained my wits.

When I finally got clear of the stream, my hair had frozen into an icicle; it stuck out behind me like a cockatoo's crest. I brushed off any further assistance—"I'm fine, I'm fine"—and skied down the last twenty-five minutes rather than wait for a wagon. But once I got to the bottom, I was frantic about a possible miscarriage.

"You'll be all right," said Patti Palmer-Tomkinson, a close friend of my mother's and Charles's. "Apples fall off trees only if they are meant to." I took a sonogram test, and the baby was fine.

At Klosters I normally skied the Madrisa run with Bruno in the afternoon, where the powder was preserved by morning shade. But that day I felt frazzled and spent, and before lunch I headed back to rest.

My uncharacteristic prudence would indirectly save Charles's life.

Since I didn't require his services that afternoon, Bruno went along with Charles's party instead, as the prince's guest. They ran into an avalanche, and Bruno—sensing it several beats ahead of the rest—yelled, "Jump!"

The Prince of Wales jumped higher than he'd ever jumped in his life and escaped injury. But Patti Palmer-Tomkinson was buried under a mass of snow and rocks until Bruno dug her out, gave her the kiss of life, and told Charles to talk to her while he got help, to keep her conscious at all costs.

Charles held Patti's head and spoke to her in the same soothing voice he had used with me that morning—and Patti survived, though her body was mangled.

Hugh Lindsay, the Queen's onetime equerry and an extraordinarily dear man, didn't make it. I am writing this now to remember him.

I always thought Charles an extraordinary person. He was a very good friend to me then; we found the same things funny, made each other laugh. We don't see each other anymore, and I miss him more than he knows.

8

Fat and Appalling

*E*arly in 1988, something happened to shake me into action, make me buck the status quo: I was going to have a baby, and where would we nest? That spring I went to everyone and said, "You've got to find me a house." But with Andrew at sea, there was no one to take charge of it, and I began to get despondent at the notion of raising my baby in the Department of the Environment.

Then I got lucky. At polo one day I sat next to Queen Noor, the American-born wife of King Hussein of Jordan, and I asked her if she knew of any cottage we might live in. She took me straight away to see an amazing place called Castlewood House, on the outskirts of Windsor Great Park in Berkshire. King Hussein had bought it for his children when they grew up, but Queen Noor said we could live there for a while.

Castlewood had a swimming pool and a tennis court and lush grounds at the edge of the park—it was my dream house. In May I moved in. Though duty bound me to the Palace during the week, my weekends in the country were liberation. I had my own garden to walk in, a fridge to raid whenever I felt like it. My own *kettle*, of all things. I had everything I needed in that big house, except for my man, now the watch-keeping officer on HMS *Edinburgh,* at sea for my entire pregnancy.

As my pregnancy advanced, I found it harder to keep the house and staff running; for that matter, it was strenuous to get in or out of a car. The more upset I grew at Andrew's absence, the more I grew in general. I drowned my sorrows in mayonnaise, sausage rolls, and smoked mackerel pâté sandwiches from Marks & Spencer's. (The food was cheaper than at Harrods.) I got bigger and bigger. My hands and ankles swelled. I felt like an elephant, ugly and grotesque. By the day of my delivery, I would weigh 203 pounds.

If I was a ship without a rudder before my pregnancy, now I was an enormous Spanish galleon, with great billowing sails.

I funneled my devotion into letters, writing to Andrew every day, never missing a batch that went out to the ships. I logged each one in my diary, right down to the bag number. And my husband wrote me back—wonderful letters, full of feeling.

On our second anniversary he wrote to me from Singapore. Each night at Castlewood I would walk out to the garden with my little dog Bendicks, a gift from Andrew to make me less lonely. I would look up at the sky and wonder if my husband might be standing on his bridge, seeing the same stars as I—but I knew he was too far away, in barely the same hemisphere, and surely his sky must be different.

I should have rested more in my pregnancy. Instead I kept running like mad, as though to flee the pain that perched on my shoulder. Every now and again—my waterskiing debacle, my accident at Klosters— the universe would signal me to slow down and listen to myself. But I was a person to speed through every yellow light and quite a few red ones. To stop the world and get off, to be *still,* might have forced me to look inside, and that I would not do.

In August, Andrew came home on two weeks' leave, and our baby was induced on the 8th to fit the Royal Navy's schedule. I had never warmed to babies much; I liked children when they were old enough to answer back. But that was before I had my own. When I looked into my daughter's sweet face and huge eyes, I felt such overwhelming pride. We named her Beatrice, after Queen Victoria's youngest daughter.

Four days later, my newborn and I were flown straight to Scotland; Andrew wanted a week to get us settled at Balmoral before he went back to sea. Time for another signal: as I walked out of the hospital, holding my baby, I skidded and ripped my stitches.

It was too much, too soon, too fast. The three of us might have had a blissful week alone together at Castlewood instead, but August in Balmoral was sacrosanct—it was what Andrew wanted and that's what we did. It would make him happy, and if he was happy life would be easier. Or so I thought.

In fact, life was dismal. We stayed in a lodge on the estate, and I cried every day when Andrew was with me, for I knew he would be leaving with the lark. And then he *was* gone, back to his ship in the Philippines. I moved into the castle after he left, feeling fat and self-conscious and altogether hideous. I holed up in my room, writing 750 thank-you notes by hand for the baby presents.

At last we got back to London, and I saw how my world

had changed irrevocably, and for the better. Our dining room/ office at the Palace was now a nursery as well. I would bob-sled through my engagements, as before, but I'd feel a new thrill as day's end approached: to come home to Beatrice, this tiny thing I could play with and be with, responding to her every need.

It was a precious time, and my sole regret is that I failed to seize more of it. While pregnant I had fallen behind in the Royal Duties Race and now felt pressured to catch up, to make my quota and not look too shabby in the year-end to-tals.

What the hell was I doing? Here was my most remarkable achievement, this beautiful girl I had given Andrew, and yet I could not pause to enjoy her. The Pleaser was working over-time, and still she was cheating the two who mattered most: the new mother and her child.

In September, when Beatrice was six weeks old, I left her with Alison Wardley to join Andrew on tour in Australia.

I had urgently wanted to take her with me; newborns are highly portable, after all. You simply strapped them to your chest, and off you went—they were happy with a smile and a coo now and then, and a bottle and a clean nappy.

But The Firm was quite firm on this point. It would be "ill advised" to take Beatrice to Australia, the courtiers informed me.

And: "You can't flit halfway around the world with a baby."

And: "The last thing in the world the poor child wants is to be dragged from place to place."

And, for me, the clincher: *"It is not done."*

Here, then, was my dilemma: Should I leave my child or my husband? I was getting trim at last, and I wanted Andrew to look at me as a woman again. (Only later would I realize that he cared far less about my weight than I did.) I could not bear the image of him turning up at port without me standing there and waiting with the other officers' wives.

Most of all, I needed to shore up my marriage. The two years since our wedding had wafted us apart; though I wouldn't dare say as much, I sensed we were in trouble. It had to be Andrew's turn now. I knew Beatrice would be well cared for by Alison, and so I left.

If I had to do it over, I would have snatched my baby up and made a run for it. Instead I bowed to my fear of whispers. What would the courtiers say about me? What would the Family think? (*Look at her she doesn't listen she doesn't take advice . . .*) I'd been brought up to do what I was told. It is a hard habit to break.

As I have said, fear will often lead you to what you fear most. The trip to Australia wound up pleasing no one. Each morning I awoke with the ache of missing a part of myself. Andrew was caught up in his job and the Navy boys' club—and six weeks cannot save a marriage, in any case. The press, meanwhile, laid the most hurtful charge imaginable: that I was a bad mother.

No one cared to remember that the Queen, and the Queen Mother before her, had once been obliged to leave their own infants and go out on tour. The tabloids can nod to history or leave it, depending on their aim, and now they aimed to do me in. I had gotten a few knocks before—for the Ascot umbrella caper and other piddling improprieties—but this attack was something different. It was heavy and enduring and mean-spirited, and soon it would spiral into something worse.

Fergiemania was dead and buried. It was my time to be the royal scapegoat. As with everything else, I would do it in a big way.

Where exactly did my plummet begin?

Many months before Australia, I'd begun to feel that some great, massive machine was pulling me down, it was set on automatic and it never let up. At the Palace I felt perplexed and helpless—not just now and then, but eight times a day. I could not ring up Andrew and say, "How do I deal with this?" I could only rely on my upbringing, on what I thought was right, but that approach had proved a patent failure. I was not pleasing *anybody.* With each mistake I lost confidence, and the more I lacked confidence the more silly things I did, till I dove into a tailspin with the joy stick sawn off in my hand.

In short, I was a sitting duck for the first tabloid in need of a potshot. The British press had come a long way since the days of Edward VIII, when they tiptoed around his affair with Wallis Simpson. The modern Royal Family was a late-edition soap opera, its members stripped down into two-dimensional cartoon characters. When I first joined the cast, the Princess of Wales happened to be out of favor. The press needed a new angel. And so was born, as Lady Colin Campbell put it, "Fergie the Real Person," such a bracing change of pace from "Diana the Birdbrain Spendthrift."

By late 1987, however, Diana had been restored to golden-girl status. Her return opened a vacancy on Fleet Street for "the bad Royal," a role filled at one time or another by Philip, Margaret, Charles, Anne, and Princess Michael. And who better to play the heavy than an overweight excommoner with a strong (now overbearing) personality and a candid (now tactless) way of talking?

The Duchess of York was declared a Loser. A major, big-time loser. And unlike Charles or Anne, who were Royals by birth, she was also expendable—no need to worry about going too far.

One thing is certain: the press could not have found a more unsuspecting target. Cruising along as the Remarkable Fergie, plumped into my feather-pillow banality, I'd been heedless of the cruelties heaped upon Diana. I surely missed some of the early salvoes fired across my own bow, for defamation starts as a subtle thing. One day your photographs are not quite so flattering—if you pull a single silly face, or flash a bit of thigh in leaving a car, that is what you will find on the next day's front pages.

The reading public doesn't see the editor poring over six rolls of film to find the most damning shot. The reading public simply thinks you are a fool.

Then the bombardment steps up. You find quotes put in your mouth that aren't simply made up, which is routine, but are also absurd or insulting or just out-and-out stupid. You go to dinner with friends for some moderate enjoyment—a bottle of red, a bottle of white—and some enterprising cub reporter has counted the number of glasses at your table, including the ones for Perrier, and implies that you have partied to beat old Bacchus.

When I stayed at Buckingham Palace, the butler brought the morning papers to my flat at six o'clock. I scanned through the lot of them but read only the bad stories word for word. If one writer called me fat and ten others thought me pretty, I would believe the worst every time and carry it with me all the rest of the day. I lived in dread of the next written rebuke, and it was never long in coming. The worst was when they called the office for some comment on Friday. I'd know they were building up to some big Sunday story, and my whole weekend would be ruined.

When you are a public figure and the press declares open season, there is no way to fight back. Respond to one sniper, one especially wild distortion, and you expose your flank to the next. And besides, I saw no cause to take on my accusers. Didn't everyone believe them? Didn't I believe them, too? If they said I was a bad person and a bad mother and this joke of a duchess, it must be so. My old self-hatred was now confirmed in black and white.

Many times I *knew* the facts were not what they'd said, dating back to my laundry weekend in Dummer. But the facts did not matter, not to me or the press; my specific guilt was irrelevant. If I hadn't committed the mischief at hand, surely I had done something else they had missed, and probably it was worse. I deserved the beating. I had it coming.

And I *was* guilty: of mental cruelty and abuse, of attempted murder. I was bent on my own destruction. I was still my own worst enemy—which in those days was saying a lot.

With hindsight, I might have got clemency had I played the shy, starving victim, the pale girl who would sin no more. But you must remember that I was unsinkable, I was Molly Brown with a vengeance. *What can we do to get this woman down?* It must have galled the tabloids to see me keep bouncing back, like a child's inflatable clown. Or like the boxer who gets pummeled into concussion but refuses to take the count and fights on into brain damage.

Other "bad Royals" had been protected from the excesses of the press. Harold Evans of *The Sunday Times* once told me that the Queen herself had asked each editor to back off and leave Diana alone back in 1982, which they did, at least for a while. Princess Anne, to name another, withdrew into silence, then came back rehabilitated.

But I would be allowed no such grace, nor was I apt to seek it. With no normal home or family life, with my husband gone and my friends shunted aside by duty, I had lost touch —you are looking at a true identity crisis here. My private self, long anemic, now was nearly invisible. Certainly inaudible. *Who was Sarah?* I could not answer, as I could not make out the question.

All I could hang on to was this baroque public figure, this messy concoction of a duchess. She might be ridiculous and contemptible, my persona, and soon the most reviled woman in the British Isles. But I could not lay her to rest; I had nothing inside to take her place.

"*I*'m just part of this day and age," I averred at one point, when my popularity had sunk lower than the pound against the German mark. "I'm just me. I don't profess to be anything else."

Why didn't they like me anymore? I was behaving like a normal person (the problem, exactly)—just being myself, whoever that was. They had found me so delightful as a policewoman on my hen night. They'd chortled along with my famous grimaces and verbal hijinks. Maybe they didn't really think me hilarious, but they would humor me, and that was all right—the dig in the ribs, the tolerant smile: *It's that good old girl the Duchess, after all, so what can we expect?*

But now the smiles had stiffened. Now they found me unacceptable, totally lacking in decorum. There was Ascot and *l'affaire* Lulu. Or the private dinner in New York where I had "knighted" our host's dog with a butter knife. Or the time when Diana and I played at pushing each other down the slope at Klosters as the photographers snapped away. We were sisters-in-law and playmates, just goofing around, and if you said we were immature you wouldn't be wrong—we were *young* then, after all.

I set store in good times. I tried to make everything fun, even at Windsor Castle, where I made sure there were games after dinner and a first-ever discothèque at Christmas. Though the Queen may have enjoyed it, there were others around The Firm who were less amused.

But I could not change my act. I was playing the fool, as I had at Hurst Lodge and a thousand cocktail parties, only now I had the megaphone of royalty at my lips. I was a Great and Laughable Wizard, and if my voice was too loud or my jokes a tad forward, I had good reason. I had to keep you trained on the megaphone, or else you might notice that dull little woman behind the curtain, and then you would lose all interest.

My first high crime in the decorum department occurred in 1987, when everyone still adored me. Prince Edward asked me for help in a televised charity event he'd organized, a game show called "It's a Royal Knockout!" to run on the BBC. It seemed just good family manners to participate, and Andrew and Anne agreed to go on as well. Everybody said it was okay. When Charles and Diana declined the invitation, I remember feeling miffed. I thought they were being most unsportsmanlike, not supporting the Family as they should.

Later I realized how smart they had been—that you cannot put your neck on the line when there's an "HRH" by your name.

The show was structured around a series of slapstick contests: races on oil slicks, water-bucket drenchings, pies in the face. Celebrities like Jane Seymour and Christopher Reeve had been enlisted to perform the actual foolishness. The young Royals were team leaders; we dressed in medieval costume and rooted from the sidelines.

The show was all in good spirit and for a good cause, but it ended as a public-relations debacle. Harold Brooks-Baker of *Burke's Peerage,* sniffing like a man with terminal hayfever, declared: "It is extremely dangerous for members of the Royal Family to conduct themselves in this way. These actions could lead to a republic."

I was ready to take my share of the heat for the show. I was *not* prepared to be cast as the villain of the piece, the pigeon *numero uno,* but that was exactly what happened. In the weeks to follow and for years to come, "It's a Royal Knockout!" would be analyzed as my first great blunder. It seemed so unfair to me. As captain of the blue team, I might have mugged and cheered more freely than the rest, me being such a fun-loving sort. I was still the new girl on the block—why should I be singled out as coarse and vulgar? What of Edward and Anne and Andrew, whose lead I was following? Why should I be blamed?

Now, too late, I see how the game was played, in the media and in The Firm. How I was suckered time and again. Everyone had a rule book but me, and when I finally got my copy, it read in pig latin, and I couldn't catch up with the class.

I had been given the rope to hang myself and had tied the knot like a scout.

I was bruised when the press chastised my behavior. I was bloodied when they condemned my taste in clothes. But what hurt most by far was when they wrote I was fat, the hobgoblin I'd fought since puberty.

When I was younger, and life simpler, I thought the road to happiness and good boyfriends was paved with a pretty face and a thin body. Dieting became an obsession. During my years in Clapham, I lived on black coffee and irregular, ill-balanced meals. The end result was a jittery wreck, completely wired up, a woman who would faint in the middle of the afternoon—I had no petrol in my tank! I got migraines every other day. I was poisoning myself to death, unless I starved myself first.

I calmed down during my courtship with Andrew, who took me as I was. In an interview before our wedding, I dismissed any battle of the bulge: "I do not diet. I do not have a problem. A woman should have a trim waist, a good 'up top' and enough down the bottom—a good womanly figure.

"I'm not going to get thin. I'm not going to change a lot. I'm just going to be me."

At the time, in truth, I was subsisting on meat and oranges and vitamins, to be slim and fine in my wedding gown. Still, I was at peace with my figure as long as my husband lived with me at the Palace. When I feel in control of my life, my weight follows suit. But when Andrew left, so did my discipline, and I own a metabolism that leaves little margin for excess—a pasta dinner will blow me up for three days.

During our marriage I would yo-yo up and down, though I'd never get so heavy again as when I was expecting Beatrice. For the most part I had an ordinary body—not perfect, but nothing to scare a small child if we met after dusk.

But that wasn't good enough for the tabloids, not anymore. They had a new cartoon character to play with—Fergie the Fat and Appalling—and Disney never did more to make one come alive. Having spared no effort or expense, the press was not about to spare my feelings. That is the quandary of a public figure—even your figure is public. Your vital statistics can be scrutinized like the national debt. You are left *nothing* as your own, least of all how you look.

And when that public figure is a woman, she is doubly vulnerable; the press can leer and mock and put her down in the lowest old-boys'-club tradition, all under the cover of "the public interest."

Of all the headlines composed in my honor, there is one that takes first prize. Set above a singularly unflattering photograph, it proclaimed me: DUCHESS OF PORK!

As awful and humiliating as these articles could be, the worst part—the most defeating part—was that all of them were smoke screens. I could have looked like Michelle Pfeiffer, dressed like Jackie Onassis, and behaved like Mother Teresa, and at the end of the day it would have made no difference. It would have forced the editors to work a little harder, to use more of their fertile imagination, but they are resourceful people—they would have found a way.

Viewed objectively, I was a sadder and lonelier person in 1988 than in 1986, but not a demonstrably different one. The main change lay not within myself but in how I was perceived.

The Remarkable Fergie was a welcome dose of new blood, the wholesome product of solid country stock, whose parents were well accepted by the Royal Family. The Fat and Appalling Fergie was a coarse and common girl from Basingstoke, the daughter of a royal retainer and a woman who'd run off with some Spanish-speaking foreigner.

The Remarkable Fergie was unpretentious, straightforward, good-humored, and exuberant. The Fat and Appalling Fergie was crass, rude, raucous, and bereft of all dignity.

The deck was stacked against me. Over the next years I would be thrashed for dressing badly, then for spending excessively on clothes; for neglecting my royal engagements, or neglecting my children; for slacking off; for being schemingly ambitious.

But my real problem was none of the above. In fact, I was damned not for what I did or how I looked, but for *who I was* —and that was something I was helpless to change. I was Irish on both sides, and redheaded, and full of zest for life, even if I knew not where to put it. I was different from the rest in Buckingham Palace, to be sure; my differentness had drawn Andrew to me, won the Queen's favor, made me a duchess.

And now it had made me a marked woman, as well.

Looked at this way, the damage was done at the very beginning. I was hopeless from the start, the wrong person in the wrong place at the wrong time. They could never make me the perfect princess.

Picture a horse that has been shut up all day in a dark stall. Finally he is taken out to a lush, green field—but he is not allowed to gallop over the field, or roll in it, or flick his head about and savor his freedom. He is permitted a few blades of grass to peck at, and then it is back to his dungeon.

I was that horse, and I would not submit to their bit. I would not stay in that narrow stall they had reserved for the Duchess of York, a place for vacant smiles and meek propriety. I would have my head; *I* would choose where I ran, and how fast.

*D*espite all I have been through with London's tabloids, I would not shoot the messenger. I know how a reporter's fair account can be twisted to match a good headline; how basically honest editors (even at the *Telegraph* and *The Times*, 'tis true) can be pushed by competitive pressure into stories built on sand.

Most editors are pragmatists, with no particular ax to grind. In my case, they made a simple judgment call. They decided that their long-term interests lay in playing ball with the System (aka business as usual) rather than with me. They assumed that the Palace machinery would grind me down, that I would surrender and then I would leave.

Given the rules of their ball game, accuracy might sometimes suffer, but at no great risk accrued, as royal duchesses do not sue. The press was grateful to get whatever tasty pint of defamation that the courtiers—with my own eager assistance—were ladling out that day. They knew that the soup bowl was deep; there would always be more food where that came from. If a publisher was especially loyal and consistent, a title might even be thrown in for garnish. (There is no more reliable member of the Establishment, for example, than the distinguished Lord Rothermere, chairman of the *Daily Mail.*)

But the press made two mistakes.

On the first count, I did leave—but I have yet to surrender.

On the second count, they missed a tremendous story. Something much bigger than any brickbat thrown my way, even bigger—if you can imagine—than two consenting adults showing affection by a swimming pool.

In my opinion, the press is still missing that story today. As yet unwritten is the tale of how some of the most trusted people at Buckingham Palace have undermined the monarchy itself.

9

Slamming the Window

The Prince of Wales once put it neatly. "We don't run our staff," Charles said. "They run us."

If the Royal Family represented The Firm's board of directors (with the Queen as chairman of the board), the senior courtiers were the operating officers, the ones who called the shots from day to day. At the top of their pyramid loomed the private secretaries, one for each branch of the Family. They ruled their fiefdoms with the assistance of their deputies and equerries (think of bureaucrats with epaulets), and they ruled with an iron hand.

These were the Grey Men, the obsequious band that shaped Palace policy and decided who got access to the Royals themselves. While the top jobs were semihereditary, the typical courtier entered the Palace only after his career stalled elsewhere. The Royal Family didn't pay well, but the Grey Men weren't looking for a big wage—they came from the good old landed gentry, after all.

Once entrenched, a private secretary might keep his job until someone noticed that he hadn't dozed off at his desk after all but was on permanent coffee break. In his inertia he was the perfect agent of the British Establishment, an exemplar of stability over talent. Prime ministers might lose votes of confidence. Royal houses might rise and then fall. But the courtiers would remain at Buckingham Palace; their faces might change, their mission never. (And after you had been there for a while, even the faces all began to look the same.)

The Grey Men were essentially well-marinated Sloane Rangers. Their suits were charcoal or navy, perhaps with a pinstripe—or, when the weather was warm and they felt especially jaunty, a gray Prince of Wales check. Striped or colored shirts, pale pink or pale blue. Conservative ties with some regimental insignia, or old school ties. Black shoes, buffed to within an inch of their lives.

These senior courtiers did their work with a certain insouciance. They went shooting most weekends, took a day off for Royal Ascot each June and for Wimbledon each July. When they managed to show up at the Palace, they followed a daily regime that was military in its precision, everything down to the minute. At 9:30 in the morning they trooped in through the Privy Purse Entrance, where a footman relieved them of their umbrellas and their overcoats, to be folded—*never* hung—just so.

"Will you be having lunch today, sir?" the footman would say.

"I'll let you know," the Grey Man might reply, a bit brusque.

Filing straight into the Equerries' Room, with its thick blue carpet, the courtiers harrumphed their way through their newspapers. (If I happened to be featured, a not infrequent misfortune, they would periodically croak out some trenchant comment, such as: "What has that dreadful woman done *now?*" When several of them got going, I've been told, the effect was not unlike Budweiser's famous talking frogs.)

Reading done, the courtiers popped into their offices, made and took a few phone calls. They knew well the first rule of any business hierarchy: that one's influence hinged on how well one controlled the flow of information. At the Palace, for example, Prince Charles could not simply ring up Princess Anne with an idea for some joint charitable endeavor. He would speak instead to his private secretary, who would pass the message down to a lesser secretary, who would call over to a secretary in Anne's household, who would relay the message back up to *her* private secretary, who would then speak to Anne.

It could all get quite byzantine. But no matter how strenuous their toil, the Grey Men were sure to get back to the Equerries' Room at 12:30 on the dot for their gin and tonic.

If they were dining in for lunch, they would stroll along at 1:15 to the Household Dining Room, the exclusive preserve of the private secretaries, equerries, and ladies-in-waiting. A second Palace dining room accommodated other white-collar staff. A third served the butlers, footmen, drivers, and housemaids—and woe betide anyone who happened to trespass into the wrong room!

Tea was served in the Equerries' Room at four o'clock sharp, and another gin and tonic at six. In between the courtiers might change and get puffed up into another wonderful new outfit—the equerries would look especially grand with all their shiny medals.

In sum, this was less a job than a cushioned way of life. Yes, the pay was not much, but it was quite a good wage for the service rendered.

*M*r. Z was The Firm's CEO. He was not quite fifty when he rose to his current post, but his age seemed indeterminate, as it often did among the Grey Men; he would look as though he'd been at Buckingham Palace forever and would stay on for all time.

Were you to happen upon him outside the Palace, you might think Mr. Z a superb bowler-hat caricature of the upper-class Englishman. Discreetly modulated, professionally adenoidal, Mr. Z could be most polite and charming when he cared to. By his own lights, I believe, he was an honest man who did his job as he saw fit.

But that job, as we shall see, was not for the fainthearted. Mr. Z was The Firm's enforcer, its soft-spoken muscle, upholder of standards and guardian of the rules. And though the rules might seem arbitrary, and at some remove from real life, any sorry transgressor would find a different side to that man with the glistening hair: abrupt, scathing, pitiless.

This courtier's courtier spoke with the Queen's voice, and he had the Queen's ear. By the time our paths crossed, he seemed to have lost sight of where the Sovereign's interests ended and his own began—he must have presumed they were one and the same. Were he to discern the faint scent of a brush fire, the mildest hint of a Palace uprising, he would turn his hose up full blast and then stamp out the last glowing ember. In doing battle Mr. Z was much more than a mandarin guarding his back; he was the Queen's paladin, the last bastion between order and the infidels.

*I*n theory, The Firm's purpose was to advise and organize members of the Royal Family, to translate their wishes into action, to temper their excesses and thereby spare them embarrassment.

In practice, The Firm's job was to perpetuate their own power. More royal than the Royals, the courtiers ran the snootiest club in Britain. Their hostility toward outsiders was legend. In Victoria's day, they referred to Prince Albert as "that German," and his aides as "German spies." More recently, Prince Philip took a try at reorganizing Palace management—and ran smack into a wall. For what good was it to be exclusive if you could not keep others out? And what was the point of a sinecure if one was now to be judged on merit?

The Firm's agenda bred pettiness and ignorance as Burgundy grew grapes. It especially bred an arrogant suspicion toward new ideas; the Flat Earth Society was alive and well at Buckingham Palace. In the narrow-set eyes of a Grey Man, to be original was to be a usurper; Queen Elizabeth might be the monarch, but one bowed first and last to King Status Quo. The courtiers buried their Palace in mothballs, encased it in amber. They would go to war to defend the Royal Family's mystique—for if Royals were seen to be no different from you and me, a cynical public might decide it could live without them.

When Diana entered the Palace in 1981, she was quickly marked as a threat. First, she was an outsider. Second, she developed her own base of public support and so became independent. Third, she was not as demure as she looked— she had great strength of will and would not yield to The Firm's petty tyranny. Yet despite their concerns, the courtiers felt impelled to carve a role for Diana. She was *too* popular to freeze out, and besides, she was the mother of the future heir.

With me they had fewer compunctions. As the second

son's wife, I was more dispensable. They could weather my early vogue as the "breath of fresh air." They could bide their time, but they knew what must eventually be done. Because fresh air can be a dangerous thing. Too much of it could make the Palace untidy, or rearrange the furniture.

Too much of it could even blow a house down.

By the time I returned from Australia, the Grey Men were itching to batten their door and slam their windows shut.

When I first came in, The Firm was run by an older, gentler school of courtiers. They seemed basically fair, and I deferred to their counsel.

But it wasn't long before these men left or retired or died, and The Firm had its own changing of the guard. There were (and are) still some good people there, but this new lot was different—more driven, more nervous, less tolerant. I think I was an electric shock to them—a different sort of animal than they had dealt with before. It didn't help that I was flying solo, without Andrew for guide or buffer. The new lot was suspicious of me from the start.

It began with a raising of the old eyebrow. Then the snide inflection, the cutting comment that you couldn't quite hear. My staff would be greeted by sniggering as they walked the Palace corridors; they were nearly as unpopular as I, because they would not trade gossip at lunch.

Soon I was getting periodic memos. They would be unbearably pompous by the end of line one and would never use one line when fifteen would do. The more pointed reprimands would be verbal and more circuitous. A Grey Man might phone our household's private secretary for a little chin-wag about my latest misdemeanor, with the tacit understanding that his point would be driven home to me—they were on the same team, these courtiers, all guarding something larger than the Royals they happened to be working for.

Had the Grey Men called me directly, I might have been more inclined to listen, even if I'd hated what I heard. But their indirectness got my back up. I liked to be frank and straightforward, so everyone knew where they stood. With The Firm, I felt like I was back at school and getting snitched on.

At bottom, of course, our conflict was more than a failure to communicate. The Grey Men and I were natural adversaries. They drove me mad, these constipated, self-appointed keepers of the gate. In their view, I was hopelessly erratic— due to some "women's problem," no doubt. I wasn't cut from the right cloth. I had this misguided fetish to be "real." I was, as the *Straits Times* noted, "bringing too much daylight into the magic of monarchy."

As Count Dracula—that grand aristocrat of blood-suckers —could attest, daylight is no good for parasites.

Swollen with self-importance, the courtiers tried to bring me to heel. But their memos and censures backfired. I am the first to seek advice and to be self-critical, but I am also the wild horse with those I don't respect—there is no dealing with me. Why should some man tell me that I can't go to Italy for an opera? Why should he deny me an extra half-hour with a Down syndrome child (or a "Mongoloid," in the Grey Men's fossilized parlance), to avoid being late for our train? Forget the train! The child *deserves* the extra time.

When I would not comply, the courtiers took it as defiance. They shed their unruffled veneer. They seemed to me insecure, like all bullies; they got instantly nervy when they found their judgment questioned. As if in echo of a royal command (in a hiccup, really), they would come down even harder—and I would resist in kind. I would not, *could* not cater to them, even when their opinions were spot-on. Because underneath, I knew, they thought that I was worthless, and I feared they might be right.

There could be no truce between us. I was getting judged all day long, and I don't take well to judging; it brings out the mischievous child in me, makes me wilder and more headstrong. The courtiers could still wound me (*Did they talk about me at lunch today?*), but they could not move me. I would always be different. I would never fit in.

Though tethered by circumstance, the Grey Men and I increasingly went our separate ways. Cut off from the traditional Palace network of advice and support, I would soon seek my sustenance from other, less official quarters.

And less than three years into my marriage, as the monarchy teetered in a new and uncertain time, The Firm would have its scapegoat, its maiden for the pyre. Always considerate, she had brought her own matches and kindling.

She would be cooked to order.

I tried to please in 1989. You could say I reinvented myself (again), at least in the externals.

In Phase One, my pre-Royal days, I had dressed as I liked and said to hell with accessories if you had a good honest soul.

In Phase Two, my Fabulous Fergie period, I made the huge mistake of listening to the people around me. *You're a public figure now and you have to look the part, and you have to do this and you have to do that . . .*

I thought to myself, *Who says?* Andrew never asked me to change the way I looked; our marriage contract had no dress code. But I listened, nonetheless. I *wanted* to look the part, but I lacked the first ounce of training to steer me through. Left to my own devices, I knew I would get it all wrong.

So I looked to Diana, as I had since Andrew and I began courting. I could never compete with her in the fashion department, but I might emulate her style, try to make it work for me.

And oh, I did toil at it. When I needed several outfits for Royal Ascot or some major occasion, I couldn't just buy them off the rack the week before. Several months in advance of the great event, I would go to a designer; we'd discuss what I wanted, then they'd make the first sketches. Then more reviews and discussions and fittings, and the hat designer and glove designer would be summoned to coordinate —everything was done to order.

The entire process was enervating, and the saddest part was that I wound up with a thoroughly ridiculous wardrobe —there are photographs I can barely look at today. From top to bottom, I was overdone: Big hat, big hair, frills and bows to beat the band. I wasn't trying to stick out; I wanted to blend with the "romantic" look of the eighties. But in trying to play safe and follow convention, I just made bigger mistakes. If I'd gone on what I felt, it would have been much better. My instincts were fine, but I was too weak to trust them.

As a result, I became a (literally) plump target for the fashion experts, who merrily slaughtered me for every faux pas. This particular Royal Family had never been famous for chic, but I became the lightning rod. One poll had me voted The Worst-Dressed Woman in the World.

I was totally confused. Hadn't I followed the rules? I had worked overtime for affirmation—I didn't look *that* bad, did I? (*Yes you did, you are hideous,* said the demon voice inside.) In my room I would read the papers and stare at my fashion "disaster" photos and cry until my face was a perfect color match for my preened red hair.

But in 1989 I entered Phase Three, my fashion makeover. I stopped trying to be like the Princess of Wales. I switched to simpler, cleaner lines. I wore more black. I imported tailored suits by Yves Saint Laurent, took the flak for using a non-British designer. Later on I had my hair cropped short, to a shoulder-length bob—and such an uproar ensued that you might have thought I was Rapunzel.

I was determined to get fit, inside and out. A nutritionist named Gudrun Johnson put me on a low-fat diet, fruits and vegetables and grilled chicken or fish, and I kept my weight down even into my second pregnancy. Three times a week I rose early to work out with my trainer, Josh Salzmann, and to swim a hundred lengths of the pool. Soon my body remembered that it once had been athletic.

I was, I think, just beginning to learn about myself—an early glimmer of consciousness. I had finally figured out that you cannot adopt another's style, not really, because style is individual to each of us.

While no one could call me an unbrushed red setter anymore, I had hardly won over my critics. Now, it appeared, I was trying too hard to curry public favor—to conform, of all things. "We have turned Fergie from a loud personality into a docile designer clone of Princess Diana," Jane Gordon wrote in *Today*. "Instead of the wild carefree Duchess flying in the face of convention we have a cautious and responsible mother-to-be . . . In fact the new improved Fergie is holding herself on such a tight regal rein right now that all her excesses—the ones we loved to berate her about—seem to have disappeared."

But never fear. The critics were only reloading, and I had a great fat ammo belt to feed them. Their next offensive would relate to the world's favorite subject, the basic building block of life for everyone but Royals, who are supposed to float above it.

The subject was money, and how I was spending rather more than I had.

My parents did not raise me to love material things, but I did inherit—from Mum, in particular—an enjoyment of the good life. It was *important* to have wonderful holidays and good food and parties done right.

I never learned to pinch my pennies, even when my pockets were light. Paddy McNally and Richard Burton were both work-hard, play-hard types, and I found it no hardship to step to their rhythm. I'd seize any chance to go off in an airplane —just the smell of aviation fuel made me feel good. Paddy hungered for experience and disdained the second-rate. I deemed his outlook wonderfully healthy, one to foster in myself.

By the time I met Andrew, I could juggle debts with the best of them. I came into Buckingham Palace with a bank overdraft of $800—a serious sum when you are making $18,000 a year and your sole asset is a ten-year-old car.

At that point, you might have assumed that my financial worries were over, that I would live solvently ever after in the bosom of one of the richest families in the world.

The reality was something else. For I had married the *second* son, and that made all the difference. While Andrew received a moderate sum from the Civil List, it went for the cost of official engagements and for staff and office expenses. As for my husband's personal income, the Royal Navy might provide free room and board and a chance to see the world, but it was no place to make one's fortune. In all our years together, Andrew's income never exceeded $50,000. Not that he cared. He didn't carry cash, anyway, and had written few checks in his life; ever since he was born, he'd had everything done for him.

But now he had a family, and finances got more complicated. We received a small allowance to cover expenses at Castlewood, but not enough for upkeep and staff. And while my clothing stipend from the Queen was kind and generous, I struggled to make do. In the rarefied strata I was now obliged to move through, where a single evening dress could easily run $4,000 and up, my allowance was soon depleted.

But I did possess one magical instrument: an account at Coutt's, the Royal Family's bank, with apparently unlimited credit.

I used that credit line liberally, lavishly—totally over the top. But it went too far to call me "an opportunistic bitch," in the words of one person high up in royal circles. I was richly traveled and had lovely things long before I wed Andrew; I didn't need to marry him to get those opportunities.

There is no question, however, that my favored-nation status at Coutt's enabled me to pile up a much more impressive overdraft—a debt that would reach six figures by 1992, when Andrew and I were separated.

Where did the money go? Quite a bit to cover costs at Castlewood and later at Sunninghill Park, the new home we'd move into in 1990. A fair amount for trips, to be sure, and even more after my daughters came along, for I would take them almost everywhere. I refused to stop doing what I had done all my life, no matter how the press reviled me for my "foreign vacations." My skiing kept me sane, and I thought it none of the tabloids' business. I paid my own way

—and if I wished to fly first-class, I paid for that, too, rather than booking in coach and presuming I'd be upgraded.

I spent money, as well, on our Christmas parties at Buckingham Palace. We'd invite everyone who had helped us during the year—not just our office and household staffs, but also my hairdressers and makeup artists, the travel agents and insurance sellers. We would get 250 people into the ballroom, and we'd give them more than the minimal Palace standard: a warm sherry and sausage roll. We would treat them to really good food and drink, maybe a play or a Caribbean theme for fun.

Not least, I spent money shopping—I was the impulse buyer incarnate. I had always been a great one for giving, going back to my racehorse wreath era. Now, with Coutt's behind me, I played Santa all year long. It was easy and convenient to do; merchants were more than happy to bring their wares into the Palace for approval.

I did not see my generosity as a fault. I got such a buzz from showing friends that I had thought of them; it was almost addictive with me. Where I really overstepped was within the Royal Family. I took pains to find gifts for the Queen or Princess Margaret that were completely original, things they really wanted but that no one else would think to get. When I found such a present, I did not care how much it cost—I took it and had the check raised out of my account.

I just wanted to make them happy, you see.

My gifts never seemed grandiose to me, but I had not reckoned with my in-laws' horror of material display. The House of Windsor was modest and humble, and I had broken the house rules. Rather than get thanked, I would be put down for overspending. *You didn't need to do all that. . . .* And they were right, I should have known better, but I *did* need to do all that, because I needed their love and I had hoped that my giving might carry the day for me.

In my defense, I was not entirely insensible to my growing pool of red ink. I tried to save money where I could. I found that some designers would allow me a deep discount in return for the publicity value of my wearing their fashions. It seemed like a no-lose deal to me, a business that served both sides and hurt no one. Wrong again—I found out that such things were *not done* by a royal duchess. The tabloids created a new cartoon strip: "Freebie Fergie," alias "Fergie the Freeloader." Freebie began popping up whenever I ventured out; I might take some girlfriends to dinner *and* pick up the tab, but I would still be Britain's biggest leech in the next morning edition.

What they failed to understand, in the press and in the Palace, was that I urgently wanted to work, to earn, to be productive. I had never wanted to stop my publishing job, though my duties forced me to taper off after we finished *The Palace of Westminster*. I missed a real job's stimulation and rested uneasy in depending upon the Royal Family. (A sound presentiment, there.) I had been on my own since the age of eighteen, and I liked how it felt to pay my own freight.

The idea for my first children's book was born at 5,000 feet. By late in 1987 I had grown bored with my helicopter lessons, and so I turned them into a childish adventure playground. I started calling my helicopter "Budgie," after the bird I thought it resembled. Before long I had infused Budgie with a full-fledged personality, just as I had with my childhood ponies and dogs. He was a freckled, impulsive, slightly disheveled boy, the type who goes out with his cap on wrong and oil spilling out of his tummy.

Rather than fly my designated circuit during a lesson, I started giving way to impulse. "I'm sure Budgie would want us to go left instead of straight," I'd tell my instructor, a Navy pilot named Kevin Mulhearn, who would indulge me.

Much later, my debt blooming by the day, I went to a prominent polo friend of Dads's. I outlined my financial straits, and then I started talking about Budgie. "This is a really good idea," the man said. He put me in contact with Mort Janklow, the New York literary agent, who in turn got me a contract with Simon & Schuster.

Soon I was scribbling out plot lines in pencil on our mahogany table at Castlewood. I gave Budgie a Piper Warrior friend named Pippa; the settings were inspired by my own fixed-wing flights over the rugged Devon coast. In October 1989, my first two books—*Budgie the Little Helicopter* and *Budgie at Bendicks Point*—came out.

It was a huge, proud moment for me—but the backlash had begun before the books reached the stores. From the start I had pledged a portion of the *Budgie* proceeds to charity. But the press deemed that insufficient, especially after they had wildly inflated the amounts going into my pocket. (Over the seven years since *Budgie* first appeared, I have received barely $500,000, in total, from the books and the animated cartoon spin-offs. Much of that has been given away.)

Later on, the newspapers would clobber me with charges of plagiarism; they said I had stolen my idea from *Hector the Helicopter,* an out-of-print book from the 1960s. I had never heard of *Hector.* I knew where *Budgie* had come from: my own eccentric head. But the accusers' message came through loud and clear. How could I *possibly* have done something original and creative? The *Budgie* books did not square with the tabloids' picture of me; rather than alter the picture, they refused to acknowledge the books.

The real issue here wasn't charity or originality. I had come up cheek by jowl with the Establishment's manicured snobbism. I had blasphemed the *Burke's Peerage* creed: that it was perfectly dignified to inherit one's money and never do a lick of real work, but unseemly for a Royal to soil her hands in the common swamp of commercialism.

Here was perfect Wonderland logic. On the one hand, I was not given enough money to pay our bills. On the other, I was told I could not earn my own. An exquisite Catch-22— not the first or the last I would encounter, but one with especially nasty repercussions.

Whenever friends of mine get engaged, I am full of sage advice. Spend all the time you can with your husband or wife, I tell them. Never go away for long. And keep a healthy distance from your families, to establish a real family of your own.

As the voice of hard experience, I know the importance of laying a strong foundation in the first years of marriage. When the winds come—and believe me, they will come— you will need that foundation for your house to stand firm.

Andrew and I were home together roughly one day out of ten. Through the whole of our marriage, discounting our Royal Marines Band honeymoon, we spent exactly five days alone on holiday, in Barbados.

That was a joy, but not nearly enough. My husband grasped the problem as well as I. "I am a prince, then a naval officer, then a husband," he would say. Those were the priorities put upon him, and one of the three had to lose.

"I just can't cope with the separations," I told the Queen and the Duke of Edinburgh. It was early in 1987, when Andrew was stationed at Portland. We were approaching his parents with a modest proposal: Couldn't I go and live in normal naval quarters, like a normal naval wife? I knew I could adapt to any situation, so long as my man was near.

Much frowning in response. It wasn't possible, they told us. The security, for one thing. It just wasn't done.

"But it's really very difficult not being with him," I said.

"Well," Prince Philip replied, "the Mountbattens managed, and so can you." Stiffen that lip, old girl. The subject was closed.

Looking back, I should have persisted. For that matter, I should have asked Andrew to leave the Navy; there were certainly other royal roles he could have filled. He might have got angry with me, but we might still be together today.

Of course I should have fought for myself, for our marriage, for what I believed was right. But I was frightened of my shadow then. I thought that a good wife sat and made the best of things—that to marry a man, much less a prince, meant accepting what he did. I didn't know how to fight that way. And Andrew, who could never forget that his mother was also his Queen, was no more able than I.

Now I can see how my old, sick patterns trapped me. I might be "HRH" to everyone else, but inside I was still the chubby teenager who cried herself to sleep, the uncertain woman who hid her qualms from Paddy and every other man. Inside I was nothing, a nobody, and nobodies don't pester the Royal Family unless they are ready to be shown the door.

And so Andrew and I carried on in our two distant worlds. By 1989 we were sharing less and less, till we lost the stitch of the fabric we'd been weaving together. A marriage is not about special events or lavish holidays; it is built by small things, all those homely, mundane moments that add up to something more. Without them we had little to talk about. Communication sputtered.

How could he know how I felt if I never told him?

How could I explain if I did not understand it myself?

There were times when I sat on our bed, convulsed with sobs, and Andrew would say, "Why are you crying?"

"I don't know," I would answer. When he put his arm around me for comfort, I spurned his touch. "I'm fine," I would insist. "I'm fine." Our solar systems had wheeled too far apart, beyond what we could reach.

10

The Plot Thickens

*L*oneliness was an old friend of mine. It had crept to my bedside each night at Hurst Lodge, moved in to stay at Dummer Down after Mum and Jane left, loitered nearby in Clapham and Verbier.

Yet never was I so lonely as when I was a duchess. For years I hauled the emotion around as my own furtive burden —the hard gauge of loneliness, after all, is the lack of someone in whom you can confide. But I was losing control over what feelings I showed and where I showed them. My private anguish began seeping into my public persona, that glossy shell that was supposed to be all-right-Jack at all times.

Charles would say, "There is a public person and a private person." And I would reply, "Why should I be any different outside and inside?" But Charles understood that public figures need some line of demarcation between their image and their soul, lest their soul become just another image for the media's digestion.

In my case, however, the public and private persons were on different planets. The one was manic and invincible, the other frail and malnourished. They had diverged too far. They were pulling me apart.

(A definition of someone with a disturbed mind: a person who is lying all the time with a smile on her face.)

And so I tried to make myself whole, bring my two parts together. I tried to rescue my private self before I lost it altogether. As usual, I botched the job. By April of 1989, I was seeping out into my interviews, speaking publicly of my loneliness and of how I'd been hurt by my critics. This was sheer lunacy, no question. At best, it would be taken as self-pity; at worst, it might egg my foes on to finish me.

I can only explain that I was starving for attention. As a Navy wife, I had no male companion. As a duchess, I had few people to call on. My oldest friends stood by me through all of my melodramas; I have never seen loyalty to match theirs. But I knew that last night's dining companions would be the next day's tabloid fodder. They had huge pressure on them, my friends; they had to stay silent to the grave on my behalf. Add in my grinding schedule, and the rigmarole of royal security, and I saw fewer and fewer people as time went on.

I'd made plenty of new friends, of course. When your home address is Buckingham Palace, you ascend to every A list in town. But after the press turned against me, it was funny, the invitations weren't so forthcoming. Increasingly I turned to other celebrities for company—not to join "the jet set," but because they understood what I was going through. They had been through hell themselves. They wouldn't judge me by my press clippings.

On November 2, 1989, four months pregnant, I arrived in Houston to pay tribute to that city's Grand Opera. I stayed at the home of Lynn Wyatt. For five days I attended to duty: a performance of *The Mikado;* a visit with the mayor; a tour of the NASA Space Center; a traditional Texas barbecue.

I also met Steve Wyatt, Lynn's son, and a friend of his named Pricilla Phillips. We fell to talking—about the mountains, I think, which they loved as much as I did—and within minutes we seemed like old cronies.

Steve and Pricilla were less inhibited than the people I knew in London, more open to matters of the spirit; they both meditated, which I found intriguing. When they were around, the darkness lost its power.

No longer did I feel like an abandoned pregnant woman, a morose combination if ever there was one. I had two new confidants, two pillars to lean on. Steve and Illa cared nothing about my title or the baggage of my past. They saw me at face value and accepted what they saw.

On the way back to London, I stopped in New York for a *Budgie* promotion. At a dinner party thrown by Mort Janklow, I found myself seated next to Tom Wolfe and opposite Norman Mailer. I asked Mailer to recommend one of his books to me; he proposed *Tough Guys Don't Dance.*

"What is it about?" I asked.

Mailer looked at me deadpan and replied with a single word: the plural form of the slang for the most private part of a woman's body.

The assembled literary lions were dumbstruck. But I was a hard case to shock. From Paddy McNally I had learned the art of staying unflappable, of defusing a situation without putting the other person down.

"You know, Mr. Mailer," I said, breaking the silence, "the most interesting thing for me right now is watching everyone's face at this table."

* * *

As soon as I got home, I hopped in my car and drove three hours to surprise Andrew in Portland. I longed to be with my husband. Our bubbles had been drifting ever farther apart, and I missed our old closeness. But Andrew was busy with work, unable to go to dinner. I left Portland still gnawed at by our estrangement.

Some time in the winter of 1989–90, a friend asked me to receive Dr. Ramzi Salman, who was head of marketing for the Iraqi state oil interests. It would be a Palace courtesy call, a friendly drink and no more.

Three years in the system had taught me to take precautions. I asked a senior courtier to double-check that it was all right and to make the arrangements. The courtier came back and said everything was fine but that it might be nicer to meet in the White Drawing Room rather than in our dining room.

When you are spinning on your own merry-go-round, as I was, it is hard to see what is going on around you. Six months or more before the invasion of Kuwait, I did not realize that Saddam Hussein was already deemed a threat by the West.

I was just doing a favor for a friend who had been good to me. And though I had asked for advice, nearly begged for it, no one in The Firm chose to brief me that I was tramping through a diplomatic minefield.

The courtier instructed Dr. Salman to come through the Sovereign's Entrance, which I assumed was appropriate for any visiting official. We met in the White Drawing Room, had a drink and a chat. Our conversation was too innocuous to remember—small talk about the Palace, a few polite questions about my guest's children.

The senior courtier was with us every minute and looked appropriately bored. There was not the faintest signal that I might have jeopardized the Queen's close ties with the Emir of Kuwait, who would soon be living in exile in London. But that is just what I had done—and worse, I had rubbed everyone's noses in it. Had I met with Dr. Salman in my flat, as originally planned, and had he come through a lesser entrance, our meeting might have been less conspicuous.

But I hadn't, and he hadn't. My self-sabotage had taken another great step forward. I did not know it at the time, but that casual drink in the White Drawing Room might have sealed my fate.

On Friday, March 9, 1990, I took a call at the apartment. It was Mr. Z. He wanted to see me in his office at eleven o'clock. I cringed at the sound of his voice; there was menace in those low and cultivated inflections. Though we'd have occasional social contact, Mr. Z never met me face to face on Palace business; that just wasn't his style. Nor was he the type to offer a "well done" after you had shone.

I panicked—I had been called in to see the headmaster! *What have I done? Oh my gosh, I am going to get told off. I'm sorry, I didn't mean it . . .*

I was eight and a half months pregnant. Mr. Z's office lay half a mile away, and it took me some time to traverse the red runway of a corridor. I got there promptly at eleven and was ushered into an office with three hard faces: Mr. Z; Mr. Y, his deputy, a shambling, rubber-lipped man with a permanent pleat in his nylon trousers; and a third courtier in reserve.

Without further ado they piled on; they had been looking forward to this seminar for some time, I believe. "We don't like your behavior," Mr. Z began, drawing himself up into the royal first-person plural.

When I asked for an example, they were off to the races—

they had a laundry list of violations, and all three men were well rehearsed. The meeting with Dr. Salman had been entirely improper; to have him come through the Sovereign's Entrance—reserved for the Queen, I now found out—was inexcusable. And what *had* I been thinking when I used one of the Queen's luggage cars to help a friend move his furniture to a different flat?

And while they were on the subject, the Grey Men kept on, these new American friends of mine weren't "the right sort of people," and I would be well advised to see less of them.

"You have made a *huge* mistake," said Mr. Y, who was working himself into a fine froth. He was quite frightening to behold, flailing about in this state. His arms moved mechanically, as if they were on pulleys.

"Didn't you know what you were *doing?*" Mr. Y continued. "You have abused Her Majesty and her kindness."

Their barrage lasted a full hour, and it was brutal to the end. With hindsight, the courtiers must have regarded me as a lame duck, dead in the water, or they would not have dared speak to me that way. The Firm was washing its hands of me, then and there. I was an irredeemable loose cannon, a total idiot and buffoon: case closed.

The Grey Men's whole reason for being lay in doing things "the right way." I persisted in doing them wrong. How could we possibly coexist?

If their rebuke seems like overkill in the retelling, it was because of how they viewed me: as this loud and fearless person who just didn't give a damn, who went about blithely hurting others with full malice aforethought. They couldn't see that I had beat myself up a hundred times before they'd lent *their* fists to the chore; that I was loud for lack of confidence, not its surfeit; that it had taken all the courage I had just to creep into their room that morning.

For the most part I just bore their harangue, too numb for tears. *(When I tell you off, why can't you just accept the criticism and say you are sorry, and then forget all about it?)* But as I staggered out the door, I managed to ask, "Does Her Majesty know that you are telling me this?"

"We have Her Majesty's full authority to tell you this," one of the courtiers said evenly. (I cannot remember which one; at that point the three men were a single hostile blur.)

Distraught, almost dizzy, I wobbled my way to the lift and back up to the second floor. I started to hike the red runway, but it seemed that it stretched for miles. Never had I felt such turmoil. My hormones were up the spout anyway, and now I had been blasted by the monarch, by my beloved "Mama" —I felt like I wore the mark of Cain. It was my worst nightmare turned to flesh, the final absolute rejection.

I was still a good eighty yards from the flat when I reeled and nearly fainted by a grand piano. That was where Jane Ambler found me. She somehow gathered me up and got me home to Castlewood, where I would lie in bed for two days.

On Sunday I finally got back on my feet and went to see the Queen at Windsor. I asked her why she had sent her three men to rebuke me—why hadn't she voiced her concerns to my face?

My story surprised the Queen; she had been unaware of my pummeling.

A sad postscript appends this story. To that point my pregnancy had been smooth and easy. The sonograms showed the baby to be well positioned; I'd assumed I would have a natural childbirth, as I'd had with Beatrice. But after her mother's going over that morning in the Palace, my baby did something rare for a fully grown fetus. She turned herself around in the womb, into a breech position.

She had heard what the outside world was like and quite sensibly wanted no part of it.

Two hundred press photographers, many perched on ladders or scaffolding towers, would camp outside the hospital for a week before the birth. But Andrew arrived only just in time from Plymouth, where the frigate HMS *Campbeltown* had docked. The obstetrician had tried to turn my baby but failed. She was delivered by cesarean section at 8 P.M. Friday, March 23. We named her Eugenie.

I still carry the scar, a memento from the Grey Men.

$\mathcal{T}$he more I learned about motor neurone disease, the more work there seemed to be done. As royal patron, my job was to raise both funds and awareness to fight this little-known killer. The MND Association spent more than $3 million a year—and received less than $20,000 from the government. The money went toward bed elevators and motorized recliner chairs, loaned free of charge to individuals; a telephone helpline, to answer people's questions and steer them to other services; a network of regional care advisers, furnishing each family with an advocate; subsidies for respite care; and, not least, funding for drug trials and other medical research.

MND devastates whole families at a blow. Charleigh was eight years old when I met her, but childhood had already passed her by. Her father had the disease; a former boxer, he was furious all the time at what had happened to him. The family lived in a fourth-floor council flat, where the lifts kept breaking down. When Charleigh's parents came home at night, her mother wouldn't be strong enough to pull her father up the stairs. She would wake Charleigh up out of bed for assistance—it was either that or leave the man on the landing for the night.

Such tragedies were commonplace, but the MND Association also gave me great inspiration. I wouldn't soon forget the first time I met Stephen Hawking, the Association's patients' patron and one of the great brains of our time. The professor was locked into his wheelchair, but he had not lost his sense of humor. After clasping my hand, he tapped for several seconds on his keyboard, and a voice synthesizer intoned: "Excuse my American accent."

After one encountered a man like that, it was infuriating to see people with MND treated as though they were drunk or mentally deranged—as people to be avoided on the street. The disease can be crushingly isolating. Friends and relatives tend to be frightened or embarrassed; they don't know what to do with a person who can't talk, and so they pull back.

When I attended an MND conference, I'd be struck by its brimming energy. The room would feel charged, like the air before a thunderstorm. All of these silenced people would be packed together, and they'd be straining to push out so much feeling and information to me through their subconscious. I felt washed by a huge, great wave; Peter Cardy, the association's director, called it *the fire*.

No matter how large the gathering, I would speak to each individual before I left. I refused to be rushed off; I'd be late to my next engagement if I had to be. These people were all so desperate to be understood, to leap the chasm of their speechlessness, and somehow I could read into them, and we would have this very intense, one-way conversation. It is difficult to explain, but I would experience their wheelchair, their sense of entrapment, as though I were inside it myself.

I might be introduced to a man who was once a civil servant, and the first thing I would say is, "Please don't get up" —I'd make a joke of it.

"Right, I know exactly what you're trying to say," I might go on. "The first thing you want to do is get rid of this beastly chair, and to stand up and shake my hand."

And it would seem that the man was thinking, *Phew! She's understood that I'm feeling like this.*

I never looked down at these people. I would get to their level, either by crouching or having a chair set for me. One time I got up to say something from the middle of a conversation, and Jane Ambler thought I was ready to move on to the next person. She moved my chair—and I made this tremendous pratfall when I tried to sit down again. Everyone thought me a regular Charlie Chaplin; it worked very well.

Once I went to a psychotherapist directly after an MND meeting. "I'm not sure I can treat you," he said gravely, "because we don't deal with people on drugs."

"But I'm not," I said.

"But look at you—you're high," he insisted.

The therapist didn't grasp that I was high on *the fire.* Here I was feeling lost and alienated from all around me, and depicted in the press as some contemptible Looney Tune, and once or twice a week I met these people who saw me for who I was—who knew that I wasn't such a bad person. I listened to them, and we understood each other, and no one could take that away from me. These were my secret, private moments, my rare connections. My small rewards.

I wasn't satisfied to be another public face with a pitch; my friends needed more than a figurehead. Most of all, they needed a cure, a goal that could seem maddeningly abstract as we awaited our first real breakthrough. In February 1990, I organized a meeting at Buckingham Palace of half a dozen leading researchers, in the hope that their exchange might spark some new ideas.

On my way there, I got a call from Mum. Hector had felt ill for months, and now they knew why: he had cancer of the lymph glands. He would be treated with chemotherapy at Memorial Sloan-Kettering in New York.

I would be there to meet them.

To keep the press at bay, they put Hector on the ninth floor, among patients with face or neck cancers. But now they had another disturbance to put up with, this very pregnant duchess with her entourage of British bodyguards and U.S. State Department security men. When I apologized to the nurses for the upset, one of them asked me, "Would you mind visiting the other patients? It would do them a lot of good."

There were people on that floor without tongues or noses. I sat very close to them and held their hands and chatted. I felt quite comfortable around them. The good thing about being a pariah is that you lose all squeamishness. I knew what it meant to be untouchable, to be judged each day as unworthy and *believe* it myself, and so I treated these people as the equals they were. I took them as they came.

(A small dose of kindness can be powerful medicine. Mum told me afterward that no one on the floor asked for extra morphine that day and that an older woman declared, "I'm going home tomorrow, nose or no nose, because I spoke to a princess and she said I looked great!")

I shuttled to New York several times that spring. Between his treatments, Hector stayed at White Birch Farm, the Connecticut home of his best friend, Peter Brant. It was hard to see *El Gordo* so gaunt and listless. One day I organized a baseball game on the lawn with the security men, just to break the heavy mood—I think Hector enjoyed watching that.

That summer Mum called from Argentina. It was a matter of days now, she said, and Hector had asked to see me and Beatrice one more time, and to meet little Eugenie. I had to ask the Queen's permission to go; no member of the Royal Family had visited Argentina since the Falklands War, and only recently had Britain restored its ambassador. Her Majesty wished me Godspeed, and the three of us left for El Pucara on July 28.

Hector rallied enough to be driven out to watch us ride his wonderful ponies, out past the cedar trees I'd helped plant a decade before. I held Beatrice, not quite two, in front of my saddle: her first horse-riding lesson.

Hector and Mum had moved into a new hilltop home just weeks before, but he knew he had no future there. "I'm not living, just existing," he would sigh. He had hung on to see us, but now his strength ebbed again. On August 7 he checked into a hospital in Buenos Aires. We left the next day, on Beatrice's second birthday, but not before Hector and I had one last talk.

"Be careful," he told me. "Don't get stuck in the situation that I am in now; don't do things in life that cause you to regret." I understood his meaning—that there were other ways than cancer to be inextricably cornered and destroyed.

And Hector said, "I love your mother more than any woman in the whole wide world—will you look after her for me?"

And he said, "Remember that Andrew is a very good man, and that he'll be a very good man in the future. Stay with him."

Two days after we left, Hector died at the age of fifty-one.

I went into total and utter head-down. I didn't feel like I had lost a father, or a stepfather. I felt like I had lost a friend —my best friend.

Castlewood was my nest and I felt safe there, but I knew we couldn't stay forever. With two children in tow, it was time for Andrew and me to find a permanent abode; it would be a gift from the Queen, as per tradition. I would have loved to have had an older home—I was ready to live anywhere feasible. Unfortunately, all the houses nearby had been rented or sold; there was no empty royal residence nearer than Yorkshire.

So we decided to build our own house, with the Queen's full support. We chose a site at Sunninghill Park, close to Windsor Park and near a lake, and soon were caught up in layouts and room plans. Andrew and I made all the big decisions together—another layer of stress in my life, another escape hatch. The more I had to do, you see, the less I had to feel. After the earthquakes I had suffered of late, emotion seemed safer when salted away.

As Sunninghill Park neared completion, I got more excited. Built in the modern ranch style, it had sun and air that made up for what it lacked in Victorian detail. It offered freedom and space and five acres of wooded garden. Each day brought my girls and me closer to what I hoped would be our last move.

Until one day we were pulled up short. The money people at the Palace had signed off on the plans for Sunninghill at every step, but now they shut the budget. The pool and tennis court were yet to be built—luxuries, granted, but a big house must have its finishing touches if it's not to look half baked.

The garden was not done. And it wasn't just the grounds—there were cornices on the walls left incomplete. We had no funds for *curtains*.

By the time the last worker left, I would draw more than $500,000 out of my own account to finish Sunninghill. Some of it came from *Budgie,* but we needed quite a lot more. Plus Hector had left Mum with considerable debt; she would be fighting to hold on to El Pucara, and I had to help her. We were all in a fix. We needed a financial infusion, and fast.

The solution—the only one that presented itself—was a deal with *Hello!,* a Spanish-based magazine that doted on fluffy photo spreads on royalty. In return for what they'd term a "privileged glimpse behind the public image," *Hello!* would pay us some $350,000. The photographs would be taken at Castlewood by a friend of Andrew's.

When the magazine came out that August, I was flabbergasted. Rather than devoting its standard five or six pages to us, as I had assumed, our family was splashed across seventy-five candid photographs on forty-eight pages. It was much too much—like bringing an Iraqi minister through the Sovereign's Entrance.

Taken one by one, the pictures were not very shocking. Andrew paddled in the pool with our daughters, threw a tennis ball to our dog; I smeared sun lotion on Beatrice, bathed and fed four-month-old Eugenie. (Eugenie, naturally, was naked—a great to-do for certain individuals with that peculiarly British terror of the human body.)

My family looked happy and loving and altogether normal, no different from anyone else—and that was our crime, exactly. The *Hello!* spread had pierced the central myth of royalty: that they are of some different species. Those bland domestic photographs would be food for scandal on the dinner-party circuit for months to come. Once more I had ignored the ramifications; I had leapt in where Royals fear to tread.

"One of the most dangerous things perpetrated by members of the Royal Family," declared the ubiquitous Harold Brooks-Baker.

"We don't want the Royals behaving like *EastEnders*," added author Barbara Cartland, chanting the Establishment's theme song with perfect pitch. "We might as well have pictures of the Queen Mother taking her clothes off and climbing into the bath.

"If the Royal Family lose their mystique, they will go altogether. The younger ones don't seem to understand this. It's all very well them wanting to be liked, but this is taking the common touch too far."

Andrew was off on his frigate when the magazine came out. I would have to talk to his mother, he said; he just couldn't deal with it.

I screwed up my courage and joined the family on HM Yacht *Britannia* for ten days of penance. Ten days of telling off by The Firm for my execrable judgment and astounding impropriety. "This is most irregular and very strange of you to behave in such a way," a Grey Man might say, finding my knuckles with his titanium-plated ruler. "It is really not right, and I don't know if it pleased Her Majesty very much that you behaved like that."

And when I wasn't being disciplined, I was being excluded; you would have thought I was carrying some distasteful tropical ailment.

There was no question as to who would take the rap. Andrew was the Sovereign's son and had to be protected. Never mind that it took two to tango, that my husband's grinning face shone out from *Hello!* next to mine. The party line could not be challenged: I was the greedy bewitcher, and he a mere dupe of a duke. We were playing "It's a Royal Knockout!" all over again.

The Castlewood photographs were not another nail in my coffin. They were a thick lead spike into my forehead.

But I had not *meant* to be so bad—why couldn't they see? My motives had been good (as usual); I was trying to show initiative, be self-sufficient, only my methods were scatter-shot. A scheming witch? They kept giving me too much credit. I was a Ferrari with no brakes then, whizzing too fast to think ahead; I caught sight of my trail of destruction only when I found the rearview mirror.

Looked at more coolly, my sin was more of context than of content—less what I did than who I was, or was not. A few months after my latest disgrace, BBC television began taping an unprecedented documentary. Called *Elizabeth R,* it depicted a year in the life of Her Majesty. Along with footage of state visits and high ceremonies, the public would enjoy several more intimate vignettes, "behind the pageantry": the Queen inspecting a racehorse at Sandringham or rooting for her pick at Epsom Downs; the family joking about on the day of Eugenie's christening; the Queen taking Beatrice on a pony ride at Balmoral.

No one shuddered or recoiled when this video was broad-cast. No cry went up from *Burke's Peerage* or Barbara Cart-land. A little daylight was not so terrible, it turned out, when the Queen was adjusting the blinds.

As moving day approached, I was overwhelmed. With An-drew away, all the logistics fell to me, and I had taken on too much. I felt angry all the time and never expressed it. I cried endlessly. (I was on another intense diet, which didn't help.)

I could not shake my skulking fear—that my life had nothing to do with who I really was.

On Friday, October 5, I began my day with a hair appointment at eight, then drove two hours to Hector's memorial service in Gloucestershire, near *El Gordo*'s home pitch. Grummy had given me a reading, and my voice shook as I began:

"Death is nothing at all, I have only slipped away into the next room. . . ."

I believed every word of it; I had as many fears as the ark had pairs, but death was not among them. I missed Hector terribly (and miss him more today), but I've always felt content with people who were dying. They were passing on to another, better place. And I agreed with the American Indians —that if you lived fully, any day was a good day to die.

Then, too, death must have seemed inviting at the time, if only for the peace of it. Because no sooner had I returned from Hector's service than I was back on my spinning treadmill. I ran out to say good-bye to Castlewood and finish our move into Sunninghill Park. At 4:30 I had my dress fitting and makeup and hair done, again. At eight o'clock I was grinning my most hospitable grin to two hundred people in black tie.

It was time for our housewarming, and I cared so much that everyone should have a good time.

If ever there was an exercise in criminal insanity, this was it. We had not finished moving until that afternoon. The choir's last notes still echoed in Gloucestershire. And here I was, all jacked up and turned out in my stunning party dress, playing the Gracious Hostess for one and all. I was quite sharp at charades, mind you, but this time I had outdone myself.

We could have changed the party date, of course, but I

would have none of it. *I can handle anything—who says I can't?* Deaf to the cries inside, blind to my inner pain, I was a perfect pinball wizard. I kept racking up points for a game without purpose, or end.

The next day, October 6, I attended a sports foundation dinner and Andrew went back on duty. The game played on.

I had known we'd take some criticism for Sunninghill, but I was caught short by its ferocity. The tabloids delighted in calling it "South-york," after the grandiose Southfork in the TV show *Dallas*. One more time I bore the brunt of the onslaught, as though the place had been my idea alone. But that was not even the point. Sunninghill was our dream and creation, our fair prerogative, and why should anyone have the right to pull it apart?

Meanwhile, my debts kept rolling up like the digits on a petrol pump. A larger house meant more staff: a valet and a nanny, a cook and a butler, and weekend staff as well.

People would say I should roll up my sleeves and carry the weekend load myself, but I had other obligations: my quota, for one thing. In 1989 I had soared to near the top of the standings, with 327 official engagements. (I would have taken a bow, but there were no prizes to be had in this business, except of the booby variety.) In 1990 I dropped to last with only 108—ten fewer, the tabloids noted, than the Queen Mother, who was ninety years old at the time.

My apparent slump inspired a whole new raft of headlines: THE LAZIEST ROYAL; THE DUCHESS OF DOOLITTLE. I was a shameless Switzerland ski bum, or a brain-fried Riviera sun worshipper, take your pick. No one seemed to notice that I'd been busy that year, in my own small way. I had given birth to a child, lost my stepfather, organized our move to Sunninghill.

Moreover, I was doing more duchess work than advertised; I was charging along, in fact, at a breakneck pace. By 1990 I was serving as president of four charities and patron for twelve others, including the Chemical Dependency Centre, the Sick Children's Trust, and Action Research for the Crippled Child. There might be briefings five times a day—I was getting briefed as I prepared to deliver Eugenie.

Much of my activity wasn't charted by the Court Circular: private visits to the homes of MND patients or to Trinity Hospice in Clapham; visits to charity headquarters and dining-room meetings at the Palace; telephone briefings or the river of obligatory letters. I refused to be just a name on a letterhead, I was more hands-on than the traditional Royal, and my "numbers" suffered for it.

At times I would commit to something utterly daft, but my promises were ironclad. When my sister wanted me for an MND function in Australia, I flew straight there from Portugal, then back to London the next day.

If I told you I wasn't keeping score I would be lying. I always wanted to excel, to be *perfect;* the more they perceived me falling short, the more I would be driven to prove the critics wrong. No one would be busier than the Duchess of York; I would not allow it. To slow down would prove their case—would convict me as that do-little fraud. (To slow down might force me to face the void inside.)

Every now and then, a mote of sanity would struggle to the surface. "We're both chained to our stupid duties and ruining our lives together!" I once exclaimed to Andrew. Somehow I had retained this odd notion of being a wife, if only part time. For example: A week after our housewarming, I was in London all day with my MND people, then flew out the door to support my husband at a shooting weekend—more jolly japes with Bunty! We came back on Sunday, but Andrew had a short leave, so we flew back out the door and hauled up to Northampton for two days.

The children weren't with us on outings like these, nor would they see me much during the week. I always felt cheated of time with my daughters, felt permanently torn and guilty. It wrenched my heart when Beatrice asked her nanny, "Oh, why couldn't we go and live where Mummy lives sometimes?" Meaning the Palace, where I burrowed in for days at a time. *(Maybe you are a bad mother after all you cannot do anything right. . . .)*

Now Hector was gone, and I had this huge new house to maintain . . .

The whole world seemed to be slipping away from me, and I could not find my grip.

11

Making a Break

*F*or the Merry Wives of Windsor, as the press called Diana and me, 1991 would be a year of unrest. The two of us were groping in the dark—we were the blind leading the blind out of our Brothers Grimm nightmare. We had no idea where we were headed, but we knew that we could not sit pat.

It was the year we first put words to the unspeakable idea that had been nudging us in the ribs for some time: that one or both of us might leave the Royal Family. We burned the phone wires into the night, trading secrets and jokes that no one else would understand. The Firm was aware of our potent confederacy and did what it could to divide us. The courtiers had to insulate Diana, who might yet be the future queen. So they hatched a new scenario—that Diana, like Andrew, was an innocent dupe, the victim of my wiles. I was the sinner, she the saint; I the bad witch, she the good. (Such power I had then.) It was an absurd construction, as anyone who knew Diana also knew that she was her own woman.

The more alienated we felt, the more outrageous our conduct. One summer night, as everyone sat down to coffee and chocolates at Balmoral, Diana and I were feeling rather bored. We slipped out the front door in our long dresses and piggybacked on one of the quad bikes. Undaunted by the pitch darkness, we proceeded to zip through the golf course, ruining the greens for the next day's play—by accident, I assure you. At one point we found ourselves at the lodge occupied by Mr. Z and his family and rang the bell, giggling at our nerve. It wasn't much before midnight, and Mr. Z was not amused when he came to the door. Another black mark for me, I suppose.

By that point Diana and I had fallen into hysterics, which was typical for us—either you laughed at The Firm or you cried. We rode back down to Balmoral Castle and liberated the Queen Mother's Daimler, this huge antiquated car with storefront windows. Diana got in front and drove, with a chauffeur's cap to top off her long dress. I sat in back, screwing lightbulbs as we rolled along the deserted gravel drive.

"Faster, Smithers!" I commanded. Diana sunk her foot down, and we did gravel spins all the way around the castle. We eased the Daimler back into the garage—no one had seen us, we never got caught for that one.

As you might suspect, my court jesting failed to endear me to certain members of the Family. On the way to dinner at Windsor Castle one evening, I passed the green baize door, the traditional barrier between gentry and their servants. I looked through its round porthole and saw a butler I knew, and I waved and called him by his first name.

Well, that was simply *not done.* You would never see other Royals greeting a butler in this manner. Some of them, in fact, did not know the names of the people who worked for them.

The Duke of Edinburgh looked at me askance, and said, "Surely you have outgrown flirting with the staff."

I knew that he was right to upbraid me. It didn't matter that I had just been trying to be polite; I was out of line, again. At dinner that night I felt as though I were back at Sandringham, that first time, when I had mixed up kings with counts and kept tripping over the corgis. I was sitting next to Prince Philip, of course, and felt totally tongue-tied, for I'd made such a bad blunder and how could he not have contempt for me? To make amends, I asked him if he had driven his horses that day—an imbecilic question that deserved the retort it fetched, since Philip drove his horses most every day.

At times like that I was one great ball of fear. I ate this and drank that, tried to follow instructions, but I never got anything right. I was either too big or too small, too much or too little. Like Alice, I could never please the Queen of Hearts.

The tragic thing about being ostracized is that it keeps getting worse. You come to be the focus of all negative attention. As the family's cream-colored dog, the house numskull, I was easy to blame when something went wrong. When someone leaked the address of Edward's girlfriend, Sophie Rhys-Jones, to the papers, Edward just *knew* who had stabbed him in the back. He shot off a letter to Andrew, the gist of which was, *Can't you keep your wife under control?*

In fact, it wasn't me; I did not play those kinds of games. But families can be kangaroo courts in the best of times.

During that winter of 1991, I thought quite a bit about the most famous female outcast of them all, the one who had led a king to abdicate and ultimately brought Elizabeth to her throne. There were yellow roses strangely growing in my garden at Sunninghill at the time, defying the cold. I picked a bunch and took them to Frogmore, the royal mausoleum.

And I laid those stubborn flowers on the sparsely kept grave of Mrs. Wallis Warfield Simpson, another woman who could never fit in.

The Firm was getting more aggressive. I was "advised" to cancel a ski trip because it "wouldn't look good." I saw my life disappearing and got in a panic. When cornered I lashed back. I would *not* be told by some fat-bellied man that I could not take my children to Switzerland—I would go anyway!

Though I might win the occasional skirmish, I was readily outflanked. When the Gulf War appeared ready to explode on January 15, 1991, I cut short a trip to Klosters and immediately flew home with my daughters. Three days later, as the news showed bombs raining on Iraq, the press dusted off a picture of me on the slopes, to "document" their story that "Fergie couldn't be bothered to come back." I looked like a callous fool, like a blithering social butterfly. I knew the truth, but the British public would believe what they read—why should they question it?

I was fighting a two-front war, against the press and The Firm, and you do not win many of those. It was only a question of when I would surrender—and whether I'd escape with my hide.

Grummy was a big hit with the Royal Family. Recognizing a soulmate, the Queen cherished her straightforward ways, her utter lack of airs. Grummy had come to my wedding in her running shoes—her feet were too sore to wear anything else, she insisted—and did the same when we shared a carriage at Royal Ascot.

When I lived in the Palace, before my daughters were born, I drove out to visit Grummy and her black Labrador each week, at her home in Wiltshire. Then well past eighty, she hadn't changed since my girlhood. She had never stopped laughing, or tending her garden, or making her beautiful tapestries. She had the same impeccable manners, except when she bit into one of the hard digestive biscuits from the orange tin beside her bed. It was her nightly ritual, and it never failed —her false teeth would tumble out.

Grummy used good Irish linen sheets, and she kept her house so cold that I spent the whole night freezing whenever I slept over. But I never minded, because my grandmother was a person who made everything all right. When I felt terminally disgruntled about my life in the Palace, she would offer her time-tested wisdom.

"To get something good in life, you have to make sacrifices," she would say.

And: "Be content with knowing what you know."

And: "The mere fact that someone in this world loves you means more than anything else." I liked that one the best, because I knew that Grummy did love me, always had and always would. As long as I stayed in that icebox of a house I felt safe.

Grummy had broken her pelvis as a young woman, when she rode sidesaddle and a nervous horse ran backwards over a wall. Later on she was in two motor crashes, and developed osteoporosis; at the end she was living on steroids. She suffered immense pain all her life but would never complain. Once they operated on her hip and the surgeon shortchanged her on anesthetic. They were about to begin when she looked up and said, "Good man, I think you need to give me a little bit of something else—you are not cutting the ham for breakfast, you know."

When you have known a person all your life, and she has always seemed old to you but always so vital, you cannot conceive of the day she will not be there. With Grummy that day came in May of 1991.

From that day on I was on my own.

*T*he events of *annus horribilis* were a long time germinating. In May of 1990, I had taken a brief holiday on the Moroccan coast with Pricilla. We flew out on a plane lent to us by Peter Palumbo, and stayed at a public resort called La Gazelle d'Or, where I paid the bill. The locale was idyllic, our five days there uneventful and unobserved—or so I thought.

I had no way of knowing that an anonymous tipster had called the London tabloid *Today* and reported that Steve Wyatt was with me in Morocco—an absolute falsehood. After Steve left London in 1991, the danger of a frame-up seemed real enough to lead me to have his Belgravia flat searched, top to bottom. It was clean.

Several weeks later, a window cleaner entered the flat to spruce it up for the next tenant. In the guest bedroom he spotted several plastic packets on top of a shelving unit. Inside were more than a hundred photographs.

The pictures ultimately found their way to the *Daily Mail.* On January 15, 1992, the *Mail* ran this front-page headline: MYSTERY OF FERGIE PHOTOGRAPHS. Over that day and the next, the major tabloids would devote a total of more than forty pages to the story. (*The Times* and *Telegraph* showed little interest, while the BBC ignored it entirely.) The Palace press office, not quite rushing to my defense, offered a stiff no-comment, which only whetted the papers' appetite the more.

The gist of the tale was that Steve had flown me to Morocco in *his* plane, and had been there with us throughout. In support of this fable, the *Mail* reproduced several watercolor replications from the window cleaner's find. (The originals had been turned over to our equerry by New Scotland Yard.) The most "damning" illustration showed Steve and me on a wooden swing chair, dressed in sweatshirts and shorts, the way a woman might pose with her father-in-law. In another, Steve was with Beatrice; according to the newspapers, Andrew had been "enraged" to see his paternal role usurped.

The whole invention was flimsy and ridiculous, a web of fabricated "facts" and harmless pictures. The photographs discovered in Belgravia were actually taken on two different occasions, at two different places. (It was no surprise to learn that they'd been developed on different dates.) The snapshots featuring Steve originated at a house party in Gloucestershire, where I had popped in for lunch.

A "mystery," indeed. New Scotland Yard was called in to investigate, and came up with nothing. But one police source told the press the obvious—that the photographs might have been planted to embarrass me, "as part of a conspiracy to tarnish her image and destroy her marriage."

While the "Morocco" photographs were trifling of themselves, they set in motion much larger events; they were the head of the match to a cache of dry powder. For me they were the proverbial last straw. Hemmed in by innuendo, mocked by the press and harried by the courtiers, fettered to a schedule which never let me exhale—I had reached my limit. My brain felt like it was about to explode.

I had borne the strain and gotten on with it, just as Dads had taught me, but now my private fears were leaking badly. I was making a spectacle of myself, one thing a Royal must never do. Even worse, I was saying what I really thought, a quirk given only to fools (see *King Lear*) and to heretics (see the Tower of London). In my last interview before bailing out, the seepage was all over the lot.

"It is very difficult to get any privacy," I told the freelance journalist Georgina Howell. "In fact I don't have any. Oh, there are times when I don't have anybody in the house [at Sunninghill] and we can just be a family together. I sometimes give everyone the night off and go into the kitchen and make a cheese sandwich. But you have staff, you have security, you always have to be aware. You're always on show, twenty-four hours a day; you've just got to accept that.

"The life I lead isn't for real. Modern life isn't the pomp and circumstance of Buckingham Palace. I cannot stick to the guidelines because . . . we are not being *real*.

"At the end of the day you die alone . . . and as long as you're kind, and you get up in the morning, and you're happy to look at yourself . . . and you're straightforward and thank God for everything you do . . . because He knows. And the journalists can write what they want to write."

Finally, in a half-strangled cri de coeur, I burst out with my yearning to "get away from the System and the people saying, 'No you can't, no you can't, no you can't.' That's what the System is."

Not your typical royal interview, to be sure. In spite of my rambling incoherence (for I was a woman on the edge of a breakdown), I had somehow issued a manifesto, my personal call to arms. It was my futile attempt to explain myself directly to the British people.

Ever since childhood, my whole life had been a cowering—a repression of discontents, an evasion of desires. But now something truthful had crystallized inside of me, in *spite* of me. I was taking my first baby steps toward confronting the damage I had done—to others, and most of all to myself.

At the Palace, I now realized, I had sold myself into a package deal. To be married to Andrew was to be wed to The Firm, and I had to get out. No longer could I feign to respect, honor, and obey *that* institution. It was one thing to live in a gilded cage; people trade freedom for security all the time. It was another when they electrified the bars of that cage and aimed their heartless sights your way, as though it were Saturday at Sandringham and you were the prize pheasant.

There was no point in fighting on. To persist could only inflame my enemies, embarrass the Queen, harm the people I held dearest, and push my own tattered psyche past the point of no return. I had no clarity about the path I should be taking, but of one thing I was sure: If I remained in the Royal Family, the best part of me would die. It would be a slow death, no doubt, for I was stubborn and strong, but a sure death nonetheless.

On January 21, six days after the Belgravia photos came out, I told Andrew at dinner that I thought we should separate. We were both very sad; it was the last thing we had wanted. But he saw my resignation and did not try to argue: "If this will make you happy, then I still stand by you."

The next morning we went up to see the Queen in Sandringham. I walked in gripping my rosary for strength. "I am so sorry," I said, "but I think this is best for you and your family—I can't go on letting you down."

The Queen looked sadder than I had ever seen her. She asked me to reconsider, to be strong and go forward.

But I was resolute. After returning to Sunninghill, I offered to resign my title as Her Royal Highness. I wrote that I could not maintain the standards that the title demanded, that my behavior was not fitting. I had the letter taken to Her Majesty that day. It was mostly a symbolic gesture, but an important one; I wanted to show her that I wasn't trying to have it both ways.

With a general election coming up in April, I agreed to "play down," to not rush into anything publicly. Just as my engagement had been deferred to suit affairs of state, so would my separation—not that I minded. Why not go with the flow awhile longer? I had put up with The Firm for six long years. What harm could come from waiting a few weeks more?

Word got around to a few trusted people, however. Those who loved me were worried. I was cutting a new path, through a jungle thick with spiders, and who knew whether I would make it through? Friends told me to be cautious, go slowly. A well-known religious official advised me to stay in the marriage and be "selfless to duty."

That was the way of the old-school aristocracy, the way of the Queen and of Grummy—to be selfless to the grave. But I had detoured from that course. I was more literally *self-less* than anyone knew, and I could see where it had led me: straight to the cliff's sheer drop. I needed to harvest *more* of my self, not less—more self-awareness, self-expression, self-love.

Andrew understood me better than the rest. His concerns were of another stripe. "If we go through with this," he told me, "you will be physically destroyed as a human being. I am just warning you—please be careful."

I knew what he meant, because I wasn't really leaving Andrew. We had been living a de facto separation for years, and the caring we shared would endure. I *was* divorcing The Firm, however. Like other abusive spouses, it would be most dangerous when deserted.

As any student of British history can tell you, women leave the Royal Family in only one mode: with their heads cleaved from their shoulders.

"What do you want me to do?" I asked Andrew, after we'd come home from our meeting with the Queen. I had proclaimed my independence, yet I remained at Sunninghill; I was a woman in limbo and had no idea what people expected of me.

"You are still Your Royal Highness," he replied, my letter notwithstanding. "You're still my wife—carry on."

Nothing had changed. But everything had changed. Within days of our trip to Sandringham, I was cut out of the Court Circular. Engagements were canceled without notice or explanation. The flow of invitations from the lord lieutenants, the counties' liaisons to the Palace, trickled to a stop. There would be no more shopping centers to open, no more factories to visit.

The Firm was sending me a message, in its own subtle way: *Don't let the door hit you on your way out.* The courtiers moved with ruthless dispatch—they weren't such sluggards when their heart was in their work. There was no policy for what they did to me, no rule to be followed. When Diana separated from Charles later that year, her calendar was unaffected.

But you must remember: She was the Good Witch. I was something else.

In February I fulfilled my last official engagement as a member of the Royal Family: a memorial service at the Tower of London, an apt site for my swan song. Then I heard from a diplomat friend of mine that the Grey Men had rung up their contacts at the U.S. Embassy. I was no longer Her Majesty's representative, at home or abroad, the Americans were told. No assistance was to be rendered me.

Apparently non grata throughout the Western World, I was an absolute nonperson in Buckingham Palace. A month before, the courtiers might have smirked behind my back, but at least they bowed to protocol and gave me a proper greeting. Now they snubbed me cold, wouldn't even speak to me. That was a major cruelty, that silent treatment—I felt like Peter Pan without his shadow. In their eyes I saw a mirror of my own self-loathing. *(You are worthless, we don't want you, go away. . . .)* I was beyond the pale, and no longer would they hide their hatred for me.

I still had plenty to do in that period; I could still run myself ragged. On one typical day—February 10, 1992—I ran out to my first appointment at 7:30 A.M., proceeded to a hospital function at eleven, a charity engagement at three, and a sports foundation dinner that evening.

At night, after the children were to bed and the staff dismissed, I would overeat and take a sleeping pill and hope it worked.

My relationship with the British press was a variable affair. The *Guardian* and *Independent* just ignored me, as they did the rest of the Royal Family. *The Times* and *Telegraph* were generally impartial, though they might twist a fact or two in the heat of their latest circulation war.

Among the tabloids, the *Sun* stood out for its wonderfully trashy headlines and farfetched articles; they could be quite entertaining, in the manner of science fiction. The *Express,* the *Mirror, Today, News of the World*—I'd had my ups and downs with them all. But the most insidious, far and away, was the *Daily Mail,* Fleet Street's command center for right-wing gossip, where Mr. and Mrs. Aristocrat went slumming. For years the *Mail* had served as the Grey Men's weapon of choice against enemy camps. It was there that they broke the stories that served them; it was there that they planted their acid-dipped quotes, their radioactive rumors.

(To wit: a *Daily Mail* story which suggested that a film project I'd embarked upon would feature graphic sex scenes between Queen Victoria and Prince Albert. The account was absolutely bogus and likely originated with the Grey Men, one of whom had already made the same report to the Queen.)

Even before my Australia trip in 1988, the *Mail* had pursued a vendetta against me. Its attack began to escalate by mid-1990, right about the time that the Queen appointed a new press secretary. Mr. X was considered quite a catch for the Palace. He was somewhat younger than the average Grey Man, sportily well dressed, good-looking in a self-satisfied way. Though he could be gruff and officious, he was not easily ruffled.

As intermediary between Her Majesty and the public, Mr. X was valued most for his discretion and unfailing prudence. It was widely reported that his predecessor as press secretary had lost his job after suggesting that the Queen was displeased at Margaret Thatcher's abrasiveness. Mr. X would never make that sort of rash mistake, the insiders agreed. He always saved himself an out. He would err on the side of caution, if he erred at all.

On Wednesday, March 18, three weeks before the general election, the dam burst. In a front-page exclusive by Andrew Morton and Richard Kay, the *Daily Mail* reported that the Palace "is preparing to announce the separation of The Duke and the Duchess of York." The story went on to disclose sketchy details of our lawyers' discussions, and mentioned a private conversation with the Queen at Sandringham.

I was more shocked than anyone when I saw the paper that morning; I'd had no advance word. I knew only one thing for sure: that no good could come of this.

With the election reduced to a sideshow, the Palace's hand was forced. On Thursday, March 19, the sixth anniversary of our engagement, a half-dozen court correspondents filed through the Privy Purse gate. A red-liveried doorman led them to a spacious ground-floor office. Mr. X handed each reporter a brief press release, which left no doubt as to who was initiating the separation:

"In view of the media speculation which the Queen finds especially undesirable during the Election Campaign, Her Majesty is issuing the following statement: 'Last week lawyers acting for the Duchess of York initiated discussions about a formal separation for the Duke and Duchess. These discussions are not yet completed and nothing will be said until they are. The Queen hopes that the media will spare the Duke and Duchess and their children any intrusion.' "

The Palace is well known for understatement in family

matters, and the correspondents took their three bland sentences and prepared to write their stories. They couldn't see the red faces behind the closed office doors, couldn't hear the courtiers snarling as they hunted for the leaker. As one senior official told the press, "Everyone is certain that somewhere —and we are not sure by whom—this has been orchestrated. It was a put-up job."

Just after noon, a veteran BBC radio man named Paul Reynolds returned to Mr. X's office for a private chat, a bit of clarification.

Twenty minutes later, Reynolds emerged with the royal story of the year. "The knives are out for Fergie in the Palace," he announced, somewhat breathlessly, over the BBC's *World at One.* Then came the bombshell allegation: that I had hired a public-relations company to leak the separation story to the *Daily Mail.*

And there was more. "I have rarely heard Palace officials speak in such terms about someone," Reynolds said. "They are talking about her unsuitability for public life, royal life— her behavior in being photographed in *Hello!* magazine. . . ."

Mr. X, it would seem, had gone slightly overboard.

For all of the intrigues and corridor wars that have inhabited Buckingham Palace, no one had ever heard the like of this: the public denunciation of a Royal by The Firm itself. "I was absolutely flabbergasted," said Sue Crewe, who covered the Royal Family for the magazine *Harper's and Queen.* "It's without precedent that the Palace should exhibit an emotion."

By late that afternoon, as I sat in a theater with my daughters, watching *The Wind in the Willows,* Reynolds's story led every broadcast in the land. To loyal readers of the tabloids, not to mention the Grey Men themselves, the BBC report made perfect sense. I obviously wanted out, their logic ran, and didn't care to wait, and so I engineered a leak to bring the matter to a boil. It merely proved their point—that I was willful and selfish and perpetually out of control.

Unfortunately for The Firm, Mr. X had got carried away; he had been too explicit to save his out. By the end of the day, the public relations company in question had categorically denied any involvement in the leak. Sir David English, the *Mail*'s editor, backed the company up. (Flying as I did by the seat of my pants, I could never have devised such a Machiavellian plan—it was beyond my meager resources.)

On Friday morning, Mr. X issued a rather mealy retraction: "I very much regret that what was said should have been interpreted by the media to the detriment of the Duchess of York. . . ." He also distributed copies of the notes he had sent to the Queen and myself, including his "personal apologies for the distress that this episode has caused you."

The retraction, one columnist wrote, was "like applying a tourniquet to someone's neck after they had been guillotined."

Mr. X submitted his resignation, but the Queen rejected it.

At the risk of seeming ungenerous, I would submit that Mr. X's tears were crocodilian. *Because The Firm did not stop.* Far from going and sinning no more, the courtiers drove their dagger in deeper. It mattered not that one of their cohort had been exposed. In fact, he had done the team a great service; his remarks had established a new benchmark for fair commentary. Now the Grey Men could say out loud what they'd been muttering in the Equerries' Room. Now they could tell the press how they *really* felt.

In the days that followed Mr. X's outburst, when I was at my most vulnerable, the courtiers circled in for the kill. "She has been a complete disaster," one Palace source told the

Mail. "She has let everyone down and made Prince Andrew very unhappy. Quite honestly, the Royal Family have done their very best for her, but now they're washing their hands of her."

I had long suspected that Mr. Z and Mr. X worked in tandem, as Tweedledee to Tweedledum. It was not surprising, then, to read that I had been "placed on probation" by the Queen's private secretary well before the leak to the *Mail.* Quite a revealing choice of phrase, I thought. For months they had been ready to lock me up—or, more precisely, lock me out—at my very next slip.

It was the courtiers, not I, who had tired of waiting for my departure. It was Mr. X, not I, who had rushed to a resolution —and I do not think he did it by impulse, or by accident. I believe that Mr. X had a game plan when Paul Reynolds returned to his office, however clumsy his execution of it. The Firm's best interests could not be served if I went gently into the night. They needed to cut me off at the knees, abort my future options, destroy my standing with the Queen.

They also needed to send a warning to Diana, to keep her in the fold and shore up the monarchy. My public vivisection would be a pointed reminder: *This is what happens if you cross us.* (They did indeed scare the daylights out of my sister-in-law, who was now afraid to be seen with me, and I could not blame her.)

Dads found Mr. Z's role in all of this insupportable and demanded that he apologize. One day I picked up my ringing phone—and winced, by reflex, when I heard that modulated voice. "There's been a terrible misunderstanding," said Mr. Z, "and I'm sorry for any inconvenience caused to you."

"It's all right, I understand," I said blankly.

I could not be angry with Mr. Z. I could not fault The Firm for sharpening its knives, because I knew they were right about me—even when their facts were wrong, they were right. I was a despicable human being. I had failed the monarchy single-handedly. Now, at last, the whole country was onto me. They knew exactly how awful I was, and how could a whole country be wrong?

12

On the Outs

The consequences came swiftly after my separation was officially announced. The very next day I lost my royal protection officers from the Metropolitan Police. I was devastated—those officers had become great friends to me. They were people I could talk to and laugh with when I felt most alone; John Askew, in particular, supplied better jokes than most men I knew. They had shielded this fearful woman from Clapham and made her feel safe. Would I ever feel safe again?

There could be no question of staying at Sunninghill; the girls and I would leave, and quickly. My in-laws proposed that we move down the drive and into the keeper's house, a two-room cottage with a bathroom outside. "A lick of paint and it will be fine," the Duke of Edinburgh said.

I might have been blown away by recent events, but I wasn't *that* defeated, not where my children were concerned. I rented a house nearby called Romenda Lodge, on the Wentworth Golf Course. My housing allowance wouldn't cover our expenses, and my overdraft would bulge like an old bicycle tire, but so be it.

I kept up my manic pace. I still had my office at the Palace, and no shortage of appointments to buzz around to. On March 23, Andrew and I threw a party at Sunninghill for Eugenie's second birthday. It wasn't so easy to put on my happy family face, but I managed. I could always manage those things.

Inside, however, I was terrified. My dread was a living thing, like Yeats's rough slouching beast, and I knew that my center could not hold. Having cast myself adrift from the Royal Family, the emptiness swelled inside me, and my terror along with it. My old questions started catching up to me: *What am I doing? What have I done? Am I really the person I read about in the papers—and if not, who am I?*

My new life was laden with many fears, but none more frightening than my freedom. With freedom came choice, and accountability for one's actions—an awful concept for someone with no confidence. For escape I reverted to my old compulsive behaviors. My diet went haywire, until I felt like a blob. I spent money as though I really had it.

And then there was the binge that cost me most dear: John Bryan.

Andrew and I first met John at a London dinner party in 1990. He had been exploring high-technology investments with his father, a shrewd businessman. I was impressed by John's boldness and energy; he was a fountain of fresh ideas. After he outlined some ambitious possibilities for Budgie, I asked him to represent me in any film or television opportunities.

On February 20, 1992, John asked me to dinner. I was needy and full of doubts; he was attentive and breezily self-assured. John had a rare gift of the gab—he was one of those people who could sell snow to the Eskimos. I swallowed everything he dished up for me. I believed he was a fabulous tycoon, this brilliantly cosmopolitan man. I had no desire to peer beneath the surface, to *understand*. I believed it all, as a child believes.

By that spring, after the knives came out for Fergie, I was a shell-shocked and assassinated person. I couldn't have called directory assistance. And in swept Mr. Worldly, who knew what time it was all over the globe. "Leave everything to me," he said, and I did. John organized our move into Romenda Lodge. When we went skating he looked after the children—he was marvelous with my daughters, and it wasn't long before I thought that none of us could live without him.

The more he did, the more he wanted to do. My intensity filled the sails of his self-importance; he played off my hyperactivity. He would come in and say, "Okay, this is how I can help you: I'll talk to the bank, I'll pay for this, don't worry about that. . . ." And I would think, *Ah, I can relax*. I was putty in his hands. When you are a breakdown person, there is nothing finer than someone who wants to take charge of your life.

In June, John would ask for my power of attorney, which I willingly granted. I would have let him choose my dresses and plan my breakfasts if he'd cared to.

One of my best friends took me aside and said, "Can't you see what he's doing—can't you *see*?" But I was blinded by need. "You're wrong," I responded. "He's a wonderful man." In truth, John could be generous to a fault and a joy to be with. It never crossed my mind that he might be using me, as *Today* would assess years later, as "a meal ticket, a trophy, a passport to a social circle . . . whose doors would otherwise be not so much shut as triple locked."

And whenever I betrayed the slightest reservation (for sanity can be starved and beaten but is hard to kill), John would rush in to soothe me. "Don't worry, it will be fine," he would tell me. "I'm looking after it for you, don't believe anything you hear."

Then he would sucker me with the flattery I needed. *"You,"* he would say, with force and sincerity, *"are a little heroine."*

But for all of John's excesses and power games, he was not "Fergie's Rasputin," as *The Sunday Times Magazine* would later call him. That gave him too much credit, and me too little responsibility. He did not drug me or physically coerce me. With hindsight, that master teacher, I can see that we used each other. The trade may have been perverse, but not unfair.

John's bluff command, I see now, cloaked his own insecurity. He was desperate for a big financial score, and a secure niche among the glitterati; I was desperate for approval and affection. We were two people stuck in quicksand, immobilized by terror and confusion. Too weak or scared to reach out for a saving branch, we clung more tightly to one another, and we were doomed.

$\mathcal{B}$eatrice and Eugenie were invited to the Royal Family's Easter gathering at Windsor Castle, but their mother had been deleted from the guest list. I decided that none of us would attend; I was feeling sensitive about separations.

As an alternative, I had a friend book us on an Asian holiday, as far from The Firm and the press as we could get. On

April 9 we flew to Zurich and then straight to Thailand, to the island resort of Phuket. I hadn't invited John along—I wanted a total break and seclusion. But he insisted on coming and followed us out; it is hard to exert control over someone seven thousand miles away.

Throughout our trip, we managed to stay a jump ahead of the tabloids. (The editors' frustration provoked one memorable headline: WHERE THE PHUKET IS THE DUCHESS?) The press did get hold of one photo from Thailand, after the fact; someone had recognized me walking with John in the hotel courtyard and snapped us for a sale.

That picture should have warned the wise, but my warning systems were shut down tight those days. Looking back, it seems as though John was courting exposure, with a willing coconspirator in tow. "You can't imagine what you were like then," said a friend of mine who had joined us for part of the trip. "I kept telling you that you weren't behaving right and you couldn't understand what I was saying. You thought everything you were doing was okay."

My friend believed I was having a breakdown, and she may have been right. But breakdowns are double edged— they signal the birth of the new as well as the death of the old. (As the saying goes: You cannot make an omelet without breaking some eggs.) I had been swimming about in my unreal world of duty and protocol, and for the first time in my life I was smelling the smells around me. *Wake up!* went the small lost voice inside, waiting for someone to answer.

I was miserable back at Romenda Lodge, missing Andrew and Sunninghill. Then, in June, I received a welcome invitation: to visit Leonard Cheshire, who was afflicted with motor neurone disease.

Lord Cheshire was a special hero of mine. The most decorated bomber pilot of World War II, he completed one hundred missions when the odds were but one in three that a pilot would live through thirty of them. He kept coming back to help his crews survive.

As an official British observer, Lord Cheshire witnessed the unimaginable devastation of the atomic bomb upon Nagasaki. Later in life he became one of the world's great humanitarians, founding the Cheshire Foundation Homes for the disabled and incurably sick. His work had grown until there were more than 250 homes, in forty-eight countries; they allowed thousands of people to end their lives with dignity and proper care.

Now the founder himself was dying, and I was flattered that he had agreed to see me. As I walked in he was lying in his bed, and he said, "I knew something good was going to happen today because a little bud came out on my tree as I looked out my window."

We talked for a while about how I might help fill a gap in the services his homes provided. I felt a strange calm as I sat with him—it was great encouragement to think that such a fine man could like me. A few days later, he wrote me of his confidence "that a major lifetime's work waits ahead and that it won't be too long before you discover what it is."

The following week was Royal Ascot. A year before I had been part of the royal procession, riding in a carriage with the Queen Mother. Now I watched the parade from the sidelines, by the road in Great Windsor Park, with my daughters standing by me as I had once stood with Mum. I gave Beatrice and Eugenie handkerchiefs to wave to the Queen as she passed; I wanted them to know what their granny did. Through all of the chaos of the past six months, the Queen and I had stayed consistent. She still took my calls, and I still brought her grandchildren to Windsor for tea on Sundays. It was an unspoken pact we had, and I would not let down my side of it.

On the second day, Andrew joined us by the roadside. Just a small token of solidarity, but it reminded me of why I had loved him, and why I loved him still.

There were many more trips that summer, with John always at the helm. Never had I run so hard from my pain. But the pain was more resourceful than the cleverest paparazzi, and in each new place it found me, and tapped me on the shoulder, and I would move on to the next rush of novelty.

Until August, when my fugitive feet would carry me to the south of France, and I would demonstrate for all time that running and hiding are two different things.

*T*o review the bidding: John Bryan had booked our pink villa near St. Tropez under an assumed name. We flew in on a chartered plane. We were more than two miles off the road. There was no public access to the villa; we were sheltered by woods and hills, halfway up a private gravel track that led to an isolated vineyard.

How, then, had I landed at the wrong end of a telephoto lens?

Three days after the photographs came out, the *Sunday Express* published a story headed, WAS SARAH SET UP? It posed the following questions:

How did Daniel Angeli, the paparazzo known as "the hitman's hitman," know when we would be at the villa?

How did Angeli escape detection as he worked?

And, most intriguing, *who had tipped him off?*

John found a partial answer the following week, when he returned to the villa and discovered a large trench within a hundred yards of the villa and its pool. Judging from the size of the trench, and the fact that Angeli had shot me in several different bathing suits, the photographer and his assistant must have dug in and bivouacked there for at least three days, clicking away to their hearts' content.

This was an extraordinary find. It made tangible what we already knew: that the most basic rules for royal security had been breached. While I had forfeited any special treatment by separating, my daughters remained part of the Royal Family, in line to the throne. Whenever they traveled abroad, the host nation's security apparatus would automatically be notified to take appropriate steps.

We had no such protection in the south of France in August 1992. After the scandal broke, French authorities reportedly voiced astonishment that they had received no word of our presence—such negligence was unheard of.

But the French were no more startled than I, because I knew that I had followed standard protocol. Several days before leaving for St. Tropez, I informed the Queen, as I always did.

Circumstances suggest, therefore, that some paragon of bureaucratic efficiency failed to make the normal security arrangements. My suspicions further told me that The Firm colluded with the press by leaking details of my whereabouts. The press then tipped off the French photo agency, and the deal was struck.

As a result, our traveling party was next to defenseless. While my daughters had their personal protection officers on hand, there was no one to patrol the grounds of the estate. Had we been stalked by someone with a rougher agenda than Angeli, we might have seen a different sort of headline.

Cheering Prince Charles on at polo. I modeled myself after Andrew's every public move.

At the Windsor Horse Show with Andrew, the Queen and Sir John Miller. I felt happiest in my moments with Her Majesty—she is loyal, steadfast and consistent; the qualities I most admire.

Seeing Andrew off, again, to his duties with the Royal Navy. Throughout our marriage, Andrew averaged forty days at home per year.

In Hector Barrantes, Mum found the love of her life in Argentina, then lost it too soon.

With newborn Eugenie. Like so many people, I did not fully appreciate babies, until I had my own.

Beatrice and Eugenie en route to the stables at Balmoral Castle.

Our daughters as bridesmaids at the 1993 wedding of their former nanny, Alison Wardley—someone who took care of me, as well, through hard times.

A family visit aboard HMS *Cottesmore*, July 1994.

Teaching Eugenie to ski, as Mum had taught me. I seek
the tonic of the mountains whenever I can.

Eugenie and Beatrice, who make my life sparkle.

Above: Picking Beatrice up from school on the day that my separation from Andrew was announced. My sadness was plain on my face.

At the Windsor Horse Show in May 1992, two months after our separation—when I did not know what day it was.

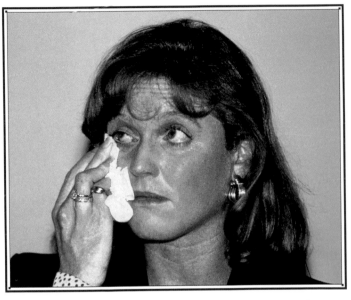

Just weeks after the John Bryan photographs came out, I received a
tremendous welcome from the Motor Neurone Disease Association
caregivers and patients. It was too much for me—
I feared I had let them all down.

In retracing Queen Victoria's journey through Germany,
I made a sketch outside Stolzenfels, high above the Rhine.

With the luggage in Stolzenfels. Like Queen Victoria, I found traveling a welcome relief from the pressures and constant scrutiny at home.

With Paul Sillitoe, 20,000 feet up in the Himalayas.

In Kenya, October 1994. When I meet children around the world, and share their high spirits and see their great need, my own troubles seem very small.

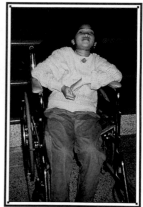

When Chances for Children helped Rhonda regain her sight through surgery, it was one of the most moving things I had ever witnessed.

In Bucharest I met a self-sustaining community of orphans who had fashioned a home out of a garbage dump.

Our family has remained close-knit and loving.

Parents' Day at Upton House School, 1992. I always try to finish first—and once nearly broke my kneecap.

Ascot Race Course. Show jumping in
an event for the Princess Royal's charity.

At the King
George V Gold
Cup. I present the
1995 trophy to
Robert Splaine on
Heather Blaze—
an Irish rider on
an Irish horse. No
one knew it at the
time, but I was also
one of the horse's
proud owners.

My first visit to Qatar, in January 1996, when I attended a charity function that raised funds for Children in Crisis.

In March of 1996, I competed in the International Qatar Horse Marathon. Twenty-six miles across the desert, which I survived because I trusted my horse.

13

At the Hickstead Horse Show with Beatrice, May 30th, 1996, the day the divorce came through.

In our daughters, Andrew and I will have an unbreakable bond, forever.

I have come to terms with the pain of my past;
now I look to the future with hope.

To paint is to try to absorb the world's color and light—to live in that
natural moment. This watercolor came out of my trip to Stolzenfels.

The security breakdown "was no oversight," wrote Lady Colin Campbell in *The Royal Marriages.* "It was done deliberately. . . . The idea of Sarah's enemies at Court was to discredit her so thoroughly that she could never be readmitted into the Royal Family as a fully fledged member. Diana would get the message that if she persisted in traveling down Sarah's path, she would go her way in more ways than one. So they set Sarah up. . . ."

If Lady Colin Campbell is correct, The Firm won the lottery with the St. Tropez photos. If they had put the press onto us, the Grey Men had guaranteed my embarrassment. At the very least, my trip would document yet another spendthrift extravagance. John's poolside presence, in addition, would make for spicy innuendo. But the courtiers could not have guessed that I would load my own murder weapon for them —that I would display myself in hugs and nuzzles with a bald American in bathing trunks. They had gotten a huge bonus.

In sum: I gave my nemeses all they could dream of to sabotage, and more. *But they did sab-o-tage. . . .*

As I saw it, The Firm had done a job on me and done it well. I was routed and disgraced; I'd been flung into exile. But one question remained: had The Firm done its *duty?* Had it truly served its Sovereign if it instigated "the biggest scandal since the abdication of 1936"?

For Buckingham Palace to survive the knocks of the modern era, the senior courtiers must do more than sip their G and T's and fulminate about foreigners. They must guard the Royals from every kind of public harm, including the harm Royals do to themselves. With me—a hard case, granted— they did the opposite. I believe that they preyed on my frailties and used the press to do me in.

The irony is that I would have left anyway—they didn't

need to go so far. They expelled me with a pipe bomb when a small shove might have sufficed, and the monarchy still shakes from the aftershock.

"There was a faction within the queen machine who never thought Fergie was the right stuff," Bob Houston concluded in *Royalty* magazine. "So the idea was give her enough rope, and she'll hang herself. She shot herself in the foot several times along the way, but she should only have been allowed to shoot herself in the foot once."

By the time I returned from Balmoral to Romenda Lodge, I was like an ethered butterfly, pinned under glass: quite interesting to look at, but very much dead all the same.

Though I was no stranger to sadness, this was the low point. I was in shock; I did not know what day it was. I had no idea of what to do from one moment to the next. If I needed to meet someone for lunch on business, I'd ask half a dozen people—my secretary, the butler, my daughters' policemen —what type of restaurant I should choose.

Twenty minutes later I would ask them all again.

In the evening I curled up in a corner and cried. I cut myself off from all but a few closest friends. I wanted to be alone.

I tried, as before, to lose myself in excess: buying, eating, even smoking. (I hadn't touched a cigarette since my courtship—Andrew hated the smell of smoke—but I was touching them now.) I was one great open wound, like the gaping mouth in that painting, *The Scream*: just a mindless maw of pain.

In truth, I was not fit to be around. I was terminally sad and moody and incommunicative. The only people who could lift me were Beatrice and Eugenie—having children may have saved my life then, I do not exaggerate. The best part of my day was the morning, when I dropped them at school. Although I would shrink from the other parents' stares, for what must they think of me?

I wouldn't bother wearing makeup on the school runs; I was often en route to a workout and didn't care how I looked in any case. (Josh Salzmann, my personal trainer, kept me sane.) One of the tabloids took an especially terrible picture of me in my sweatshirt and running shoes and captioned it "The Bag Lady Goes to School."

The next time we went out to Windsor Castle, the Duke of Edinburgh admonished me, "Could you take your children to school looking a little smarter?"

My skin was rubbed thinnest where my daughters were concerned. One reason I drove them each morning was for fear they would be stolen from my custody. My general paranoia aside, there were men in high places who might have favored such abduction. At Balmoral, a day or two after the photographs came out, I passed a room where a couple of Grey Men were huddled, making no effort to be discreet. "Yes, she's an unfit mother," I overheard one of them say.

As usual, The Firm was a fair barometer of Establishment thinking. David Williamson, coeditor of *Debrett's Peerage and Baronetage,* pronounced that he "would be very surprised if the Queen would let [me] keep [my daughters], as they are princesses of the Royal blood . . . They may have to be made wards of court."

The point was plain: Such a harlot as I was unsuitable to raise the Queen's grandchildren. I might have been entirely unhinged had Andrew not reassured me that our children were *our* children and would go to no one else.

In point of fact, David Williamson was one of the more

mannerly hounds to be chasing this redheaded fox. I was fair game, now more than ever, and the scent of blood had drawn the pack. In the wake of the *Mirror*'s lucrative coup, the tabloids were out sniffing for the next great exclusive. Eight investigative journalists trailed me everywhere I went. To the video store. *(Does she rent adult movies?)* To the butcher. *(Does she buy the cheap cuts or the dear ones? Does she pay her bill on time?)*

With no place safe, I hid in my house. But even there I could not screen out their poison darts; I still had the bad habit of reading my press and believing what I saw in the tabloids' fun-house mirrors. I was THE DUCHESS OF YAK, THE FIRST ROYAL YUPPIE, THE MUCHNESS OF YORK. I was, most hurtfully, "the fat white woman whom nobody loves."

That jeering chorus would grate in my ears all day—it would grind me down, till I fell into bed for relief. But there, in the dark, the real horror started. Every night, off and on all night long, I would see the Men in Black creeping through my bedroom window. They wore black masks and black jerseys, and they were silent and sinuous as snakes. There was no way to keep them out—they could slip through the smallest crack of the window, the slimmest parting of the curtain.

Each of the men was armed with a camera, and I wished they'd had guns instead. I never saw a flash, never heard the click of a shutter, but I knew I would be humiliated, again. I knew these men were out to do me great damage, to bear me into the flames of hell, and I would scream because I did not want to go there . . .

Four years later, I understand that vision for what it really was: the first sign of my healing. In the depth of my horror I had come to the pivot point of my life, the first real grappling with my pain. For so long I had kept squashing it down inside of me, but now there was too much to repress, and it flooded the banks of my consciousness like a rainy-season river.

That first encounter was involuntary; I was not nearly strong enough to shake hands with my pain and meet its open gaze. I was not ready to dive into my pool of hurt —I wasn't yet sure if I'd come out the other side.

Still, I had found my new path—that slower, broader road. I would not turn back from it. But before it took me home, there were other places I must visit. Much like Dorothy in the Land of Oz, and just as Grummy had promised, I would find myself by serving others.

"*I* can't come," I told Peter Cardy. "I'll resign. I *can't* come —I'm so ashamed and embarrassed."

On September 19, 1992, one month after the St. Tropez photos broke, I was scheduled to address the Motor Neurone Disease Association's annual conference in Birmingham. I hadn't made a public appearance since leaving Balmoral; I was a walking corpse, the Duchess in Disgrace, and I was acting out the part each day. How could I possibly face the people who had trusted me—*given* me—so much? I had dishonored their gratitude. I had let them all down.

But Peter held me to my commitment. I went to Birmingham and walked into the lobby—and stopped cold at the doorway to the large hall. I turned to Kevin Langdon, a good friend, and I said, "Kevin, I can't walk in there."

Kevin was a man to be reckoned with. He had been told he would never walk again but refused to believe it—he is still walking today, by force of will. He looked straight at me and said, "If you don't bloody well get in that door, you have got me to deal with. What do you think most of the people here would give to walk into that room?"

That shut me up. It was one of the blessings of being around people with MND; more trivial problems were put in their place.

I went out on stage to hear Peter Cardy introduce me, and his speech was so moving, so generous, that I barely held my composure. And at the end of it those five hundred people, most of them in wheelchairs, began to applaud. It can be a great effort to put your hands together when you have MND, but those people kept on clapping. Then they rose, one by one, propped up by their carers, exhausting themselves in tribute.

They did not care about my scandal, or my trail of destruction. They were connecting with *me,* the person who'd always met them at their level, and now they were returning the favor.

I was seasoned enough on the public stage to know it was a ridiculous place for crying, but I could not stop myself. I let down my guard, and the tears streamed down my face. I felt more guilty, and humble, and contrite, than ever in my life. These people were dying, yet they had rallied to make me feel better. They had forgiven me when I felt unforgivable, when I could not forgive myself.

The tabloids would be typically brutal the next day: *"Fergie weeps for affection, she must think her tears can make us love her again, she uses MND patients to get better press."* But they could not erase what I'd had that night in Birmingham, when my friends stood up and cheered for me, and *the fire* blazed into conflagration, and it lit the night.

13

Seeking to Understand

$\mathcal{F}$or the Royal Family, *annus horribilis* ended as it had begun: with calamity. In November, a fire at Windsor Castle caused $80 million in damage. In December, Diana and Charles finally announced their separation—a huge blow to the monarchy, even though everyone knew it was coming.

But for me the year ended with a whiff of grace and opportunity. I attended a polo match to benefit Angels International, where a woman named Theo Ellert told me about the charity's work in Upper Silesia, the industrial center of Poland. By the time the match ended, I knew that I wanted to help.

There are many bad places for children to live in this world, but Upper Silesia ranks high on any list. Whole forests have been killed by the sulfur and coal that spew from countless polluting smokestacks; death wafts through the very air. The region has the highest infant mortality rate in Europe. In the Katowice area, half of the four-year-olds are chronically ill.

Just before Christmas, Theo invited me to join her in an inspection of the leukemia ward at Zabrze Children's Hospital. It was a place of terrible want. The young patients had no blankets or sheets, no medicine or bandages, no toys or posters or the least bit of color in their life. They had nothing—*nothing!* There were two makeshift incubators, and if a third baby needed one, that baby died—end of story.

Little love could be found at Zabrze. As it was the sole children's hospital in Poland, many parents had to travel great distances to get there, and their visits were sporadic and brief. Yet the children were so courageous in adversity. There was a little girl I shall call Katie who needed chemotherapy, but the hospital had no child-sized needles. So the nurses would use these gigantic bone marrow needles, with no anesthetic. Katie would try hard to be brave, but at last she would cry desperately as they stuck into the vein in her hand.

For a person who cannot bear it when her daughter gets stung by a wasp, this was a life-changing experience. In Poland I was baptized into a larger world. I had found greater need than I'd ever seen before, a great scandal of need. I had to rethink what "scandal" really meant—my own now seemed laughable, much ado about very little. What could all my crises matter next to the plight of a girl like Katie?

Upon returning to England I began working with Angels on a major fund-raiser. A month or two before the event, however, the organization withdrew; some of its officers feared they might get tarred by working too closely with me. They wanted to pull the plug, but I was stubborn. The children at Zabrze still needed that money. If Angels was unwilling, I would do it myself. I would start my own charity.

That was the genesis of Children in Crisis. Theo left Angels to join me, and we scrambled to get registered in time for our March event. We raised nearly $50,000 that night—and that is when our real work began.

More than 180,000 charities are registered in the United Kingdom, and a goodly number focus on children. But my experience in Poland pointed to a gap we might fill. There were children out there to whom nothing was given, not even tomorrow, and yet they were being overlooked. Disasters have a brief shelf life in our volatile world; today's front-page war zone is next month's forgotten news. But within the limits of our resources (and in cooperation with larger, more experienced agencies), Children in Crisis could be constant. We could stay the course after the klieg lights had dimmed. We could last and make a difference.

We set our sights high. Our mission, we wrote, would be "the relief of hardship, distress and sickness of persons in need, particularly children, in any part of the world."

I had broken with tradition once again. While members of the Royal Family are expected to serve in good causes, they generally come to charities by invitation, or by finding a group in need of a boost, as I had with the MND Association. They are *not* expected to spit on their hands and perform the heavy lifting that any new organization requires.

But I was patterning after a different role model, a man who once said, "For of those to whom much is given, much is required." I thought John F. Kennedy was onto something. I had been given so much—in experience, most of all—and just now I was learning how best to give back. Children in Crisis was my second chance in life, whether The Firm liked it or not. I *was* different, and my days of false conforming were done.

Over the next three years, Children in Crisis would raise $7 million. We spent just 7 percent on administration and overhead, one-third the industry norm. In those early months

I underwrote any shortfalls myself. If we had promised to send out $4,000 a month in fresh fruits and vegetables to Bosnia, we never missed a shipment, regardless of our bank statement. The giving was a gift to me, as well—I still felt my old buzz, but now it had focus and foundation.

As chairman, I conferred with Theo and Deborah Oxley, our charity manager, several times a week. I presided at our monthly board meetings and brainstormed along with the rest —I'd always loved belonging to a team, and we had a very good one. No matter where I went or whom I saw, Children in Crisis would be uppermost in my thoughts—I brought it into everything I did. I got little public recognition (our work was too serious for a good cartoon), and honestly didn't care. I had found something real in my life, and that was enough.

In Poland we sent medicine and disposable nappies to Zabrze, but the children needed more. We wanted to give them strength and hope, but how could they hope when every breath they took was another dose of cancer? We somehow had to find them respite. When a woman named Sophie Lillingston came to us with her idea for a mountain haven, we jumped at it.

Today the Mountain Haven Centre welcomes thirty children with cancer or chronic respiratory ailments at a time, more than seven hundred each year. Based in a modern chalet at the foot of the Carpathians, near the Czech border, the haven is ringed by pine forests, like something out of *The Sound of Music*. There is a playground and a swimming pool, a garden and farm animals. The children play and laugh together, and most of all they breathe clean air. Soon they are gaining weight and strength, and the morale to fight through their next treatment. They stay for only two weeks at a time —but those two weeks, experts say, can extend their lives by two years.

By 1998 our work in Poland should be self-sustaining, fully staffed and funded by the people who live there. Which in turn will free our London operation, the mother ship, to move in somewhere else.

*I*n April 1993, our staff team visited Croatia to assess what we might do there. As bad as we thought it would be in that war-torn country, it was worse—far worse. Our people found overcrowded camps short of food or water, and children crying for parents who would never return. Worst of all were the hospitals that functioned without drugs or even electricity. They were less hospitals than morgues, really, especially for the babies who'd been abandoned there.

One month later, following the able lead of a group called Feed the Children, we had organized our first humanitarian aid lorry as part of a monthly convoy to Split and over the border into Bosnia. Over the next year we would fill our trucks with more than a thousand tons of aid, including 8,000 pairs of children's shoes and socks.

After discussions with the United Nations High Commission for Refugees (UNHCR), we also joined the effort to keep war victims alive through the coming winter. Children in Crisis would concentrate on one simple but essential commodity: the candle, a source of both light and heat. With enough candles, refugees might cope with the pervasive loss of electricity. Hospitals could operate in belowground shelters. Children could be read to after dark.

To begin, we commissioned the design of a manually operated candle-making machine. Subsidized by the British government, we bought and distributed twenty machines to scattered sites in Bosnia and Croatia. When supplied with wax powder, it would take a man thirty seconds to make a candle that burned for fifteen hours. Within three months more than two million candles were produced.

The best part was that the refugees were doing all the work, and getting paid for it. When the war moved, we consolidated most of the machines in one place and established a small factory. We hope to leave that behind us, as a permanent source of income and dignity for the people who thought they'd lost everything.

*E*ven as I immersed myself in Children in Crisis, a little gnat would come buzzing by my ear. Every now and again I'd be reminded that The Firm was not done with me—that while I might have lost my royal perquisites, I could still be put under the courtiers' thumb. In February 1993, I was told to cancel a paid-for trip with my daughters to the Caribbean. Diana had recently been snapped in a bikini there, they lectured me, "and we don't want photographs of you swanning around on the beach." *Plus,* I thought, *my body doesn't look as good as hers.*

I wanted to accommodate the Queen, so I acceded.

It was right around then that Diana and I were characterized as "two bad women" by one of the tabloids' "Palace sources." The Grey Men were troubled, you see. The erstwhile Merry Widows might soon be Gay Divorcées; we'd be out of the family, and good riddance, but also outside the courtiers' control. To keep us from flexing new muscles, The Firm did its level best to isolate us. Any friends seen in our company suddenly appeared in the papers, in articles that were less than flattering. One wealthy American was explic-

itly warned *not* to see us—he must treat us, he was told, as
though we had AIDS.

Then there were the actions that spoke louder than words.
Going back to 1990, according to *Today*'s Chris Hutchins,
tips about my whereabouts abroad had been fed to his newspaper over the phone or via clandestine meetings. In Hutchins's view, the informants were uniformly "well-dressed,
well-spoken, and obviously well-placed." He pegged them
as members of the Secret Service.

I know that MI5 tapped my phones and analyzed the re-
cordings at their "listening centre" at Cheltenham. (As confirmed by a former MI6 officer, the Secret Service had a
special unit to monitor the Royal Family—all, of course, "in
defense of the realm.") When their taps came up empty, they
had to trap me by some other means, fair or foul.

Now and then I would get a wave of gooseflesh, the same
creeping sense I'd had in the south of France. *Someone was
watching.* Was it The Firm? The press? The Secret Service?
The distinctions had blurred for me. A spy is a spy, and you
know he is not your friend.

Early in 1993, I paid a secret visit to my lawyer in London,
to discuss a divorce and how it might play out for me. A few
days later, the lawyer's office was burgled.

Some weeks later I came across a strange-looking worm
under the wicker fence at Romenda Lodge. Upon closer inspection, the worm turned out to be a miniature camera, fixed
to the end of a doctor's proctoscope—the symbolism is all
too obvious—and aimed at my house.

No corner of a Royal's life was safe from prying or exposure. I had given up keeping my diaries. (For a time I had
kept them in a bank, but I feared the bank might be robbed!)

Before my separation, my movements could be traced
through my security officers; loyal and wonderful men

though they were, they could not stonewall point-blank questions from their bosses. Later on, after I'd lost my protection, I had reason to believe that my car was bugged with a tracking device.

At first Andrew hated it when I talked about these things. He'd grown up in the Palace as the fair-haired boy, after all: massively indulged, massively protected. The courtiers had always seemed so benign and solicitous, like well-dressed family retainers. How could The Firm wish to harm me? Why was I talking such nonsense? "Don't be so suspicious," he would say. "It wouldn't be like that." Or even: "You are oversensitive and paranoid, you are completely and utterly wrong."

(The Grey Men took a more clinical view: my conspiracy theories were figments of some hormonal malady. I had postnatal depression, or premenstrual syndrome, or posttraumatic stress—just pick the one you liked.)

Much of the time I feared that Andrew might be right. Was I paranoid? Had I lost my grip? When you have lived for years in a Lewis Carroll fantasyland, where truth seems no more fixed or tangible than the Cheshire cat, it is hard to be sure of things.

Gradually, however, Andrew's skepticism would soften. After the Squidgy tape, and "Camillagate," and the divulgence of one of our own tapped phone calls, my charges no longer seemed farfetched. Over time, as my husband faced The Firm's ruthlessness firsthand, he would come to share my suspicions, and arrive at the same conclusion as James Whitaker in *Royal Blood Feud:* "That forces were at work to destabilize the Royal Family suddenly seemed to be distinctly possible, in fact very probable."

* * *

One still had to live one's life, regardless of who might be listening in. I had gotten thick-skinned since the St. Tropez photos—I could block more things out, shrug them off. I had my new calling, after all. I had work of my own, and it lay beyond the reach of the courtiers' pale soft hands.

One day I heard from Pida Ripley, the founder of Women-Aid, who was raising money for rape victims in Bosnia. Her appeal touched me, and I responded with enthusiasm. It was only a phone call, but it set a mighty ball rolling.

At the time, the United Nations High Commission for Refugees was casting about for a goodwill ambassador, to fill the vacancy created by the death of Audrey Hepburn. Pida put my name forward, and on June 10, 1993, the appointment was confirmed; I would be taking my place beside Sophia Loren and Barbara Hendricks, the American opera singer.

I was "an ideal choice," Sadako Ogata, the UNHCR commissioner, told the press. "We have been very impressed by the work the Duchess has already undertaken on behalf of refugee children in Bosnia. We are anxious for her to join us as soon as possible."

Sylvana Foa, an agency spokeswoman, added: "The Duchess has kept her head up despite all her personal problems, and you have to admire her for that."

Or as another UN source put it: "When she goes around, everyone knows who she is. If she asks for something, they will hesitate before saying no."

My first engagement came that night, when I accepted a WomenAid award on Mrs. Ogata's behalf in London. Shortly, I was told, I would be summoned to Geneva to collect my flak jacket and blue beret, and my symbolic contract. (The going rate for a roving ambassador was one pound per annum.) Soon I might be dispatched to visit children in Mozambique and Bangladesh.

By all accounts, my appointment was popular among the field-workers; I was perceived quite differently outside the dank, cloistered world of the Grey Men. For my part, I thought it was about the most wonderful thing that could ever happen. The UN post would break the chains of my past. People would come to see me as I really was. And with an independent base, and a diplomatic passport, I could pursue my work abroad without Palace interference.

I might not be Audrey Hepburn—for who could match her sleek elegance or serenity?—but I knew I could do a good job.

What I had not counted on, in the giddiness of the moment, was how hard The Firm would balk. I had notified the Queen before the appointment was made public. But the UN had failed to consult with either the Palace or Downing Street, and must have given the Grey Men the shock of their lives. They had seen how Diana's trip to Zimbabwe had stolen Charles's thunder and propelled her to international superstar status—and effectively out of their control. They had no wish to see the same thing happen to me.

"They have had their fill of Fergie," said one Palace insider. "It is simply a case of saying enough is enough."

A beheading, after all, is not a partial affair.

The backlash erupted within twenty-four hours of the UN's announcement. My selection, fumed the *Daily Mail,* the Grey Men's favorite newspaper, bordered "on the grotesque. . . . The Duchess is hardly representative of the caring, self-sacrificing traditions of this nation's charitable conscience. . . . If ever there was a time when the Foreign Office needed to have a discreet word in someone's ear at the

UN headquarters, this is the moment. The Duchess should be grounded."

For the record, a Palace source noted, the appointment was "a matter between the Duchess and the UNHCR. She now operates independently from the Palace." But it was also reported that Mr. Z had discussed "the problem" with Foreign Minister Douglas Hurd. And off the record, the courtiers hissed and whispered all the old magic words:

Inappropriate.

Ill-judged.

Unsuitable.

My confirmation stalled. I knew I was in trouble the first week of July, when Douglas Hurd approved my pending trip to Croatia for Children in Crisis—and then canceled it two days later for "security reasons." (Although, as the *Daily Express* noted, "the only risk the Duchess faced in Split was sunstroke.")

Three weeks later, the Establishment moved in for the kill. "Such an appointment would be entirely undesirable," one cabinet minister said, and then added a twist of his stiletto: "There is no Shirley Temple role available."

But first prize for chivalry must go to Sir Nicholas Fairbairn, a Scottish MP and former government minister: "I can't think of anybody else I would sooner not appoint to this post than the Duchess of York.... She is a lady short on looks, absolutely deprived of any dress sense, has a figure like a Jurassic monster, is very greedy when it comes to loot, has no tact, and wants to upstage everyone else."

As the witch-hunt accelerated, it would offend even some of the newspapers. The campaign against me was "not just vindictive," said the *Sunday Express*. "It is plain stupid. She may not be perfect and she may have made mistakes. But she has done no worse than many of her detractors, and the person she has hurt most is herself. She deserves another chance."

That chance would not be forthcoming, not this time. Sylvana Foa called Pida Ripley and tearfully gave her the bad news. The Foreign Office had set its terms, Pida told me. Britain would withdraw all future support from the UNHCR unless my appointment was killed. Moreover, Pida said, the Commission must deny ever asking me in the first place—it would all be framed as a mistake, a vain fantasy.

When blackmail is well crafted, it quickly carries the day. Sadako Ogata's operation was running more than $100 million in the red. It depended heavily on British funding and goodwill—and on British troops in Bosnia. There was no choice to be made; it was only a matter of scripting the press release.

The UNHCR, Sylvana Foa told the press on July 29, had invited my participation at the WomenAid award dinner, no more and no less. "At this stage," she said, "no other joint initiatives are planned."

I just had to let it go; there was nothing I could do.

No, that wasn't quite right. There *was* something I could do—I could get on with the work at hand. In February 1994, I finally made it to Croatia. Working in partnership with a UNHCR airlift, we boarded a cargo plane filled with blankets and baby food. After we landed, I personally delivered the aid to various hospitals. The press responded; it brought the people's plight temporarily back to the forefront.

And it opened my eyes, wider than before. Though my own life had been sheltered, I could imagine what it was to be displaced—I could taste the terror of it as I met with these refugees, though we had no language in common. It tore my heart to see the human destruction of this war. I met a twelve-year-old Muslim girl quaking with fear in a Catholic hospital;

she had been shot below the waist by Serbian troops (a common tactic among ethnic cleansers), and left to bleed to death by the side of a road. I saw children living in railway carriages, needing someone to answer their questions: *Why is there no television? Why can't we go outside and play football? Why are Mummy and Daddy gone?*

In June of that year, Children in Crisis established a refugee center for more than five hundred people in Tasovcici, a devastated village near Mostar, in Bosnia. We housed our families in private, prefabricated huts, and furnished the essentials of life: food, clothes, safety.

But we didn't want our center to be just another hopeless way station to nowhere. We wanted to create a *village,* instead. Given support, the refugees were eager to reclaim some small part of their lives. They formed a committee to help run the place, and then there was no stopping them. They staffed our kitchen and our counseling center, the preschool and the first-aid clinic. They worked in cottage industries to make candles and soap. Refugee druggists ran the pharmacy; refugee dentists operated a mobile care unit.

Soon you could see how much more positive the adults had become, and how their confidence infected their children. They all *belonged* to this community, and it to them.

Tasovcici worked because we dealt with needy people as *people,* not as patients or victims. Rather than presume to know what they needed, we listened to what they wanted— and if that meant getting them Doc Marten boots, we'd try to do it. (The same principle applies in my other organizations. At the Teenage Cancer Trust, we have helped create special hospital units for teenagers, where they can be together with their music and video games and blue jeans with holes in them. Nurses are out of uniform, and pop posters adorn the walls. We treat them as teenagers, in short, rather than as

Poor Tragic Children—and their projected survival rate has risen by 15 percent.)

In recognition of our efforts, the UNHCR rated Tasovcici as one of the three best-run camps in the whole of the former Yugoslavia.

I'd like to think that Audrey Hepburn might have been proud.

14

Peaks and Valleys

*I*n October 1993, I collected my friend Aly Brown and flew to Nepal. As president of MacIntyre Care, a group that promotes independent living for the disabled, I would be joining a trek to the top of Pokalde Peak, more than 19,000 feet high.

There were thirty-eight climbers in all, eight of whom had physical or mental disabilities. We were out to dramatize the fact that these people can lead productive, challenging lives —that they don't need to be locked up in institutions. They may do things a little more slowly, but they can reach the same places as the rest of us.

The rest of the group had embarked several weeks earlier, to allow for a gradual acclimation to the thinner air. But Aly and I didn't have that kind of time. We had budgeted ten days up and four days down—and without oxygen masks, we would be pushing our limits. We'd get by on anti–altitude sickness pills and two gallons of water per day.

The climb would be rigorous and then some: eight hours a

day up a steep grade, with no stopping for lunch. But the weather was perfect, the air like blue glass, and it warmed enough by day to let us shed our parkas and go on in T-shirts. Depending on our position, we could see the top triangle of Everest. And it was fantastic to be completely away from one's normal day-to-day, totally absorbed in physical activity —it was a smelling salt for the soul.

By night I shared a tent with Aly, one of the very few people in the world with whom I could survive for two weeks in such close quarters. By day I climbed with a well-built young man named Paul Sillitoe, whose mother had got a whooping cough injection while she was pregnant with him.

Paul is a baker, and he has a girlfriend, and he is simply a hero to me. He has the most marvelous attitude toward stuffy Establishment types; he is a natural-born subversive. Once I took him to a prestigious award ceremony, where I'd been booked to hand out the prizes, and we had to meet a long line of generals. "Paul," I said, "this is General Holland."

"General—oh hello, yeah."

"And his name is Graham," I added.

"Oh well," Paul said, "I'll call him Graham, then," and so he did. My friend made formalities superfluous. On our trek he took to calling me "Duchess Crisps," mainly because there were no crisps to be had in the Himalayas, and Paul missed them. Whenever I flagged he would encourage me: "My Duchess Crisps, come on, we can do it."

On my ninth night, at the Everest base camp, the temperature plunged toward zero. The next morning we were given helmets and roped together; this would be the steepest part of the climb, and we'd have to watch our footing. Two hours later, Paul and I reached the summit of Pokalde ahead of the rest. Paul breathed in the panorama. "Crisps," he said, "this is the closest to God I am ever going to get alive."

That was too much—the most innocent statement, and the truest one. Tears poured down my cheeks. In that moment with Paul, near the top of the world, I felt a great calm. My self-absorption melted. Life seemed so much larger, and more important, than the sum of my own travails.

Aly and I stayed at the summit for twenty minutes, then began our race down. We had a plane to catch, to get back in time for our daughters' school holidays. I wasn't sorry to leave. Once I've achieved something, I am not one to dwell on it. I am ready to move on.

A week after returning from Pokalde, I turned on the BBC—and caught a vision of hell. The subject was a state orphanage in Albania, and its nightmare images were out of Hieronymus Bosch. In an unheated building, where people's breath frosted the air, naked children were tied to filthy cots. They drank from the drains and ate off the floor; excrement was everywhere. Babies lay neglected with bulging rags around their bottoms; their bodies wept with sores. Rats rustled underfoot, unafraid.

I was staggered by the program. Before it had even ended I rang the news reporter, a man named Bill Hamilton, and said to him, "I cannot bear this—are there really children going through all this?"

And he said, "Yes, there are."

"Can we go and see it?"

"We're going in three days."

"Yes, I'm coming."

Albania is the poorest country in Europe. Per capita, its Ministry of Health spent ten dollars per year. But even Albania was not impervious to pressure. By the time we arrived, the government had closed the state orphanage. One child was dead from exposure; the rest had been dispersed to slightly less horrendous places. Packed into a rattletrap mini-bus, we tracked each of those children down—they were okay, just.

It was past 7 P.M. when we finished our last inspection, deep in the rain-sodden Albanian countryside, hours from the capital, Tirana. I was about to board our bus when I heard the strangest sounds coming from a barnlike building fifty yards off. Ankle-deep in water, we approached it down a concrete path. Soon I could make the sounds out: they were screams and wails, high-pitched and haunting, a chorus of torment.

We had driven bad roads for two days, and the crew was exhausted. I turned to the cameraman and said, "We have got to go in there—I don't like the sound of it." One of the men and I started banging on these big wooden doors—we were ready to bash them down if a nurse had not opened them. "You can't come in here!" she said, but we pushed right by her, camera and all, and we were in.

How do I express what I saw in that barn? More than fifty women with shaved heads were crammed into three rooms meant to hold perhaps ten of them. It was cold and damp but the women were unclothed, save for a few shreds of night-gowns. They lay on iron beds, and they used the floor for a toilet. These women had bruises everywhere; the nurses were broad-shouldered, and apparently free with their fists. The conditions were so wretched that the patients had to be con-tinuously sedated. There was only one needle, so everyone shared.

The facility was supposed to house the mentally ill, but I am convinced that political prisoners were mixed in as well. (One woman spoke fluent English, which was rare in those parts.) With not enough beds to go around, most of the patients got what little creature comfort they could by having sex with one another.

I felt chilled in my sweatshirt, and knew the naked woman in front of me must be freezing, so I took it off and gave it to her. "Don't do that," the nurse scolded. "She'll get beaten up for that shirt—she's better off not to have anything." She was harsh and pitiless, that nurse, and I guessed who might do the beating.

Eventually we were thrown out, though not before we had enough footage for another BBC exposé. I learned then and there the value of the impromptu visit—that if you do only what is scheduled and officially permitted, you run the risk of legitimizing some shameful situations.

In Tirana I met with President Berisha and told him what I had seen. He seemed glad to know of it, but I think that I startled him, just a bit.

I might still be a coward in fighting for myself, but for others I could be as brave as Leonard Cheshire.

*I*n June of 1993, Andrew and I were seen together at dinner, and then the press snapped him kissing me at Balmoral. The papers were full of stories about our rumored reconciliation. The Firm was all aflutter—why couldn't I just limp off into the sunset like a good little victim? Suddenly, without consulting either of us, the Firm put out a release to announce our "formal separation." Which did absolutely nothing, except to reveal the depth of the courtiers' concern.

In fact, their worries were misplaced. While my husband and I were feeling easier with each other, if only because the pressure was off, we were essentially playing for time. We had no set plan for our future—and no intention of expunging our past.

I was never one to erase a man from my life after a romance was done. People cannot be reduced to "girlfriend" or "boyfriend"—when they share something good and real, it lives on in both forever. Eight years after we broke up, Paddy McNally remained one of my closest, most trusted friends. More than a year after our separation, Andrew and I still loved each other, and we didn't care what the world thought.

I knew well the lasting power of love; Queen Victoria had proved it a century ago, as she kept on loving Albert for forty years after his death. My interest in Victoria had taken wing sometime after my wedding. I saw how Sir Michael Timms led Palace guests on private tours after dinner parties, and I thought it looked like great fun. I asked Sir Michael to teach me, which he did, donating a set of his white index cards for reminders. Soon I began leading people around myself; Andrew loved it, because I knew so much about the place where he'd grown up.

You cannot learn about Buckingham Palace without learning about Queen Victoria. Our apartment, for example, was part of the wing added by Albert—a gift to Andrew from his great-great-great-grandfather. The creative prince of Saxe-Coburg also designed the oversized balcony where we waved; Albert's Queen had needed a grand stage for reviewing her troops come home from the Crimean War.

The more history I absorbed, the more kinship I felt with the greatest of queens. I discovered that Queen Victoria had proposed to Albert (a Sovereign's prerogative) in the Blue Closet at Windsor Castle—on the same date as my birthday. Her eldest daughter, Beatrice, married Prince Henry of Battenberg on the same date that I would wed Andrew. Each strange connection, every little fact excited me, especially those I unearthed about Osborne House, the love nest created by the Queen and her consort on the Isle of Wight. I was beguiled by the aura of that seaside refuge, now preserved as a convalescent home and museum. Following the example of Victoria's Beatrice, I obtained a sprig of myrtle from Osborne's garden for my wedding bouquet.

But the published accounts of Osborne were mostly cursory and disappointing. The house was invariably painted as a mausoleum, where the widowed Victoria, draped in black, would grieve through four decades of lonely wedding anniversaries. I knew that a large part of the story must be missing, especially after I visited Osborne in 1988. I noted the friendly scale of its chambers, and how close the nursery was to the master bedroom, a departure for Victorian times. I sensed that Osborne had been meant as a *family* home, a cheerful place where Victoria and Albert could enjoy their nine children: a place of their own. It must have been a huge escape from the creaking corridors and beady eyes of Buckingham Palace, and—as the Queen herself noted—the intrusions of the press: "God knows how willingly I would always live with my beloved Albert and our children in the quiet and retirement of private life, and not be the constant object of observation, and of newspaper articles."

The embryo of a book about Osborne House dated back to before my marriage, when Richard Burton approved it as my next project after *The Palace of Westminster*. Royal duties had forced me to shelve the idea, but three years later I was keen to pick it up again. Now I had one great advantage, by Her Majesty's permission: access to the Royal Library and Royal Archives at Windsor Castle, and hence to Queen Victoria's diaries.

The Royal Library is a magical place. Its tall windows scan

a broad swath of countryside, where the river Thames sweeps by on its way to London. Inside it is a time-warp machine. Shadowy walls are lined by glass-fronted cupboards and rows of old books, some of them inscribed in Victoria's own emphatic hand. When I opened these volumes and loosed their faint aroma, I felt hypnotized, transported—as though the past were retrieving me, rather than the other way around.

As I read on, I gained a clearer picture of Albert, at great contrast to the stereotyped stern German. The prince was, in fact, a gentle, loving father, even a playful one; he encouraged his children to bathe in the sea (then quite avant-garde), and built a scaled-down replica of a Swiss chalet for their own retreat. I came to have great sympathy for this royal outsider. Love and circumstance had snatched him from a private life in the countryside and hurled him into mid-nineteenth-century London, with its congestion and coal fumes and periodic cholera. When Albert stayed at Osborne, he recaptured the clean air and light heart of his youth.

Most of all, Osborne was the place where Albert could love his Victoria as *she* really was. The common depiction of Queen Victoria is two-dimensional at best; the historians portray her as the head of the world's greatest empire at the age of eighteen, then fast-forward to the bereft little lady in black. They tend to rush over the richest two decades of her life, her married years with Albert.

In her diaries, the young Victoria comes alive as a woman full of humor and zest. At balls she would squeeze her feet into tiny pumps and dance until three in the morning, declaring that such "dissipation" did her good. She liked horses and dogs, and a good game of cards. When given the chance at Osborne she would run on the grass with cornflowers in her hair, and with her dresses cut to show off the bare shoulders that Albert so adored. She learned German and painted and played the piano, with the prince sitting in for duets. Most of all she loved her man.

"It was with some emotion that I beheld Albert—who is *beautiful,*" the twenty-year-old Victoria wrote, after beholding the prince from the top of a Windsor staircase at the outset of their courtship. Her frank and passionate attachment to Albert never faded. A fearful romantic myself, I got swept up by this tremendous love story—by the idea that an all-consuming love will transcend any obstacle, including a Sovereign's duty.

Even the end of the story was darkly romantic. Prince Albert died in Windsor at the age of forty-two; retrospective diagnoses suggest cancer of the stomach or liver. Feeling utterly lost, Victoria wanted to die with him: "*Can I—can I be alive when half my body and soul are gone?*" She mourned not just a husband, but also a "father, mother, friend, companion, advisor, lover, guardian angel. . . . *He* did everything —everywhere!"

The Queen carried on, of course, for forty years more. She never left her grief; she never deserted her duty. And every night through all that time she would wind Albert's watch and put his nightshirt out. She would climb into bed but never would she turn to the other side, where Albert slept. That was Victoria's world, from that point on: a bed only half slept in, a life only half lived.

As published in 1991 (with some proceeds going to The Prince Andrew Charitable Trust), *Victoria and Albert: Life at Osborne House* was a critical success. The book had turned out just as I had hoped: relaxed and informative, and filled with vivid photographs and art. It was, in fact, *too* good for me to claim as my own creation. The original idea had been mine, and the book's language and editing as well, yet I'd apologize to Benita Stoney, my cowriter and researcher. "It's your work," I kept telling her. "You did the whole thing." I put myself down by reflex.

But my second *Victoria* book would bear my stamp throughout. In the course of doing *Osborne House,* I uncovered Victoria's love of travel abroad. Benita and I went back to the Royal Library, to the albums as large as paving slabs. We began plotting the routes that the Queen had taken, from her first trip to Albert's native Coburg in 1845 to her final holiday in the Côte d'Azur, just two years before her death. My idea was to retrace the Queen's travels as closely as I could. I wanted to see what she saw and smell what she smelled, and thereby come to know her better.

That journey would sate my curiosity and exceed my expectations. I left for the Rhineland in November 1992, only three months after my humiliation at Balmoral. Shame had rubbed me raw, made me unnaturally susceptible to new impressions. When I reached the hills of Coburg, where Victoria had run barefoot, I felt brushed by a force larger and stronger than myself: the presence of that fabled Queen herself.

I strove to replicate her experience, to the smallest detail. At Albert's birthplace, the Rosenau, where he and his brother would puncture their bedroom wallpaper while fencing, I put my fingers into the same holes that Victoria had once examined.

As we continued, and I came to trust my instincts, there were eerie developments. Inside the Ehrenberg Palace I was drawn to a window that looked down a narrow street to the market square, and I took time out to paint the scene. In the square itself I was captivated by the smell of bratwurst smoking over fir needles. In Cap Ferrat I found a perfect breakfast spot, a terrace shaded by an umbrella of pine trees. In Potsdam a full-blown migraine struck me; en route to Nice, I was seized by impulse to detour down a winding mountain road.

Of themselves, none of these incidents seemed remarkable. But when I returned to Victoria's diaries, after the fact, I found that the Queen had painted the same street, from the same vantage point. She had sent someone out to buy the same sausages in Coburg; she'd breakfasted under the umbrella trees of Cap Ferrat. Victoria had made the same French detour—she had even complained of "racking headaches." (She was as allergic to central heating as I.)

I do not pretend to be anyone other than myself, but in the course of that journey I escaped *into* Victoria, until I felt the rattle of her horse-drawn carriage. With each leg of my trip, her presence grew stronger. Benita had accompanied me, along with a photographer and my executive assistant, but there were days when I felt entirely inside myself, enmeshed in a private quest. Victoria was all the company I needed.

Out in September 1993, *Travels With Queen Victoria* won another warm critical reception. It was easily the high point of my publishing career . . . and I felt like a gigantic fraud.

I had hoped *Travels* might win back the approval I had squandered—that I might come off as a serious person, a student of history. But now the compliments rang hollow; I knew better than the reviewers. Take, for example, my artwork. Victoria had painted *real* landscapes in Europe; my watercolors were rushed doodlings by comparison. My pictures were fraudulent—and how could they be otherwise, given the source?

For the first time, I believe, I understood Queen Victoria. And through her, Her Majesty, our present Queen. I understood what duty meant to them, and sacrifice. I was plagued by that understanding, because I had not merely let down Her

Majesty. I had, as I now saw it, betrayed this great tradition of monarchy. *(Look what the Queen has done—duty and more duty for so many years. But you haven't done your duty. . . .)*

I had made history, all right. I was a failure of historical proportions.

Better than any psychoanalyst, *Travels* helped me comprehend the damage I had wrought. It was another small step toward consciousness. And it hurt.

15

The Duchess
of Cork

On a Sunday in November 1993, I was working at home
and half watching the British Grand Prix, a show jumping
event at Hickstead. I glanced up at the television—and
dropped everything. A remarkable horse was in action, a
huge gray ballerina of a horse, clearing each jump with daylight. But what had stopped me was the rider, a silver-haired
man in a green coat. He was that rarest of performers: a styl-
ist. He rode with elegance and ease, and you could tell by his
body that he *listened* to his horse—they moved in perfect
rhythm. You could not determine where one left off and the
other began.

Their teamwork reminded me of a passage from one of
my favorite books, Nicholas Evans's *The Horse Whisperer:*
"Dancing and riding, it's the same damn thing. It's about
trust and consent."

The silver-haired man at Hickstead held the grace of life in
his hands, I knew that as I knew my name. I had not ridden

for a very long time; I'd lost my feeling for horses, the kind of thing that happens when you stop listening to yourself. But I knew I wanted to meet this man. I sensed that he might help me retrieve something.

Then a phone call distracted me, and I missed the end of the round—missed the calling of the man's name! I rang up Jane Ambler and said, "Here's a challenge for you." I told her what I knew—gray horse, green jacket—and asked her to find the rider. It took Jane two days, but she succeeded. The rider's name was Robert Splaine, and he ran an equestrian center in Belgooly, in County Cork.

That November I boarded an Aer Lingus flight to Cork. Two hours later I was shaking hands with Robert Splaine and his wife, Eileen, at their home in the rich Irish countryside. Heather Blaze, the ballerina, was calmly munching her clover in a small field; she pricked up her long rabbit ears when I approached.

The Splaines were charming people—down-to-earth, relaxed, no different with a duchess than they'd be with a dairyman—and we became fast friends. With their encouragement, I bought a horse and started show jumping again. I'd fly out once a week to Robert's place to ride and train, and when I thought I was ready I entered some Irish country shows. Show jumping was always saved for the end, after they had beribboned the best soda bread: *And here is the Duchess of York, on her horse Coolcorran Willow!*

We won a few rosettes, Willow and I, and were very proud of ourselves. The people there were fantastic. They were delighted that a member of the Royal Family had come out of her way to be with them and cheered me like a favorite son. After a while they took to calling me "the Duchess of Cork."

I have always felt comfortable in Ireland. I could be free there, and natural; I blended in with all the other redheads. I could go to local restaurants with no press on my heels. The Irish people were my security, and I felt safe.

One day I arrived at the equestrian center and could tell something was wrong. The people who owned Heather Blaze were selling her to a U.S. interest, Robert told me. Soon he would be losing her.

For Robert it was a body blow. Heather Blaze was an almost freakish mix of talent, heart, and temperament; a horseman could go a lifetime without finding her like. Without that long-eared horse, Robert could no longer compete at the top international level, and this seemed to me a crime, a waste of brilliance and grace.

Though my account at Coutt's hovered somewhere between scarlet and crimson, I vowed that I would raise the funds we needed to keep Heather Blaze. Everyone was saying, "Look after yourself," but I had to help Robert; I couldn't let him and Eileen down. Somehow I put together a sufficient sum—not a match for the other bidder's purchase price, but enough for a down payment to forestall the sale. It was too thrilling for belief, that I actually owned such a marvelous horse.

Heather Blaze was jumping in peak form in 1995, winning with regularity, but I knew that her acid test would be the King George V Gold Cup in July. As the most coveted trophy in England, the King George lured the very best horses from throughout the world; no Irish rider had won it in thirty-five years. Then again, no Irish rider had been riding the likes of Heather Blaze. Before the competition, I walked up to my horse and said softly, "The next time you are up there, don't be afraid of the planks."

Robert had supreme confidence in his mount that day, and it showed in the first round. Of more than thirty competitors, only five jumped clear—and of those five, Heather Blaze was the quickest, sailing over the fences as though immune to gravity. Her good time allowed her to go last in the jump-off, exactly Robert's plan.

In that second round, the first four horses knocked down one rail apiece. The safer strategy for Robert—the one urged by friends on the sideline—would have been to get out quickly, giving Heather Blaze a chance to win even if she faulted. But as Robert walked toward the in gate, I could see him shaking his head; he had a different, bolder notion. Rather than speed through the jump-off, he took it slowly, deliberately. He was banking on a clear round; he had the best horse, on her best form, and he trusted her absolutely.

And after Heather Blaze delivered that clear round, winning the day, the low-key Robert Splaine took off his hat and punched it in the air, to punctuate the high point of his career. Presenting the trophy to that Irish rider and Irish horse was a proud half-Irish woman.

No one at Hickstead realized that I owned Heather Blaze except Robert and myself. The secret made our feat the more special. Perhaps we would sail incognito all the way to the Olympics in Atlanta—and wouldn't that be a lesson in unity, for a royal duchess's horse to win a medal for Ireland?

Some weeks after the King George, Robert entered Heather Blaze in the Grand Prix of Ireland. She was midway through the round—jumping clear, with daylight—when she stumbled on the water jump and fell upon landing. Her left foreleg shattered. There was nothing to be done but to spare her more pain.

Robert was uninjured, but I knew how badly he was hurting. He had ridden Heather Blaze for four years; she was part of his family. We cleared a fair amount from the insurance, enough to give Robert a second chance. My intuition had gotten us this far, and I would ride it a while longer. I gave the money to Robert and said, "You find the horse."

The one he found seemed unlikely. Though a handsome brown thoroughbred, Ballymoss seemed poorly fed; I could count his ribs when I first met him. But Robert liked his potential, and we took the chance.

After a few months of Robert's care amid the thick, nutritious grasses of County Cork, Ballymoss blossomed. Today that horse competes on the international circuit, a worthy teammate for the most inspiring rider I have ever seen.

America is a special land for me. I find the people there incredibly giving, and forgiving—they are disinclined to judge. If you are pleased to be with them, then they are pleased to see you, as simple as that. When I toured the States on official visits, people seemed to respond to the person I really was. They'd call me Fergie or Sarah or Princess Ferguson, whatever worked for them. Protocol didn't matter— they were just happy to see this mass of red hair come flying through their door. (As I look back, I got similar receptions in Australia, and almost everywhere else. It was only at home that I felt a stranger.)

After years of fund-raisers, I came to feel embarrassed about going to America for British causes; it was too colonial for my tastes. I wanted to give something back to a country that had supported me through thin and thinner. In December 1994 we established Chances for Children. To make sure the new baby stayed afloat, I pledged my own money to help cover costs for the first year.

Although Chances for Children was based in Manhattan, I wanted it to break the bicoastal mold and get beyond the social glitter of New York and Los Angeles. I like to find less-traveled places, where you don't have to stand in the queue. When I visited Oklahoma City just after the bombing there, I pledged to raise $150,000 within a year to help them build a pediatric center. I had only Christine Ward to help me, and it was touch and go for a time. But I am a stickler for follow-up, and for keeping promises. We made our goal two weeks before the year was up and returned to Oklahoma with the check.

Our first case was on a smaller scale. Rhonda Armstrong, a fourteen-year-old immigrant from Guyana, had been blinded by a brain tumor pressing on her optic nerve. Unless the tumor was removed, doctors warned, she might be dead within days.

Chances for Children donated $15,000 toward Rhonda's operation at Montefiore Medical Center, where they removed a tumor the size of a chicken egg. A few days after the surgery, I came to visit her. Rhonda had just been moved from intensive care. Almost as I walked into the room, she opened her eyes and said, "Dear God, I can see!"

A handful of moments are indelible: the birth of one's children, the death of a parent. My moment with Rhonda was one of those. We had given that sweet girl an extra year of life. I still keep her picture by my bed; I can still hear her greeting the light, as if she were seeing for the first time.

In the summer of 1995, I flew to Bucharest for a three-day tour sponsored by Scottish European Aid, a frontline charity in Eastern Europe. I'd brought along a photographer; our plan was to sell his pictures back in England and donate the net proceeds to SEA and two Romanian charitable trusts.

After an official reception, our tour began with a visit to Leagen Orphanage. The children slept three to a bed, but their rooms were heated, the windows unbroken—it didn't seem a bad place, all in all.

It was 11:30 at night, the end of a very long day, when we passed near a tall brick building at the top of a hill: the Camin Hospital for Handicapped Children, on our schedule for the next morning. Something disturbed me about that building. It looked so institutional, so somber.

"Please stop the car," I said. "May I go there now?"

"It's not possible," our guide protested.

"I want to go there *now*," I said.

I was one step through the door when I was almost knocked over by the rotten-cabbage smell of urine; it is a smell that carries with me today. Then I saw where it came from. The ward was filled with children, ranging from small toddlers to teenagers. Many of them were roped down in sheetless beds—a measure to prevent them from scratching and biting one another, the nurses explained. Urine was everywhere; the patients had no way to get to the lavatory.

I stayed in the ward for a time, talking to the children. I was never uneasy with them, though they stank of wee and might wee on you too if they sat on your lap. But that was fine with me—that's what blue jeans were good for.

Then I went down to the washroom and found the root of the problem: no laundry machines.

The next morning we returned for our official visit, and I saw what a difference a day made. Clean sheets were everywhere, and the children were tidy; the smell was still there, but not nearly so bad. The staff was doing what it could to restore their charges' dignity and to keep them busy with activities during the day. But at night they were overwhelmed; they just didn't have the manpower to cope.

Before leaving Romania, I asked to spend a night on the streets in Bucharest, to see how the homeless children fared. A Renault van took us to a large garbage dump behind the train station, in the shadow of the intimidating Ceauşescu government building. Having no place else for shelter, my escort explained, more than a dozen orphans had built their domain within the dump.

My photographer and I bartered our way in with some cheeseburgers and Cokes, to behold a scene that both crushed and amazed me: a self-sustaining community organized out of refuse and rubbish. Ranging in age from ten to eighteen, the residents pooled what food they could find and slept in cardboard boxes—all but a boy named Gabriel, who used a doorless refrigerator for his bed, sharing it with five dogs. These children had to be tough to survive; deserted by the world, they trusted only one another. When you came into their home, you had to treat them with respect.

The head honcho was an eighteen-year-old named Noley, who spoke fluent English and smoked like a chimney, though he wouldn't let the younger ones touch a cigarette. We got on very well, Noley and I—he was smart and caring, and could make a mark in this world if given a chance. The saddest child there was the only girl, Romana. She was on the edge of puberty and must have been terrified of it.

When I left, Romana was crying, and I said to Noley, "You promise me you will look after her."

"You promise me you'll come back," he replied.

I promised, because I knew I would miss him. Noley was a great teacher to me that night.

A world removed from the halls of Hurst Lodge, I was finally getting my schooling.

Back home, we didn't raise as much money as we had hoped. The magazine we'd contracted with paid about

$13,000 for our photographs, and the trip's expenses had exceeded $11,000. As the children needed the help, I donated approximately $25,000 out of my personal account, with most of the money going toward industrial clothes washers and dryers at the Camin Hospital.

The trouble was that my office sent all the money to SEA, rather than dividing it among the three organizations. It did not seem an issue—we had helped the Romanian children, after all, and wasn't that the point?

But the press found out about the two smaller trusts and decided that we had reneged on our pledge, a story televised on *World in Action.* SEA went on record as being more than happy with our donation, and we furnished our side of the story, but that was not what came out on the air.

There were times that it seemed for every step I took forward, I would slide two steps back, or three or four.

*I*n the twelve months ending July 1, 1995, *Majesty* magazine would report that I had traveled more than 200,000 miles for my charities, nearly three times as far as the "second-place" Royal, the Duke of Edinburgh. In fairness, the other members of the Family were working at a disadvantage. They still had to attend to their official engagements, state occasions, Royal Ascot garden parties, and all the extended holidays at the Queen's various residences.

I, on the other hand, was banned from all of the above— and for perpetuity, it would seem. In October 1995, *The Mail on Sunday* confirmed my never-ending exile: THE QUEEN WILL KEEP FERGIE OUT OF LIMELIGHT. I knew what had induced the story; Andrew and I had recently taken our daughters to Spain. The Firm was doubtless stewing over the "R" word, as in *reconciliation*.

By that point, the Grey Men need not have worried. Andrew and I could never be together, I'd resolved, because he would always be a prince. He would always represent a package deal.

It wasn't so bad to be an exile, most of the time—it made life a lot simpler, not to mention one's wardrobe choices. But there were times when it made me feel lonely unto death, and the worst was at Christmas. Ever since my separation, I had dutifully taken Beatrice and Eugenie to Sandringham at Christmastime. I would have loved for us to spend a Christmas with Mum in Argentina, or with Jane in Australia. But I thought it right and proper that my girls be with their father and their grandmother, the Queen. I thought they needed to understand how the Royal Family worked; they needed to understand it better than their mother had.

I suppose you might say that I was still seeking approval.

As Christmas of 1995 came knocking, I crept to the door with more than my common dread. Normally we spent a week at Sandringham. This year, too strapped to make it to Switzerland, we would be there for two. As usual, we stayed at Wood Farm, a comfortable, open-beamed cottage two miles from "the big house." At 4:30 in the afternoon, snow or shine, Andrew came to pick up Beatrice and Eugenie and take them to the big house for tea with their cousins and the Queen. When they came back to me, my daughters had an air of haughtiness; it would take me a while to get them back down.

Over two full weeks, I was not invited once to the big house—not for tea, nor a drink, nor a bowl of breakfast porridge. "Mummy," Beatrice said one day, "why are you not good enough to go up there?" I tried to explain that their granny would love for me to be with them, but that I wasn't so well thought of by certain other members of the Family. My daughters seemed satisfied with that. As long as I was always there for them when they came back, they were fine.

For me the roughest time, as you might expect, was the holiday itself. According to tradition, the Family gathered round the tree to open gifts on Christmas Eve. They went down the road to church the next morning, and had their big feast that afternoon. Ever since 1992, I had been excluded from all these events—they couldn't keep me from the church, of course, but I wouldn't go and rub their noses in it.

By now, the fourth year of my segregation, I surely knew the score. But I couldn't help thinking: *Isn't this a time of forgiveness and good tidings to all men?*

Andrew and I kept our own small holiday tradition. After lunch, when I had my standard Christmas turkey and trimmings with the two policemen and the cook, my husband came down to Wood Farm. We watched James Bond films and had great fun. At 7:30 he got up to leave, grousing about having to change for dinner, and I was, again, alone.

As I have noted, I was always a good spender. I kept on spending after my separation, and my six-figure debt soon added another zero. Given my accustomed lifestyle and the level of my income, a certain deficit was built in. Given my state of mind, and the proclivities of the people around me, my overdraft flourished, mushroomed, metastasized.

In January 1995, my daughters and I moved from Romenda Lodge to Kingsbourne. Our rent stayed the same, but our new home had been vacant and damaged by rain, and I had to invest quite a lot to make it habitable.

I might not have sunk so fast, so far, if I'd had money coming in on the other side of the ledger. But that was the rub: from 1992 to 1995, my business income had sunk into negative numbers. John Bryan had negotiated a contract to exploit Budgie on television and in merchandising. He continually talked about future ventures, waiting just around the corner, which would make the company I'd started years earlier—ASB Publishing, for *Andrew-Sarah-Beatrice*—into the second coming of Disney.

John's favorite demonstration was to write out columns of prospective deals, attaching to each one a dollar figure surpassing the gross national product of Luxembourg. "It's no *problem,*" he'd say. "This one will clear the whole overdraft."

It was all very heady and wonderful—until I asked a question, or betrayed the slightest doubt. When challenged, John would rival the most venerable Grey Man. "You've just got no *idea,*" he would tell me.

I would hate getting slapped down, so I stopped asking questions. I *wanted* to believe that John was this immensely successful businessman who was putting his genius to work for me. With my power of attorney, he didn't even have to consult me before signing a contract—and I thought that was great, it made life so much easier.

Except for one problem: John's big score never materialized. ASB generated some small sums but incurred far greater expenses. There was staff to pay, and John would be jetting all over for high-powered talks, and he wasn't the sort of man who flew in economy. At the end, ASB was a six-figure loser.

John left England for good in the summer of 1995, and we would sever our last business ties by August of that same year. By that time my overdraft had reached the stratosphere.

It wasn't unusual for Coutt's to carry long-term debt for members of the Royal Family; the bank figured the Royals would be good for it, sooner or later. And I *was* the Queen's daughter-in-law, wasn't I? But by late 1995 I might have been pushing the perimeter fence a tad, considering my collateral, which was zero, and my debt, which now exceeded $5 million.

It so happened that I was getting healthier at the time; I was taking control of my affairs. I had trimmed my home expenditures, been obliged to lay off some staff. On the income side, several strong projects were in the pipeline. I was growing more conscious by the day—and, quite sensibly, more panicked. It was as if I'd been napping on the railway tracks and bestirred myself with the locomotive twenty yards away. I was *aware* of the danger, no question, but had I awakened in time?

By November, I had to get approval from the bank to issue checks to pay the florist or the grocer. I seriously thought I was about to go bankrupt, and it was at that point that I rang an American friend of mine and said, "I am in the mud, I am about to sink, and I am holding my hand out. Will you take my hand?" Where others had wavered, or been scared off, this man said he would be there. In return for future considerations on *Budgie,* he would try to save me.

By December a rescue was in motion to restructure my debt. By January a three-way deal had evolved among Coutt's, the American group, and myself. The Firm assured us that they were with me and supportive of the deal.

Maybe that is the point where I should have smelled a Palace rat. Because on January 17, just before the deal was set, The Firm released the following press statement: "The Duchess's financial affairs are no longer Her Majesty's concern. These are matters which The Duchess of York must discuss and resolve with her bankers and other financial advisers. . . . The Duchess's business ventures are conducted quite separately from any Royal duties."

That statement triggered a bank run on my account. To that point, my creditors might have been anxious. Now they were hysterical, alarmed that they would not collect. Everyone from the butcher to the airlines demanded immediate payment. My office phones rang like a telethon; stern letters from lawyers flooded the mails.

But my American friend held firm through the storm. On January 20, my office made public an agreement "which provides for a solid base for the activities of Her Royal Highness The Duchess of York, and ensures the payment of creditors." I still have a big overdraft, but I am paying every penny back.

The Firm, it would seem, had done its best to torpedo my rescue. It had tried to ram me down so far that I would never break the surface, never gain my own power.

But The Firm had failed.

The rest would be up to me.

16

The End
of the Beginning

*B*etrayals are a part of public life, no more to be escaped than zoom lenses or false rumors. I would like to tell you that I've hardened to them, that they are water off my back—but I haven't, and they aren't. It is one thing to be pounded by some anonymous newspaper editor. It is another to be broadsided by someone you have known and liked and trusted as a friend.

When I was a newlywed and marooned at Buckingham Palace without Andrew, there was no one kinder to me than Lord Charteris, the former longtime private secretary to the Queen. He would dine with me at the Connaught Hotel, and hear me out in all my loneliness; he was like a patient, sympathetic uncle.

So I was wounded when Lord Charteris made some televised comments to the extent that I was a "splendid girl, but basically unsuited to the task of being a royal princess in *any* time." And I was positively lacerated when my old dinner partner expanded on his remarks in *The Spectator,* in January 1995: "Quite simply, the Duchess of York is a vulgarian. She is vulgar, vulgar, vulgar, and that is that."

The dailies picked up the quote for a story of their own, and came after me in Klosters for a response. "Everybody's entitled to their opinion," I said. But what did I *think* of my detractor? "I think he is a great man," I said. "Actually, I like him very much." I wasn't trying to sound high-minded. I just said it automatically, because I *do* think Lord Charteris is a great man. (And when I am eighty-one years old, I hope to be granted similar dispensation.)

The most damaging betrayals can come from former employees, if only because they know so much. I am a challenging person to work for—I am quick and abrupt, and give my staff a run for their money. When my life caved in on me in the early 1990s, I am sure that I could be quite impossible. But the people who stay with me know better than to take my outbursts personally. They know that I am loyal, and they have showed me great loyalty in turn; they have held my hand through some very bad patches. They have honored my trust throughout—with two conspicuous exceptions.

The first was a butler I had known since my Palace days, who had stayed on with me into Romenda Lodge. After he left my staff, he went straight to the newspapers—and the papers were so appalled that they tipped me off. They printed five lines of his keyhole revelations, enough for me to prevent him from any further disclosures. (Anyone entering the royal employ must sign a confidentiality agreement.)

Theo Ellert was more sophisticated, and more harmful. After Children in Crisis was reorganized in the summer of 1994 and she was asked to take a different position, Theo quit instead. A few months later, she sold her version of my "intimate secrets"—FERGIE SAYS BALD MEN ARE GOOD IN

BED!— to the *Mirror* for $15,000, to fund her latest charity. Then she set up a number where people could call in and eavesdrop on two gushy recorded messages I'd left for her: 49 pence a minute.

Given my sensitivity to phone taps and spying proctoscopes, that last piece of ingenuity *really* upset me. I did not need this. I already had London's top investigative journalists bringing to ground my Romanian manicurist in New York *(How does she treat you?)*, or spending days to ascertain whether I packed tissue paper in my suitcases. Nothing was apparently too vacuous or trivial to arouse the tabloid press. Which meant that I had nothing to myself. My very essence was being held up to the light and poked at with sharp sticks.

The terrible thing about living in a fishbowl is not just that people are watching, but that they distract from what *you* need to do. Theo sold our friendship to the press at a fragile time for me. While I'd made progress on my slow road to self-awareness, I still had far to travel. I needed to keep looking inside myself, and more deeply than before, but the observation deck was getting rather crowded.

And that was before my dear father elbowed his way aboard.

In October 1994, excerpts of Dads's new autobiography— *The Galloping Major, My Life and Singular Times*—were published in the tabloids. In addition to sundry nuggets of polo lore, Dads had written a fair amount about his celebrated younger daughter—the kind of material he needed to earn a sizable advance, and to cover some pressing debts. *The Galloping Major* took on the "backbiting toadies" at The Firm. It also weighed the trials of being a Windsor wife and speculated about my future with Andrew.

That book left me feeling totally forlorn, irretrievably alone. It wasn't the content of what Dads had written. It was the fact that he had traded upon our relationship for a few thousand pounds, without so much as consulting with me. He had taken my most cherished possession, my privacy, and auctioned it off, as though it were his seigniorial right.

"What do you want me to say?" he asked me, after realizing how upset I was.

"Nothing, Dads," I said wearily. "There's nothing you can do."

When you war with a parent, you lose twice: first from the conflict, then from the alienation. You are cut off from a person who gave you life. You are cut off from a part of yourself. I ultimately forgave Dads, but for a time his book carved a deep rift between us.

We were still estranged in January 1996 when I visited Qatar, on the Arabian Peninsula. The emir invited me to return in March for their annual "Festival of the Horse"—and, most intriguingly, to ride in the International Qatar Horse Marathon, popularly known as "Desert Storm."

This was not a proposition to be taken lightly. The race, I knew, was one of the most grueling in the world. It asked everything from rider and horse alike to go twenty-six miles over sand. With more than $100,000 in prize money, the Marathon drew the Middle East's most experienced jockeys, professionals who trained all year to withstand hours of competition in hundred-degree heat. I was reasonably fit at the time from my workouts with Josh Salzmann, but I wasn't riding fit. I had not been on a horse since Heather Blaze died —it felt too sad to go back to Ireland, plus I had pared back my hobbies to save money.

Still, I was tempted by the emir's proposal. If I rode, an oil company would sponsor me and donate a significant sum to Children in Crisis. Plus I knew that I could get the perfect manager in my corner, an expert in the art of desert hydration:

Major Ronald Ferguson, formerly of the Life Guards. I thought it was time for Dads and me to make peace.

As soon as I declared I would race, the cynics fell over themselves. The conventional wisdom—i.e., the press—pegged me as a mad and frivolous publicity hound. (Never mind that there are easier ways to get your picture in the paper.) The previous year's celebrity rider, Patrick Swayze, had finished dead last, and *he* was one of Hollywood's aerobic marvels. The betting was that I would pack up a quarter of the way through, pose for the cameras, and thumb a ride to the nearest oasis.

Under the headline, FERGIE RIDING FOR A FALL, the *Daily Express* quoted a race organizer as saying, "Poor Fergie is felt to be most unlikely to finish and could end up embarrassing the Queen by looking ridiculous."

Even Dads and Robert Splaine, my equine consultant for the race, had deep reservations about my "unknown venture on an unknown horse," as Dads would put it. But they knew better than to try to talk me out of it. I had given my word, and the more that I heard I couldn't do it, the more intent I became. It was like the Hampshire Horse Show, or my Canadian canoe trip. Whenever I felt underestimated, I would rise.

Only this time the platform would be larger, the stakes higher—and the price of failure more shattering.

In England I went on a fiercely healthy diet, pushed my workouts to seven days a week. By the time I returned to Qatar, the race had taken on larger significance. Now it was a question of integrity, of my ability to stay the course and be the serious person I claimed. I could not expect to win the race, but I knew that I had to finish. Only then could I show my doubters—including the toughest one, myself—that I was for real.

When we took a look at the horse they'd assigned me,

Robert could tell straight away that he wasn't fit enough to last. Then our luck turned; we met another rider, an American jazz singer named Jean Renaud, whom everyone called "Long Legs." Sizing up our unhappiness, Long Legs introduced us to Pierre Bonnard, who happened to have available a seven-year-old chestnut gelding. The horse's name was Gal, and I like Robert's description of him: "A tall and good-looking horse, sixteen hands high, athletic and sensible."

Gal was an Akhal-Teke, a Russian breed once ridden by Alexander the Great. With their lanky bodies and thin skin, Akhal-Tekes are bred to thrive in the desert, and they are famous for endurance. "Just remember," Pierre told me, "my Gal loves to be spoken to. Just talk to him and he will help you."

The minute we met, even before we took our one practice run on the eve of the race, Gal and I had rapport. We had a little talk up each others' nostrils, and I knew that he had a heart of gold, that he was a horse to be relied upon.

We lined up the next morning across a broad expanse of light sand: forty-six ready steeds and their riders, almost all of them men. The course was only roughly marked off, with a single row of flags for a boundary. Behind the horses were twice as many cars and jeeps and ambulances—including one open-topped car filled with British press, their huge lenses bristling like monstrous antennae, and every man jack of them aching to immortalize my failure.

Minutes before we were off, a bank of dark clouds rolled in, then burst, drenching everyone to the skin.

At the starting gun there was chaos, and it was all I could do to keep my wits about me. Horses reared and motors roared and everyone charged off in what seemed like a dozen different directions. It was then that I discovered that I had saddled a racehorse, a fact Robert had withheld to keep my nerves on the charts. Gal took the bit and was gone, in a flat-out gallop, as if he were sprinting six furlongs. He just wanted to win, and he didn't know the finish line was twenty-six miles off.

I lunged to grab hold of him, but my gloves were slick from the downpour, and the reins slipped through my hands —I lost my horse complete. *When in doubt,* Robert had counseled me, *circle the horse.* My left rein gone, I put my feet firmly forward and pulled hard on the right. Gal was forced back into a circle. Finally I regained control, and we settled into a gentle trot.

Once I had been like Gal, I thought, always pushing past my limits until I flamed out. Now I knew better: Slowing down wins the race.

"Don't worry," came a man's voice. "It's going to be fine." It was Long Legs, who had decided to ride with me and help pull me through. No one could ask for a better partner; he was the kindest of men, and he never stopped smiling.

I needed all the backing I could get. I'd been prepared for heat, but not the damp of a fluke storm. The rain would lash down, on and off, for the rest of the day. It added weight for my horse, and distance to the course, since we'd have to skirt several bogs where the water had pooled. And it churned up the sand and stones till the footing was heavy and treacherous.

Early on, my prospects seemed bleak. One of my stirrups was too long, chafing my inner left knee; soon I was in real pain. I was dripping wet and scared. The rain had changed all my equations.

Some yards behind me followed my support car, a jeep with Robert in the back and Dads up front with the Arab driver. Dads had reverted to his old-school army mode, handing out orders every which way. When he gets mock-pompous like that he is hysterically funny. He makes everyone laugh—he is a very good man.

"I was stationed in the desert, in Aden," Dads would intone, as he directed the driver around the next sand dune. "I know what to do."

"Yes, Major Desert Fox," the driver would agree, and then he'd go in the opposite direction.

Dads understood that the trick in this climate was to stay "topped off"; it was easy to get dehydrated before you noticed you were thirsty. Every so often he had the jeep pull up next to me, to remind me to dip into the water bottles on my saddle. In advance of each water station, where open containers were handed out, Robert would lean out the window and shout, "Water!" When it was time to douse Gal's neck and shoulders, he called out, "Horse!"

About halfway through we reached the vet station, where the riders had to dismount and walk their horses in to be checked for soreness or rapid heart rate. Gal was in great shape, but my own legs barely functioned after rubbing so hard on the saddle.

The rain and sand were taking their toll. Horses pulled up lame, or gave in to exhaustion. With six miles left, Long Legs's horse fizzled out with fatigue. My friend told me to go on ahead, and I did, but I felt like a deserter.

Gal and I were on our own now, and the going was lonely. The wet desert stretched out before us, just as flat and monotonous as all the desert we had passed. The whole universe was brown. Would it never end? Three miles from the end, Gal slowed from a trot to a walk, then a slower one. Each step was more labored than the last . . . and then Gal stopped. *I don't want to go on,* my horse was telling me. *I am tired.*

I was used up myself, but the thought of quitting repelled me. I was part of a team of eight riders, and I could not let the rest down. I *had* to pass the line; something terribly important depended on it.

But neither could I be cruel to my horse; I could not, would not force him. "Should I push on?" I asked Robert, as the car idled alongside. "Is there enough in it?"

Under the rules, Robert could not leave the car, but he trained his keen eyes on Gal for a long moment. Then he said, "From what I can see, with the distance you have left, you're fine."

"Are you sure?"

"Yes, I am," Robert said.

Thus assured, I knew that Gal and I would go as far as our joint spirit carried us. We'd need to tap into our deepest reserves; we'd need to make our leap of faith. My horse wanted to give up, but I appealed to him as a friend, "Gal, you have got to trust me here. I know that home is the other way, and you don't know where you are, and it looks like we are going into the middle of the desert. But you have got to trust that there is something out there—you have to believe enough in me to know that I will get you through it."

By that point I was crying, and I said, " 'Cause if you don't believe in me now, we are going to fail, and we *can't* fail. Because then they will say, 'There she goes again, just being her usual stupid, crazy self.' "

Gal stayed stock still, and my heart dropped. I tried one last time: "Will you go on? When the whole world has given up on me, will you go *on?*" And then I heard the saddle creak, and I felt those weary limbs heave into motion . . . and my horse took a gamble and walked on. Gal trusted and believed in me when all logic stood against it, and he walked on.

That kindness killed me; that heart and courage laid me out. There was so much potential on this earth, so much greatness in its creatures—how could I ever feel hopeless again?

A mile or so from the finish, Gal rounded a bend and spied the grandstand. He got excited then, because he knew I had not lied to him. Half a mile out he broke into a confident canter. That was the way he went across the line, cantering freely, as fresh as a romping colt.

After I peeled myself off the saddle, I did a spectacular—if unintentional—send-up of John Wayne. My muscles were fixed in a bowlegged cowboy strut; it would be hours before I walked normally again.

I made sure Gal drank first, then took my turn. I wanted to take care of that horse forever.

My time was two hours and thirty-five minutes; I'd chopped more than an hour off Patrick Swayze's. More important, I'd conquered a course that had forced nineteen of the forty-six riders to drop out. My team finished third, and our coach wrapped me in a hug and said, "You did it, you did it for the team." That gave me enormous pleasure; I am more of a team player than most people realize.

An hour after Gal's triumph, I looked back out on the course. Through the drizzle, inching over the horizon, a rangy-framed man trudged toward us, leading his spent horse behind him—Long Legs! I wobbled out as fast as my John Wayne limbs could carry me and escorted my comrade back. He too would finish, after all.

Later I would ask my new friend why he'd stayed back with me at the start. "When you meet a great spirit," Long Legs explained, "you always have to help them through difficult times."

It was about the nicest thing anyone had ever said to me.

Foiled from blaring the story it had counted on, the *Daily*

Mail would make the best of it the next morning: SHE WAS 25TH OUT OF 27.

But *that,* I will tell you, was water off my back. How could I fret about a headline when my Dads and I were friends again? He had been so gallant all the way through, standing up and taking charge of things; he had been a real father to me. It filled me up that I'd prevailed with him watching. No son, I thought, could have done any better.

When I finished Dads came up to me in tears, and told me how proud he was and that he wished the world could know just how much I had achieved there. That meant something, for Dads was a horseman's horseman, and not easily impressed.

And I knew then he had never meant to hurt me, and we were healed.

On the surface, it seemed, my life was pulling together. With the aid of my new financial manager, I had stopped hemorrhaging money and begun to generate income; my new series of children's books would be launched in the fall. Children in Crisis was running smoothly, and would raise close to $4 million in fiscal 1996. And I was free of entanglements in the romance department—a mixed blessing, to be sure, but one that lent a certain calm.

But even as my life became simpler and more reasonable, I'd fall prey to the black dog, to use Churchill's pet name for his depression. I was like the soldier in the foxhole who alone survived the firefight: lost, benumbed, wondering why I'd been spared—and for what? My journal entry for March 11, 1996, a week before I went to Qatar: "It appears to be a vacuum inside—a hollow tube, a dark corridor with no open doors. . . . It is not fear—it is a hollow, dead piece of coral, floating lifelessly, aimless. What are the true feelings within? What is the path?

"The pain is just far too great, perhaps the word is not to care—perhaps to give up and say it is just too much.

"But I care so very much about everything, and people's feelings and attitudes. I'm really tired of worrying. I am so very tired of this long and arduous battle. Maybe the best is to just give up and realize I am in the wilderness, alone, frightened and very confused. The best I can do is just to allow this unbelievable pain inside to be there. Feel it and embrace it—maybe then I can shine and go forward with buoyancy and freedom of spirit."

Going forward would take all my courage, and something more: a clarity and closure I had yet to attain. Four years after my separation, I remained in limbo: legally, financially, emotionally. Neither Andrew nor I had wanted to make The Decision, but we could not rest on the fence forever. We had to go one way or the other, either reconcile or part, and the cards were all stacked on one side of the table.

It would be hard to divorce Andrew. We had no animosity between us; if anything, we were better friends than before. (I had to lose my prince, it seemed, to rediscover the man.) I might never find another to believe in me as Andrew did. I knew, too, that my husband would not have denied me if I had asked him to try again. Unconditional love is like that —it is always there for you.

But I had crossed my Rubicon many miles earlier. Speaking practically, I could not satisfy the bank's demands unless I became wholeheartedly commercial. As a separated mother with two children, I had a goal to be self-sufficient, and I could not get there as a member of the Royal Family. There were just too many things *not done,* from endorsements to feature film projects.

My freedom had been too hard won to relinquish. I needed to fashion a career without wavering or apology.

In the end, though, my decision wasn't swung by the bottom line. Life as a princess was just too much for me, and at the same time too little. I wanted more from a marriage than a prince could offer; I wanted a companion who would give me 110 percent, and I would give the same. But you cannot ask that of a man whose mother was the monarch; you cannot press a man for whom duty must come first, and second, third, and fourth as well. Had Andrew not been *quite* so highborn, it might have been different for us. But the facts were the facts.

Still, I *could* have given in and gone back to him. Though the Grey Men would have gone psychotic, there were limits to even their power. Andrew and I would simply have told the Queen, and that would have been that.

But too soon we would have killed each other's souls, for I could not accept the antiquated system that ruled a Royal's life. I would not let myself be judged by all the Queen's men. Not then, not now, not ever.

It had taken a small eternity for me to come to these terms, to understand what I was doing. But once I learned something, I was never one to fiddle around. I told Andrew it was time, and we agreed to do it quickly and quietly.

That Easter the girls and I stayed for six days at Sunninghill with their father. We painted eggs and had treasure hunts, all the usual things, and much of the time we simply relaxed at home. We had two sensational children, Andrew and I, and it never hurt to be reminded of it. If you had to end a marriage, this was a good way to do it.

On Thursday, April 11, I left Sunninghill in floods of tears

—I would be a spigot all day long. Andrew was outwardly unemotional as he saw me and the girls off in a car; his own turn would come later.

I had to steel myself to sign the gray document. My hand felt like some lifeless machine as it made the familiar scrawl. *You are doing the right thing,* my head told me, but there are certain acts you can't be sure of until after you have done them. I was skydiving that day. I had checked my chute a dozen times inside the plane, but who knew for sure that it would open when I needed it, when the ground would rush up to receive me?

Barely an hour later, my daughters and I were on a plane for Switzerland. I needed relief from the negativity of England, and the mountains were the place to be. Their strength would prop me up, and they'd provide neutral turf for meeting the press when the time came.

The following Tuesday, Andrew rang me in Verbier. In two hours the press would be notified about the divorce. "I am so terribly sorry," Andrew said.

I wept as I listened; Andrew was still knocking me off my hinges. He'd been doing it ever since I first pulled up to Sandringham, beset by gravel fever, when he'd ambushed me with a kiss.

On Wednesday, April 17, twenty-nine uncontested divorces were processed at the family division of the High Court in London. At the bottom of the list was this one: "HRH The Duke of York v. HRH The Duchess of York."

(A week later, Andrew and I would have dinner with both lawyers and their wives at a restaurant near Windsor. We were setting new standards for amicability.)

Andrew drove out to Portland on the seventeenth, while the children and I stayed on at Verbier in Paddy's chalet; he had given us the run of it while he was away. I was making a conscious effort to be strong. The divorce was "just a piece of paper," I told the press on the slopes that saddest day.

And: Our children were "happy and secure, because they know their mother and father are the bestest friends."

And: "I'll take each day as it comes. Each day is a new day."

But the cameras dug deeper than any spoken query, and the stress in my face streamed out of the photographs in the next day's papers. The divorce was a big-time shock, the biggest of my life. I cannot describe the sheer pain of it. It had been building within me all week, and Andrew's phone call had burst the dam.

Back home at Kingsbourne, I plunged into melancholy. I was wretched, inconsolable, well past hysterics, not far from coma. I had found my peace, of a sort: the peace of the dead. I managed to get my children dressed and off to school, but that was as much as I could handle. I just sat in my living room and rocked in my chair, lost in the feeling of nowhere. My staff would see me rocking, and ask if I wanted a cup of tea, and that would be my big decision for the afternoon.

The most sentimental grief is the mourning for what might have been.

It didn't have to be this way, I kept thinking, as I rocked like a dead person. *This didn't need to happen.*

When Andrew first came to me, he was my total hero. For somebody who needed an awful lot of love, he served. He had taken a girl who was terrified of life and he'd said, *You can do it, you're all right—go on, you can do it.* He never told me to trust myself, not in so many words, but by his actions he'd given me faith to carry on. And now he was gone, leaving this great hole inside me. He'd left a pain too large to run from any longer—for the pain was now all I had, all I *was*.

It was the pain of being born.

By itself, the divorce was just a pebble; I had been stoned by larger, sharper rocks, and lived to tell the tale. But the pebble set off an avalanche. It released the anger and soul-scarring misery I had pent up for so long. The avalanche blindsided me as I sat catatonic in my rocking chair, and soon I was sliding down the mountain with no guide to pull me clear.

Consciousness was a new medium for me. I would still get sidetracked into alleys of self-hatred or dead ends of regret. I still blanched at my old behavior. But there was something else rattling around in there, a new glimmer of understanding, even a hint of self-love. My journal entry of May 5: "I sit in a cloud of total blackness, and I think: Is this the worst now? Who was the unconscious Sarah? Who was this unreal, sordid, vulgar human? How can I have allowed such degradation?

"People may say, 'How much more can one person take? After all, she has not murdered anyone.' Well, you know, old Sarah did murder in a way. She murdered herself—to the point of extinction.

"I will never forget this time in my life—such loss, such pain. Why was I not aware as I am now?"

After months out of touch, I thought I had seen the last of John Bryan. But on Sunday, April 28, he reached out for me like some horror-movie hand reaching from the crypt, just when I thought I might be safe at last. . . .

I HAD SEX WITH FERGIE AS SHE SPOKE TO ANDY ON PHONE. That, gentle reader, was the front-page, world-war headline in the *News of the World.* The article came out less than two weeks after the decree nisi. I was still very much in my rocking-chair phase, feeling about as rugged as a robin's egg, and that headline knocked me for six. *Would everyone believe that I would do this disgusting thing?*

I called Kate Waddington, my executive assistant, and asked her why she had returned to work for me; I needed to hear someone say that I wasn't such an awful person. (I can always depend upon Kate in a crisis; like Christine Ward, she stands out for her selflessness, her dedication, and her steadfast loyalty.)

I went upstairs and washed my face, and then I sat in a chair to think for a bit. Why did these things keep happening? I could rage about John and the tabloids, but only one person had brought this upon me; I'd just seen her streaked face in the mirror. When you lie down with dogs, you can't be shocked to get fleas. When you lie down with a wolf, you must count yourself lucky to come out with your jugular intact.

Had there ever been two less-aware people than John and me—two people who'd known less about each other, or themselves?

Taking responsibility, for good and bad alike, is a salve for the spirit. It makes for a clear-eyed optimism; if a certain sort of conduct gets you into a mess, a change can get you out. You have control over what happens next.

And so I got out of my chair and found my wonderful girls. I took each of them by the hand and led them to their trampoline. As we jumped I left my anger and humiliation behind me, below me. There was no point in dwelling on the article; I wasn't about to sue and clamber into a witness box.

John's betrayal was a sad thing, but it was also a catharsis; it swept the decks clean. There was nothing left in my unconscious past that could harm me.

After we'd had our fill of jumping, Beatrice and Eugenie went to swim, and I sat by the pool watching them. Bees buzzed about the swaying daffodils. Our two dalmatians eyed the cat as it meandered by. What was more real—the crass fantasies of a desperate man, or the natural world the Lord had given us?

Yesterday's history, tomorrow's a mystery, and today is a gift. . . .

I watched my daughters swim on. The sun softly nestled on my back. And in that one invaluable, irreplaceable moment, my mind was as clear as the warm spring air.

Into the Light

On May 30, while my daughters and I watched Ballymoss go through his paces at Hickstead, a clerk at Somerset House dated a nondescript sheet of paper, then swung down a red rubber stamp.

My divorce was final.

Four days later and four thousand miles away, I received the Mother Hale Award at Hale House in Harlem. The timing wasn't ideal, but the event had been planned a year ahead, and I had to be there, more to honor the memory of the late Mother Hale than to be feted myself.

The first time I visited Hale House, I noticed that it was full of mirrors—and that all the mirrors were low to the ground, at child level. When I asked why, Mother Hale smiled and said, "The best way to give a child confidence is to say how beautiful they are when they look at their reflection."

So simple and true, I thought, and then a spasm of guilt

shot through me. Only hours before, I'd caught Beatrice looking in one of the many mirrors at our hotel. "Don't be so vain," I told her, and as soon as I said it I could hear my mum cutting me, just as Grummy had cut her. I caught myself in the act, but I hadn't done anything about it.

Back in our hotel room that evening, I saw a chance to turn things around. "Should we do your hair now?" I asked my daughter, and then: "Aren't you a beautiful girl?" A small moment, but it broke a huge pattern of put-downs going back for God knows how many generations. Ever since that day, I have consciously taught my children to love themselves first. I know what it is to go through life without confidence; it is a journey I would rather spare them.

It's no chore for me to tell my girls how proud I am, because I *am* proud, utterly and extravagantly so. I am grateful for these precious gems; I can't imagine my house without their vibrancy and laughter and grumpiness. Beatrice is musical and full of grace. She wears her heart on her sleeve, and she has a higher understanding of life than anyone else I've ever met—there is some Victoria in her. Eugenie is clever academically and appears lighthearted and easy. But she can surprise with her intensity, and she is fearlessly candid; she will go up to the Queen and say that she doesn't like her granny's lipstick.

I work hard at listening to my children. It's easy to be dismissive when you're worried about the bank or on the phone or in a rush, but I try to understand. If Beatrice complains that her shirt is itchy, I say, "That's fine, let's take it off, then," even though we're running late and the shirt seems all right to me.

Sometimes I have to remind myself that a parent is but a guardian, and that only for a time. I cannot swathe my children in cotton wool for protection. They have their own lessons to learn, as I have had mine (and will have many more). I will be honest and consistent with them, above all. My daughters have always heard the truth from their mother about the separation and divorce, and so they are not embarrassed when it comes up at school.

I never wanted a fishbowl for my children, but you cannot wish the world away. From hard experience I have found it is best to take the press in stride, that you only compound its feeding frenzy by trying to escape. When my girls go outside and see some cameras, they smile sweetly and get on with their day.

They are growing up quite normally, I think. I set limits, to be sure, but I try not to knock the stuffing out of them— you need to let children be children. We have flexible table manners: one set for tea with Granny at the Palace (totally proper); another for meals out in public (reasonably civilized); and another for dinner at home with Mummy (fun and jokes).

During the week I limit sweets and goody drinks, but come the weekend, my daughters get to do what they like—because Mummy wants to do what *she* likes! Fridays are very important. I pick them up from school and we go straight to the video shop and rent out a clutch of movies. They get an ice cream and then it's home. I stop work at 5:30, and that is all for the weekend—I am theirs. We watch movies and color pictures, and we go to fairs and on picnics. I love unwrapping the tin foil to release the smell of the sausage rolls, still warm inside.

My daughters need to see children who have suffered, to understand how lucky they are. When we held a party near Kingsbourne for Children in Crisis, they got to meet a remarkable boy from Chernobyl. At the age of seven, Igor was barely two feet tall. His legs were like little flippers, and he had only one arm, which he used to move himself forward. My children took him down to the garden, and off they went; Igor was just one of the gang.

Later, when they asked me why Igor had no legs, I tried to explain about nuclear radiation and the children of Belarus. About how their enemy was the air they breathed, and the milk they drank, and the vegetables put on their plate when the only alternative was hunger.

Children in Crisis coordinates the World Appeal for the Children of Chernobyl; it will be one of our major concentrations in years to come. Ten years after the nuclear disaster that resulted in radioactive fallout a hundred times greater than at Hiroshima, more than 800,000 children in the Republic of Belarus remain at high risk. They are prone to a grotesque litany of diseases: leukemia and other cancers of all kinds; birth deformities and Down syndrome; thyroid problems and anemia; mental sickness and blindness.

Few of these children are getting the most basic medical treatment, much less needed chemotherapy. Drugs are expensive or unavailable; a packet of aspirin costs the equivalent of two weeks' wages.

At places like Chernobyl the challenge can seem overwhelming. But we will do our best, child by child.

*I*n May I concluded a three-year term as president of the MND Association. Given my other commitments, I wanted to move on to a job with less administration attached, perhaps to establish a new research committee. I stepped down as part of a normal, planned rotation.

But the *Daily Mail* didn't see it that way. "The Duchess of

York," it reported, "is being dumped as president of one of her favorite charities following her slump in popularity."

Two months later, a financial journalist named Dominic Prince added insult to injury—or, more precisely, slur to insult. Prince had sat with me on a corporate advisory council, which supplied him with the grist for a rambling article in *The Spectator.* After lighting into me for being late to meetings and "hopelessly disorganized," Prince asserted that "some" people considered me "a no-good trollop" and wanted me off the board.

These comments were repudiated by the association, but the tabloids had their headline: HRH THE TROLLOP. Less well reported was the following observation in Prince's essay: "Most of the money our charity gets is a direct result of the Duchess's title and work."

That work, of course, is what matters, and I have no intention of letting it drop. I will always be there for the patients and carers, as they have been there for me.

I'm afraid that I still go on trusting people—it comes naturally to me, and I am happier for it. But I have got a bit wilier than I used to be. Kingsbourne has two secure phone lines, cleared all the way down to the main exchange. The house and grounds are swept for bugs twice a month, and every bit of rubbish is burnt.

Last spring, when I took my daughters on holiday to the Bahamas, I tried a new subterfuge. I told their policemen that we were going to America. I had not lied—we did spend one night in Florida before flying on to the islands. But when the officers filed their report with their supervisors in London, they had no idea of our ultimate destination.

I went the whole week without seeing a single journalist, for the first time in ten years.

*D*espite significant pressure from The Firm, Andrew has stood tall in my support. When we recently met in public, he kissed me in front of all the press; he wanted to make it clear that he had not been intimidated.

Today Andrew is totally different from the young man who teased me at Royal Ascot. He is awake, in the most vital sense; he is truly amazing. Real royalty, as my loyal friend Kenneth Rose, the biographer of George V, once noted, is not just a matter of titles or crowns. To be royal is to be compassionate, to put people at their ease, to be connected to the deeper meaning of life. By all of these measurements, Andrew is royal—not merely by birth, but by character.

Whichever lady gets him now is one very lucky lady.

*I*n July, shortly after her own decree nisi came through, Diana joined me for a holiday with our children in the south of France. The Wicked Wives of Windsor were no more, but the two of us remained a mutual-aid society, sisters under the skin. Diana had served fifteen years in the Royal Family to my ten; you might say that I'd got time off for bad behavior.

Based at Paddy's vacant villa in the Provençal hills, where magic comes up with the sun, we decompressed. The setting fed the senses. Green olive trees, blue swimming pool, and a romantic symphony of smells: pine, eucalyptus, and wild rosemary, with a grace note of cooking olive oil.

Diana left after the first week. My children had their

friends there, so I didn't need to entertain them. For five days I would lounge alone by the pool in this nirvana, my every creature need met, my external world quiet and complete.

Nothing to stop me, in short, from freaking out in style.

I was minding my own business, I thought. I awaited the slow fade of forgetting . . . but my pain would not cooperate. Rather than melt away, it bloomed out of all proportion, like James's giant peach. Gloom encircled me, enfolded me; it obscured the languid landscape, eclipsed the honey sun. I was mourning ten misplaced years, my grand boulevard of destruction.

The first day or two were very scary. I am a doer, and when my pain rose up in England I would *do* something about it. I might strive even harder to be loved and accepted. Or I might run away and deny the pain, and busy myself with work or the children—for who could fault a mother who was busy with her children?

I had run every race, and tackled great tasks; I had ventured to every continent but Antarctica. I had met the crowned heads of more countries than I could count; I had lived eight lives in the space of one.

But still there was one place I had yet to visit. I had never looked into the heart of my darkness—not full-on, without flinching.

Until now. Perhaps it was Provence, working its old disarming ways on me. Or perhaps I had nothing left inside, not even my illusions—and pain, like nature, abhorred a vacuum. Whatever the reason, I sat for hours in that chair by the bluest of pools, and allowed myself . . . to *be.* I just lay there and felt the pain of the moment, and of the next one, and the next. I didn't stiff-upper-lip myself; I didn't say, *Well, now buck up there; you're so lucky: you've got two girls and*

you're healthy and fit. . . . I just let myself feel bad. I acknowledged how I felt, and I said it was all right.

It sounds like a simple thing, but it wasn't. Not for a good
English girl who had shut off her feelings from her first toddler's tantrums. It was the hardest thing in the world, at the
start. But by the third day the pain had gained its own momentum, and I lost all thought of flight. I bounced off the
high board and gave myself to gravity. I dove up and out and
over, and then I knifed down, into . . . *what?*

Into a mass of black treacle, thick and glutinous. All the
bad things were stored there, the shame of a lifetime. Of feeling an encumbrance, and a failure, and a square peg where
there were no holes to fit into.

I dove deeper, into the gummy blackness of my loss—lost
prince, lost marriage, lost dignity, lost hope. It was a horrible
mess of treacle, a massive oil spill of the spirit.

Then I realized something strange: I was still there. I had
not been annihilated. I had broken into the dark side and was
shaking hands with my pain, looking it straight in the eye . . .
and it wasn't so bad, after all. Why had I been running so
hard, so long? There was nothing so terrible in that treacle,
not really, just the stumbles of a woman who always feared
for her next step.

Once you go deep enough into your darkness, once you
spread your arms wide to embrace it, the pain can no longer
hold you—it loses its grip. I broke through the treacle and
into a crystalline spring, sweet and clear. I knew something
had changed inside me. It wasn't so much a presence as an
absence. All the churnings I had carried—the angry static,
the dark voices—were gone. The silence was overpowering.
There was no one to tell me that I was fat and ugly and worthless. There was nothing inside me at all.

But that wasn't quite true. There *was* something inside

there, and my inner ear tuned to it, as one's eyes slowly make out a nightscape. It was the voice of creativity, and sensuality, and self-forgiveness. It was the part of me that knew I needed others and their love, and wasn't spooked by that fact. It was the very best part of me, this voice I came to call my "female," and only now was I hearing her out.

All my life I had abused my poor female. I shouted her down in my self-hatred; I sat on her until she shut up. She was stubborn, and never quite went away; she turned subversive instead, making mischief, running riot. Her great coup: the St. Tropez photographs. (*You are not listening,* she sang.) But still I turned a deaf ear to her. I bowed instead to my dark voice; it was the devil that I knew, I suppose. I ignored the gentle rapping at my door.

But now that our dialogue had opened, I could not get enough of her. I sat by that pool and simply listened. I breathed in and out, and enjoyed the calm. There were times for doing, and times to receive, and now I could relish them both.

It gets prehistorically dark in Provence at night, which used to make me anxious. But after my swim through the treacle, my old phobia flew off, and I haven't felt a twinge of it since.

I am easier with myself these days, more forgiving, more content. I have learned, for example, that there is Life After Cellulite. When I'm in the company of a model, I don't wish to have her figure. I've got my own, and it's perfectly nice—it's *me,* after all. I still punish the exercise bike for thirty extra minutes, but I also allow myself an occasional bowl of pasta. I still fantasize about running along the beach in a black bikini (partner included, naturally), but it's no longer the be-all and end-all.

I don't want to be the kindest and prettiest and cleverest anymore. I just want to be Sarah—and for those who love me, that will be enough. The Pleaser may not quite have breathed her last, but I think that her days are numbered.

I know I am a work in progress, and that I'm sure to make mistakes. But risk no longer troubles me; I am ready to stand up for what I think is right. As a free and independent divorced woman, I will do what is required to support my family. If that means writing a book, or endorsing a product, or opening a television channel for Fox, so be it.

This summer I visited my sister, Jane, in Sydney—she is the most understanding, unspoiled, unconditional woman I've ever met—and then went on to Melbourne for Fox. The morning after the opening, I drew open the curtains of my hotel room, thirty-six floors up. Down on the street I could make out a man who was rushing to work. He was fighting the wind and rain, and his mackintosh kept flaring out, because it hadn't been done up right. I thought that was very interesting—that here was a man who was late to work and getting wet, and he did not give a damn about how the Duchess of York was making her living, or whether she was fat or thin, or how the *Daily Mail* was treating her. He didn't care two hoots about that woman on the thirty-sixth floor; he had his own issues to deal with.

In other words, the day goes on.

There was a time, not long past, when my every little minute was caught up in who said what and why did they think I was so terrible—just what was going on? But now I simply don't care anymore; I move on to the next thing. When you have touched the flames of hell, a branding iron is only a mild inconvenience.

And when you squelch your toughest judge, that hanging judge at the core of you, there is very little to fear from the ones outside.

Toward the end of the film *The Shawshank Redemption,* an aging inmate named Red (played by Morgan Freeman) stands face to face with his parole board. Red has served thirty years of a life sentence; he's been denied parole so often that he is almost past caring. When a board member asks him if he regrets what he did, Red answers from his heart.

"Hell, son, I didn't need prison for that! Not a day goes by I don't feel regret, and not because I'm in here or because you think I should. I look back on myself the way I was . . . stupid kid who did that terrible crime . . . wish I could talk sense to him. Tell him how things are. But I can't. That kid's long gone, and this old man is all that's left, and I have to live with that."

Red was speaking straight to me in that movie. I still get mortified by my past. If I could shake that oblivious young woman who sowed so much destruction, I would gladly do it.

But I can't, because she is no more.

At the same time, I must tell you this: that if given the chance, I would follow my heart again, all the way into Buckingham Palace. I would not change a day of it, not even that hellish day at Balmoral, when I felt like Eve fallen from grace. I would go through it all again, to the last tabloid humiliation, because it led me to the path that saved my life. I had to be smacked down completely before I would learn and listen, not once but a hundred times. I had to be stripped bare, in body and soul, before I stopped trying to hide.

I have always sailed close to the wind, through storm and calm, and over the roughest whitecaps. I am still sailing close —only now I have charted a course to serve me, and the wind will be bringing me home.

Once upon a time, a country girl fell into public life and lost herself in the exchange. She finally had to demolish her public self, if only to rescue her private one. And that is exactly what she did, in all of her unconsciousness.

Which is to say: I had to let go of something huge to *win*, for Andrew and myself.

Lord Charteris was right; I was never cut out for royalty, even had I known what I know today. But history cannot be erased. I can never go back through the looking glass into some pristine private life. I will always be the mother of two princesses, and the second son's ex-wife; there are gossip page fixtures with slimmer résumés than that.

But today I can weather the scrutiny, take it or leave it as I please. I have something larger and more lasting than the latest three-column spread. I am my own woman now, ready to go forward. I have my life back, and I will not let go of it.

And I just might live rather happily ever after.

A Note to My Friends

> *For this I hold*
> *friendship is more than life,*
> *longer than love*
> *and it shall prove warm to the spirit*
> *when the body is cold.*
>
> —Stephen Haggard

To you my friends—and *you* know who you are . . .

You remain steadfast in your belief in me.
You are worthy of far more respect than a line on this page.
I honor your selflessness, dedication, and loyalty.
I admire your kindness and integrity.
I thank *you* for the greatest gift of all: the gift of friendship.

Sarah

Sarah The Duchess of York

INDEX